THE CATHOLIC UNIVERSITY OF AMERICA
CANON LAW STUDIES
No. 128

The Rights and Duties of the Local Ordinary Regarding Congregations of Women Religious of Pontifical Approval

A DISSERTATION

Submitted to the Faculty of Canon Law of the Catholic University of America in Partial Fulfillment of the Requirements for the Degree of

DOCTOR OF CANON LAW

BY

BENJAMIN F. FARRELL, M.A., S.T.L., J.C.L.
Priest of the Diocese of Wheeling

THE CATHOLIC UNIVERSITY OF AMERICA PRESS
WASHINGTON, D. C.
1941

NIHIL OBSTAT:
HIERONYMUS D. HANNAN,
Censor Deputatus

Washingtonii, D. C., die III Iunii, 1941

IMPRIMATUR:
✠ IOANNES I. SWINT
Episcopus Whelingensis

Whelingenii, die III Iunii, 1941.

PRINTED IN THE UNITED STATES OF AMERICA
BY THE WATKINS PRINTING CO., BALTIMORE

TABLE OF CONTENTS

FOREWORD

The juridical status of congregations of women religious of pontifical approval was not established in canonical legislation until the last decade of the nineteenth century, when Pope Leo XIII issued the Constitution *"Conditae a Christo."*

With the promulgation of the Code of Canon Law a definite norm of guidance regarding the rights and duties of the local ordinary which concern these congregations was expressed in ecclesiastical legislation, a norm which has been clarified by subsequent authoritative interpretations of the Pontifical Commission for the Interpretation of the Code.

Since, however, this juridical relationship of the local ordinary to such congregations extends to various phases of the Christian and the religious life, it was impossible to confine the expression of these rights and duties to one particular section of the Code.

The purpose of this dissertation, therefore, is to search out these expressions of jurisdictional right and obligation of the local ordinary regarding congregations of women religious of pontifical approval, and thus afford a means of reference and consultation for the ordinary.

The writer wishes to express his gratitude to the Faculty of the School of Canon Law for their invaluable supervision and to all others who have been of assistance in the preparation of this study.

Chapter I

GENERAL NOTIONS

Prior to any consideration of the historical background and development of the juridical question at hand, it will be necessary to define the terms and delineate the limits within which this study will proceed.

The Bishop is understood as the local Ordinary, governing that portion of Christ's flock assigned to him by the *missio canonica.*[1] The term "local Ordinary" includes the residential Bishop, Abbot or Prelate *nullius* and the Vicar-General of these, the Administrator, Vicar and Prefect Apostolic within their respective territories, as well as those persons who, in case of vacancy of these enumerated offices, succeed to the office by provisions of law or approved constitutions.[2] These enjoy the same authority unless one or the other is expressly excluded.

Jurisdiction in its strict sense indicates the public authority enjoyed by a superior in a perfect society over a subject. In ecclesiastical law it implies the fullness of power—the power to enact laws (legislative), to execute even by coercive means (executive), and to render judgment over controverted rights of ecclesiastical society and individuals (judicial). Jurisdiction then may be defined as a public power of ruling or governing others. If, however, the defnition is to be restricted to the ecclesiastical forum, it may be described as "a public power granted by Christ, or by

[1] Ottaviani, *Institutiones Iuris Publici Ecclesiastici* (2. ed., 2 vols. Civitas Vaticana: Typis Polyglottis Vaticanis, 1935-1936), I, 220.

[2] Cf. canon 198, §§ 1, 2; Larraona, *Commentarium pro Religiosis et Missionariis,* IV (1923), 107 ff. (Hereafter this periodical will be referred to by the initials *CpRM*); Cicognani, *Canon Law,* Authorized English version by Joseph M. O'Hara and Francis Brennan, (2. ed., Philadelphia: The Dolphin Press, 1935), p. 587.

His Church through a canonical mission, to govern the baptized to the goal of eternal life."[3]

Jurisdiction must be understood properly as distinct from the dominative power (*potestas dominativa*) of the religious superior of an institute. This dominative power, unlike jurisdiction, can be found in imperfect societies which are incapable of possessing true jurisdiction, such as communities of lay religious, and is primarily directed towards the individual good.[4]

It is not executive, judical or legislative, but a preceptive power whereby the superior can command, direct and correct the members of the society towards the achievement of the purpose of the society.[5]

The source of dominative power is disputed. Some authors claim that it arises directly from the vow of obedience. But the more common opinion is that the superior acquires this power

[3] Maroto, *Institutiones Iuris Canonici* (3. ed., Romae, 1921), I, 666; Kearney, *The Principles of Delegation*, The Catholic University of America, Canon Law Studies, No. 55 (Washington, D. C.: The Catholic University of America, 1929), 45 ff.; "Potestas vero quae Ecclesiae competit in ordine ad gubernandos homines, idest ad dirigendos auctoritative eorum actus tum quoad fidem, tum quod mores, dicitur potestas iurisdictionis, et haec confert in subiecto in quo residet proprie dictam superioritatem imperii."—Ottaviani, *op. cit.*, I, 216.

[4] Raus, *De Sacrae Obedientiae Virtute et Voto* (2 vols., Lugduni, Emmanuel Vitte, 1923), I, 65; "Dominative power comes directly from the act by which, in taking the vow of obedience in a community, Christians assume the obligation to work therein within the scope of the institute under the guidance of those members to whom the direction of the society is entrusted by due appointment or election. Jurisdiction comes directly from Christ who gave to St. Peter and his successors the right to govern the Church in all that directly or indirectly appertains to the spiritual welfare of the same Church and its members."—Papi, *The Government of Religious Communities* (New York; P. J. Kenedy & Sons, 1919), 61.

[5] The private power of a superior over subjects has been given various names by authors. St. Thomas (*Summa*, IIa, IIae, q. 57, art. 4; IIa, IIae, q. 104, art. 5 ad 1) refers to *paternal (patria)* power as that which parents have over their children; and he distinguishes this from the *dominative* power which masters exercise over their slaves, and the *economic (oeconomica)* power of husbands over wives. Today these various distinctions of power have been broadly fused into one generic term, *dominative power.*

properly and strictly through the religious profession, wherein the members subject themselves to the rule, to be governed by the general law for religious, by the constitutions and by the approved customs of the institute.[6] A superior can, indeed, be in possession of power through four possible sources, *viz.* through natural right, through the positive ordination either of God or of the Church, and through the agency of a free human act. But it may be noted that canon 501, § 1, of the Code makes explicit mention of only two powers as derived from these sources: jurisdiction and dominative power.[7]

Suarez ascribes a third power to a religious prelate, a power which arises from a vow taken by a subject (*potestas ex voto*).[8]

[6] "Unde ortum habeat potestas dominativa, non plane constat apud auctores, quod satis jam innuit cl. Piat, O. Cap. (*Prael. iur. reg.*, q. 737, I), scribens: 'Potestatem autem dominativam oriri dicunt alii *ex voto* obedientiae, alii vero rectius *ex jure naturali hypothetico,* supposita nempe tum institutione legitima Congregationis religiosae, tum *deditione peracta* eorum qui Institutum ingrediuntur.' Sed haec de solis valent religiosis. In abstracto autem videtur a lege naturali ortum ducere; in concreto, accedente vi ac dispositione legum aut contractuum, secundum Ferrari (n. 102, II) emanat saepius ex facto libero associationis et ex libera voluntate ipsorum *profitentium,* conjunctis cum promissione et obligatione obediendi juxta normas Instituti. Ex solo etiam contractu oriri poterit, ut apparet ex exemplo auctoritatis heri in suos famulos vel domini in suos voluntarios. . . . In religione deinde acquirit Praelatus seu Superior potestatem suam dominationis *proprie et stricte* per professionem suorum religiosorum, cum hi sese subjiciunt Regulae et se tradunt gubernandos ad tramitem juris communis, Constitutionum et probatae consuetudinis. Haec est verissima sententia fere omnium illustrium theologorum, et maxime classicorum auctorum, ut facile videre est ex Pirhing, Schmalzgrueber (T. III, P. IV, tit. 35, n. 59), Suarez, Donato Laynensi (II, tr. VI, q. 12, 13), Billuart (*De statu rel.*, D. IV, a. 2, VI), Pignantello (vol. III, 198, n. 4), Salmanticensibus, Card. Vives (*Compendium iuris canonici,* n. 833, VII), Aichner-Friedele (§ 141, 2, p. 507, ed. II), Berthier (Agrégé de Théologie, n. 3406)."—Raus, *De Sacrae Obedientiae Virtute et Voto,* I, 67.

[7] Canon 501, § 1: "Superiores . . . potestatem habent dominativam in subditos; in religione autem clericali exempta, habent iurisdictionem ecclesiasticam tam pro foro interno, quam pro foro externo."

[8] Suarez, *Opera Omnia,* 26 vols. (Paris, 1856-1861), Tr. VII, lib. X, c. 8, n. 1.

Since in the profession of the vow of obedience there arises a new obligation which derives from the virtue of religion, it is the power correlative to this obligation which he calls the *potestas ex voto,* and he conceives it as an entity distinct from either the power of jurisdiction or dominative power. Thus the superior enjoys the right to issue a precept, through the medium of which an actual and specific obligation arising from the vow becomes binding.[9]

Dominative power resides in all religious superiors, that is, in the presiding officers of religious institutes, whether clerical or lay, whether of men or of women. The power of jurisdiction in its fullness resides in the Roman Pontiff, and, with due dependence on the Roman Pontiff, in local bishops, in superiors of exempt clerical religious institutes, and in anyone to whom the Roman Pontiff may wish to communicate it.[10] The Roman Pontiff ordinarily exercises his power over religious through others who are extrinsic to the institute, notably through the S. Congregation for Religious. Pope Pius X in the Constitution *"Sapienti Consilio"* [11] instituted this Cosgregation on June 29, 1908, suppressing at the same time the three S. Congregations which formerly treated the affairs of religious: The *"Congregationes super negotiis Episcoporum et super negotiis Regularium"* (instituted by Pope Sixtus V in 1856) [12], the *"Congregatio super disciplina regulari"*

[9] "Suarez (Tr. VIII, lib. II, c. n. 2) regards as a mere play on words the contention that in such a case the Superior has no real power, but merely places a condition (the precept), on which the actual urgency of the vow depends. The result of this precept is always such that the person bound by the vow must obey as a matter of conscience. The power arising from the vow is, therefore, a special title by reason of which a Superior may oblige his subject. The Superior is in quasi-possession of the right which corresponds to the obligation of the person bound by the vow."—Kearney, *The Principles of Delegation,* 48.

[10] Cf. canons 499, § 1; 500, § 1.

[11] *AAS,* I (1909), 7 ff; *Fontes,* n. 682.

[12] Const. *"Immensa aeterni Dei"—Bull. Rom. Taur.,* VIII, 985. These Congregations were instituted separately, but later united by Pope Clement VIII in 1601.

(1698) [13], and the "*Congregatio de Statu Regularium Ordinum*" (instituted by Pope Pius IX in 1847).[14]

The S. Congregation for Religious has exclusive jurisdiction over the various religious institutes, including the communities or societies which have no vows but which lead a community life after the manner of religious. Their government, discipline, studies, goods and property, privileges, and dispensations from the common law of the Church, with the exception of the eucharistic fast for the celebration of Mass (which is reserved to the Holy Office), are subject to this S. Congregation. In districts subject to the Sacred Congregation of the Propagation of the Faith, however, certain of these matters come under the jurisdiction of that body. [15]

All religious are subject to the Supreme Pontiff as their highest superior, whom they are bound to obey under an additional obligation arising from the vow of obedience. [16] In addition to the obedience due to the Supreme Pontiff and the respective religious superiors, there is a further obedience due, in a limited degree, to the intermediate jurisdiction of the local ordinary. The limits of this obedience will be considered in this study in its relation to one particular class of religious—women religious professed in congregations of pontifical approval.

A religious congregation is an institute whose members make profession of simple vows only, whether perpetual or temporary.[17] The Code of Canon Law draws the distinction between

[13] Innocent XII, const. "*Debitum pastoralis officii,*" 4 aug. 1698—*Bull. Rom. Taur.*, XX, 824.

[14] Const. "*Ubi primum,*" 17 iun. 1847— *Pii IX Pontificis Maximi Acta*, I, 46.

[15] Cf. canon 251: Woywod, *A Practical Commentary on the Code of Canon Law* (4. ed., New York: Wagner, 1932), I, 98; Schaefer, *De Religiosis ad Normam Codicis Iuris Canonici* (Muenster i.W.; Ex Officina Libraria Aschendorff, 1927), n. 91; Maroto, "Annotationes"—*CpRM*, II (1921), 98-101.

[16] Cf. canon 499, § 1; Schaefer, *De Religiosis*, n. 90.

[17] Cf. canon 488, 2°.

orders and congregations on the basis of the quality of the vows professed. In orders alone solemn vows are pronounced, while the vows of members of congregations are simple. Both vows are public, that is, accepted as such in the name of the Church by a legitimate superior or delegate. The name "Religious Congregation" embraces, therefore, every institute of religious who lead a common life under the public simple vows of poverty, chastity and obedience.[18] To such congregations of women were applied at various times and under different conditions the terms "institutes," "conservatories," "societies", "sodalities", etc.

The congregations must be distinguished from those groups which, while living a community life according to a definite rule, do not, however, take public vows. These are more properly called lay congregations, and in the Code are separated from religious congregations, being provided for in a special title: *"Societies of men and women living in a community without vows"*. This treatise does not deal with such lay congregations.[19]

It may be briefly noted that the nature of the distinction between solemn and simple vows is unsettled by theologians.[20] Pope Boniface VIII (1294-1303), in answer to a question as to which vows were solemn, declared that, since the solemnity of

[18] Until the present century only Orders enjoyed the name of religions, and their members the name of religious. These members were also known as regulars. Cf. Wernz-Vidal, *Ius Canonicum,* III, n. 15; Steiger, "De Propagatione et Diffusione Vitae Religiosae. Synopsis Historica."—*Periodica,* XIII (1924), (171).

[19] Cf. canon 673 ff.

[20] "S. Thomas putat sollemnitatem votorum in quadam consecratione personae consistere, *S. Theol.* 2, 2, q. 88, a. 7; iuxta Suarez in absoluta et ab utraque parte irrevocabili traditione simulque in vi inhabilitandi actus contrarios, *De Religione,* tract. VII, 1. 2, cap. 7, n. 3 ss; Vermeersch docet sollemnitatem in votis prout in aliis actibus legitimis in eo esse quod certa authentica forma servetur, quam Ecclesia statuit ei adnectens specialem iuridicam tutelam (cf. can. 1308, § 2), *De Religiosis,* II, 13 ss." —Schaefer, *De Religiosis,* n. 264, note 2. Cf. Fanfani, *De Iure Religiosorum ad Normam Codicis Iuris Canonici* (2. ed., Romae: Marietti, 1925), n. 216; Bouix, *Tractatus de Iure Regularium* (3. ed., 2 vols., Paris, 1857), I, 86. For a good summation of the arguments cf. Raus, *Insti-*

a vow depended solely on its constitution as such by the Church, that vow alone was solemn which was solemnized by the reception of sacred orders or by profession made in one of the religions approved by the Apostolic See.[21]

In addition to the distinction growing out of the nature of their vows, religious are also distinguished by the source of their ecclesiastical approbation. An institute is called pontifical (*iuris pontificii*) if it has received approbation or at least a decree of praise (*decretum laudis*) from the Holy See. If the institute, having been canonically erected by a local ordinary, has not yet obtained a decree of approbation or commendation from the Apostolic See, it is considered diocesan. [22]

To any study of the jurisdiction of the local ordinary in relation to religious should be added a brief notion of exemption. In law, exemption has a specific meaning and technical use in regard to religious. The definition given by Ferraris describes exemption as "a privilege by which a person or place is freed and withdrawn from the jurisdiction of bishops or ordinaries, and made subject immediately to the Supreme Pontiff." [23] Orders are now granted exemption by common law, congregations only by particular concession. [24]

The independence of exempt institutes from the external control of the local ordinary is greater than if they were merely

tutiones canonicae (2. ed., Paris: Emmanuel Vitte, 1921), p. 307 ff.; Frey, *The Act of Religious Profession,* The Catholic University of America, Canon Law Studies, N. 63 (Washington, D. C.: Catholic University, 1931), p. 31 ff.

[21] C. unic., *de voto,* III, 15, in VI°.

[22] Cf. Gallik, *The Rights and Duties of Bishops Regarding Diocesan Sisterhoods.* A Dissertation submitted to the Faculty of Canon Law at the International Pontifical Institute "Angelicum" at Rome (St. Paul, Minn.: Wanderer Printing Co., 1939), p. 25.

[23] Ferraris, *Prompta Bibliotheca Canonica, Iuridica, Moralis, Theologica necnon Ascetica, Polemica, Rubristica, Historica,* 9 vols. (Romae, 1885-1899) s.v. "Regulares," art. II, n. 1; Vermeersch, *De Religiosis Institutis et Personis,* I (2. ed., 1907), n. 363 ff.

[24] Schaefer, *De Religiosis,* n. 51; canon 618, § 1.

of pontifical approval, for their ultimate obedience is transferred directly to the Supreme Pontiff.[25] For exempt religious institutes depend directly on the Holy See and not on the local ordinary except where relative to the cases expressly specified in law.[26]

It may be observed, however, that institutes of women of pontifical approval may be subject to superiors of exempt communities of men. With such communities of women this study has at most an incidental concern. The direct interest here is with those religious families of women within the Church that are non-exempt. All religious institutes of simple vows are not exempt, except when so favored by special privilege.[27]

The privilege of exemption grew by wider application along with the growth and diversification of religious orders. It is not within the scope of the present work to conduct a detailed investigation into the history of religious orders or of the special juridical autonomy they receive through exemption. However, it is not amiss to make the following observations concerning the origins of exemption:

First, during the early centuries of the Church, those who embraced the religious life remained under the power of the local bishop and his jurisdiction knew no exception for them.[28] The Council of Chalcedon (451) in canons 4 and 8 did not recog-

[25] Cf. canon 499, § 1; D'Angelo, *La Esenzione dei Religiosi Nella Vigente Disciplina Ecclesiastica* (Torino: L. I. C. E., 1929), p. 2.

[26] Cf. canon 615.

[27] Cf. canon 618, § 1.

[28] Cf. D'Angelo, *La Esenzione dei Religiosi*, p. 1; Schaefer, *De Religiosis*, n. 416; Vermeersch, *De Religiosis Institutis et Personis*, I, n. 363; Bondini, *De Privilegio Exemptionis seu De Regularium Immunitate Ab Ordinariorum Locorum Iurisdictione Prout in Novo Iuris Canonici Sancitur* (Romae: Desclée et Socii, 1919), p. 7 ff; Schiewietz, "Geschichte und Organisation der Pachomianischen Klöster im viertem Jahrhundert," *Archiv für katholisches Kirchenrecht* (hereafter to be abbreviated *AKKR*) LXXXII (1902), 454-475.

nize any exception to the general law of the Church for religious as a group.[29]

Second, when such exemption was introduced and authorized in the common law, it was restricted to the religious who were juridically recognized at the time, that is, it was understood of those who had professed vows in an order approved by the Holy See.[30]

It may be noted that some few congregations of simple vows have obtained by special grant of the Holy See a measure of exemption practically equal to that enjoyed by orders (notably in the case of the Passionists and the Redemptorists).[31] But, in the Constitution *"Conditae a Christo"* of Pope Leo XIII, in which the relations of the congregations of simple vows to the bishops were more clearly defined, real exemption was not granted generally, but rather particular provisions for internal government were made.[32]

[29] Hefele-Leclercq, *Histoire des Conciles* (10 vols., Paris, 1907-1938), II, 779, 789.

[30] "Privilegia quae a iure communi dimanant . . . ad Ordines regulares . . . spectant. . . . Ista namque Instituta (i.e. votorum simplicium) nullum ex se, et a iure privilegium habent. Cum ab Apostolica Sede approbata sint nullo eis concesso privilegio, exempta tantum sunt in iis, quae in Statutis et Constitutionibus a S. Sede approbatis continentur, scilicet subiiciuntur iurisdictioni Episcoproum, salvo eorum Instituto et Constitutitionibus ut supra approbatis. Ut igitur alia privilegia habeant, oportet ut ea a S. Sede obtineant."—*Collectanea in usum Secretariae Sacrae Congregationis Episcoprum et Regularium* (ed. Bizzarri, Romae, 1885), 742 (hereafter this volume will be referred to as *Coll. S. C. Ep. et Reg.*). Cf. also Cappello, *De Visitatione SS. Liminum et Dioeceseon ac de Relatione S. Sedi Exhibenda* (2 vols., Romae: Pustet, 1913), II, 70.

[31] Pope Clement XIV conceded many privileges to the Passionists. Cf. const. *"Supremi apostolatus,"* 16 nov. 1769—*Bull. Rom. Cont.*, VII, 73. For the privileges of the Redemptorists cf. Benedict XIV, const. *"Pastoris aeterni,"* 11 aug. 1757—*Bull. Rom. Cont.*, VI, 2111; Pius VI, const. *"Sacrosanctum,"* 27 aug. 1789—*Bull. Rom. Cont.*, X, 2111; Pius XII const. *"Qui sicut boni,"* 9 ian. 1807—*Bull. Rom. Cont.*, XI, 887. Cf. also Bernardus a Vasto, *De Communicatione Privilegiorum Praesertim Inter Religiones* (Aquilae in Vestinis, 1936), 35.

[32] Leo XIII, const. *"Conditae a Christo,"* 8 dec. 1900—*Codicis Iuris*

Canonici Fontes cura Emi. Petri Card. Gasparri editi, 9 vols. (Romae, Later Civitate Vaticana: Typis Polyglottis Vaticanis, 1923-1939) (Vols. VII-IX *ed. cura et studio Emi. Iustiniani Card. Serédi*) (hereafter this work will be referred to as *Fontes*), n. 644; "Hinc affirmanda erat Ordinariorum iurisdictio, sed simul determinanda ac definienda, et ex adversa parte exemptio formaliter denegabatur Congregationibus, sed practice et aequivalenter aliquo modo recognoscebatur."—Larraona, "Commentarium Codicis"—*CpRM,* I (1920), 171, note 1.

PART I: HISTORICAL SYNOPSIS

CHAPTER II

FIRST TO THIRTEENTH CENTURY

Article I: Early Ages of Church

The formal recognition by the Church of religious congregations of women of simple vows is of comparatively modern origin. In fact no official recognition in law was accorded them until the last decade of the nineteenth century.

The essence of the religious state draws its source, indeed, from Christ; its social organization, however, and the external and internal evolution of its government are dependent on the Church. No religious foundation obtains juridical and formal recognition until it has been approved by a local bishop or by the Holy See.[1] In view, therefore, of this ecclesiastical recognition, the Church retains the power to suppress the institute or change the rule or constitutions as she may see fit.[2]

To trace the source of jurisdiction of a local bishop over congregations of women of simple vows, it is necessary to sketch out some of the historical background of religious communities in general, and to investigate, at least briefly, their juridical relationship to the local bishop.

In His own life, as well as in His teaching, Christ gave to His Church the three counsels of poverty, chastity, and obedience, which are the nucleus and basis of the religious state, which the Code describes as a stable manner of community life in which the faithful besides observing the common precepts bind

[1] Cf. canon 492; Orth, *The Approbation of Religious Institutes,* The Catholic University of America, Canon Law Studies, No. 71 (Washington, D. C.: Catholic University, 1931), 103 ff.

[2] Pejska, *Ius Canonicum Religiosorum* (3. ed., Friburgi in Br.: Herder, 1927), 13.

themselves to the observance of the evangelical counsels by the vows of obedience, chastity and poverty.[3]

In pursuit of this life of perfection, the first religious were the *virgins* and *ascetics* of the early years of the Church. In the beginning, many who sought to devote themselves more fully to the worship of God and the practice of the counsels strove after a life of perfection in the midst of their own family circle.[4] In the course of time, however, they began to separate themselves from their families and to band together in religious communities in order to live according to a common rule of life.[5] Sometimes they endeavored to live thus in the midst of the christian community; at the period of the persecutions, however, they fled to the solitary life of the desert. Well known are the names of those first religious leaders; St. Paul the Hermit (ca. 234-347), St. Anthony the Abbot (251-356), St. Pachomius (286-346), and St. Hilarion (ca. 291-371).

Monastic life arose naturally from the practices of the ascetic and anchoretic forms of life. St. Pachomius, the author of the first written monastic rule, "gave to the cenobites, whom Anthony had governed by his oral instruction and example, a written rule complete and minute . . . He founded upon the Nile at Tabenne, the first monastery properly so called, or rather a congregation of eight monasteries, each governed by an abbot,

[3] Cf. Matt. XII: 22; XIX: 11, 12, 19, 21; I Cor. VII: 25-27; canon 487.

[4] During the apostolic age some whole communities lived a common life, not unlike the religious life of the later period. Cf. Acts II: 44, 45; IV: 32 ff.; "During the first three centuries all Christians retained the ideals of a special monastic character. They were austere and even rigid in the severity of their faith and the young ardor of their enthusiasm. . . . Their life was more or less hidden amid pagan society. They were of the old world as if they had not been."—Montalembert, *The Monks of the West* (2 vols., Boston: Thomas B. Noonan, 1872), I, 170.

[5] Smith, *Christian Monasticism from the Fourth to the Ninth Century of the Christian Era* (London, 1892), 215; Steiger, "De Propagatione et Diffusione Vitae Religiosae. Synopsis Historica"—*Periodica,* XIII (1924) (29) ff.; Frey, *The Act of Religious Profession*, p. 8 ff.; Pius XI, epist. apost., *"Unigenitus,"* 19 mart. 1924—*AAS.* XVI (1924), 133.

but united by a close tie, and placed under the same general superior. These were filled by many thousands of monks." [6]

The members of these religious communities were considered as ordinary subjects of the local bishop. In fact there was scarcely any juridical distinction made for those who had embraced the religious state. [7] Indeed, it is futile to search for any general legislation for the various communities during the formative period of the Church. For the Church was more concerned at this period with indoctrination than legislation, unless some abuse or some other specific need demanded the enactment of law.

But with the growth of religious life and the end of persecution, monasticism came forth from the desert into the cities and towns. Contact with local bishops was inevitable. Moreover, some abuses began to creep into monastic life, though indeed the great majority of religious were steadfast in their loyalty to their religious aim and were preeminent in sanctity. Legislation and clarification of juridical relationship was deemed useful and necessary.

Article II: The Council of Chalcedon (451)

The Council of Chalcedon (451) may be considered as the source of the first general legislation for religious. This Council was concerned primarily with the errors of a monk, Eutyches, and deemed it best to declare that no new monasteries should be erected without permission of the local bishop. Henceforth all religious communities were to remain entirely subject

[6] Montalembert, *The Monks of the West,* I, 179; Cf. "Regula S. Pachomii"—Migne, *Patrologiae Cursus Completus, Series Latina* (hereafter abbreviated *MPL*) XXIII, 65 ff.; Schaaf, *The Cloister,* The Catholic University of America Canon Law Studies, No. 13 (Washington, D. C.: Catholic University, 1921), 11, 12; Heimbucher, *Die Orden und Kongregationen der katholischen Kirche* (3. ed., Paderborn: Schöningh, 1933-1934), I, 65 ff.

[7] Steiger, "De Propagatione et Diffusione Vitae Religiosae"—*Periodica,* XIII (1924), (48).

to the bishop.[8] Thus any monastery built without permission of the bishop would receive no legal recognition, civil or ecclesiastical, and would have no juristic personality.[9]

In addition to episcopal approval, it seems that pontifical approval or confirmation of religious institutes was sometimes sought for the sake of procuring greater honor and distinction and at times also for the purpose of obtaining the privilege of exemption from episcopal jurisdiction.[10] There was, however, no disposition of the Holy See, during this period, requiring pontifical permission for the founding of an institute; the approval of the bishop was sufficient.[11]

Article III: Monasticism in the West

Weakened by theological discord on the part of heretical monks and enfeebled by persecution by the Byzantine dynasty, monastic life in the East entered into a state of inevitable decline during the sixth century. The enactments of the Council of Chalcedon had not exercised upon the monks of the East a sufficiently efficacious influence to enable them to maintain themselves at the fervent heights of the early centuries.[12]

[8] Council of Chalcedon, Canon 4—Mansi, *Sacrorum Conciliorum Nova et Amplissima Collectio* (Parisiis, 1901-1927) VI, 1226. (Hereafter this collection will be referred to as "*Mansi*"). It may be noted that this canon was later incorporated into the Justinian Law—cf. N. (5, 1); (131, 7).

[9] Orth, *The Approbation of Religious Institutes,* p. 18.

[10] Montalembert, *The Monks of the West,* I, 583 (monastery at Bobbio); *op. cit.* 382 (two monasteries at Autun).

[11] Orth, *op. cit.,* p. 21.

[12] "After an age of unparalleled virtue and fruitfulness—after having presented to the monastic life of all ages, not only immortal models, but also a kind of ideal almost unattainable—the monastic order allowed itself to be overcome through all the Byzantine empire by that enfeeblement and sterility of which Oriental Christianity has been the victim. One by one, those glorious centres of light, knowledge, and life, which the Anthonys, the Hilarions, the Basils, and the Chrysostoms had animated with their celestial light, were extinguished, and disappeared from the pages of history."—Montalembert, *The Monks of the West,* I, 219.

Though in the East this decline of monasticism had begun, St. Benedict gave the greatest impulse to advanced strides in monastic life in the West when he founded his Order in 529. [13] Under the wise and sympathetic jurisdiction of the bishops, monastic life beckoned to increasingly greater numbers of men and women. Monasteries multiplied throughout the West, and the centuries that followed were resplendent with the magnificent work of the orders. [14] When laxity by its inward decay threatened destruction, God in His Providence saw fit to raise up such stalwart reformers as St. Odo, Abbot of Cluny (924-942), and St. Bernard of Clairvaux (1090-1153).[15]

The reforms of the tenth and eleventh centuries at Cluny and Citeaux brought a new plan of organization into religious life. Where monasteries had been separate monastic units and *sui iuris,* the trend now veered to a union of monastic congregations.[16] This change in form of government rendered the juris-

[13] Currier, *History of Religious Orders* (New York, 1913), p. 4 ff.

[14] "The Rule of St. Benedict was the foundation of many other orders. Thus the founder of the *Calmaldolese* (St. Romuald, 1027) and the founder of the *Vallambrosians* (St. John Gualbert, 1073) adopted the Code of the 'Patriarch of Western Monasticism.' The most illustrious branch is that founded by St. Robert at Citeaux, Burgundy, in 1098."—Augustine, *A Commentary on the New Code of Canon Law,* III (5. ed., St. Louis: Herder, 1938), 8.

[15] Cf. Vermeersch, *De Religiosis Institutis et Personis,* I, n. 44.

[16] "The name of one great abbot of Clairvaux, St. Bernard, has given to the Cistercians a lustre which shall never fade. St. Bernard is said to have received two hundred novices, and in the middle of the XIV century his order counted no less than seven hundred abbeys. Their rule was that of St. Benedict, while the more detailed organization is contained in the *Charta Chartatis.* The chief superior is the abbot of Citeaux, who is assisted by four "Father Abbots" and a general chapter held every year. The powers of the chapter were extensive. It could even depose the abbot of Citeaux, though the latter was elected by the monks of Citeaux and the abbots of the other monasteries. Besides, the general chapter elected twenty-five *Definitores,* who were entrusted with the affairs of the Order outside the time of the chapter meeting. This is, if not a deviation from, at least a change of, the Benedictine rule, and, we believe, a wholesome democratic one, which the orders of the following period adopted." Augustine, *A Commentary on the New Code of Canon Law,* III, 8.

diction of a local bishop decidedly ineffective, since a congregation extended through many dioceses. This factor, together with the startling rise of the Mendicant Orders, served as an occasion for the concomitant and more insistent struggle for exemption from the jurisdiction of the local bishop.

Article IV: The Mendicant Orders

The rise of the Mendicant Orders, with their correlated Tertiary groups, followed closely upon the rejuvenation of monasticism. St. Francics of Assisi founded his "Confederation" in 1209 and the rule was approved by Pope Honorius III (1216-1227) on Nov. 29, 1223. [17] The Order of St. Dominic was approved by the same Pontiff in 1216 and the organization proper was established at a chapter held at Bologna in 1220. [18]

A new governmental organization consisting of provinces and local houses was instituted by the Mendicants. [19] Since these provinces of the Mendicant Orders were destined to extend over many different dioceses, exemption from the jurisdiction of the local bishop was sought, for it was alleged that diocesan jurisdiction was indeed inadequate to cope with the supra-diocesan problems.

When this exemption was extended to the Mendicants, the privilege became general to the orders, particularly through communication or participation in the privileges enjoyed by others. But the extent of the exemption could be determined only by the wording of each specific decree, since there were yet few general principles of Canon Law to govern the relationship between exempt institutes and the local bishops. The I General

[17] Bulla *"Solet annuere"—Bull. Rom. Taur.* III, 594.

[18] Honorius III, bulla *"Religiosam vitam,"* 22 dec. 1216—*Bull. Rom. Taur.*, III, 309.

[19] The organization of the Franciscan groups is somewhat similar to the Cistercians in as much as the Minister-General is elected by the general chapter, which may also, upon unanimous vote, depose him. Under the Minister-General are the provincials, and under these are the *custodes.* Cf. Augustine, *A Commentary on the New Code of Canon Law,* III, 11.

Lateran Council (1123) had laid down some general rules of direction to govern the relations between diocesan bishops and religious living in their territory, but these were not sufficiently specific to clarify all points of controversy or to prevent abuse.[20] The Council of Trent (1545-1563) strove still more earnestly to modify some abuses, but did not touch the nature of exemption and what it really implied.[21] Consequently, the controversies continued unabated. Various pontifical Constitutions restored, at least in part, the episcopal jurisdiction over some of the monasteries, especially concerning the matter of visitation.[22] However, after the institution by Pope Sixtus V (1585-1590) of a Congregation of Bishops and a Congregation of Regulars, these two Congregations were united at the beginning of the seventeenth century and formed the most effective means of settling the disputes engendered by claims of exemption.[23] Since that time, the major portion of the affairs of religious in relation to the Holy See and the Church as a whole was dispatched by this Congregation of Bishops and Regulars, continuing thus until the suppression of the Congregation by Pope Pius X, June 29, 1908.[24] And it is to this Congregation that one must trace the source of the greater part of the ensuing legislation for religious.

[20] Cf. cc. 4, 17, 19—*Mansi,* XXI, 285. (Canon 17 was taken into the *Decretum Gratiani,* c. 10, C. XVI, q. 1); Wernz-Vidal, *Ius Canonicum ad Codicis normam exactum,* III: *De Religiosis* (Romae: Universitas Gregoriana, 1933) n. 397. It may be noted that an entire title of the *Corpus Iuris Canonici* (X, *de privilegiis et excessibus privilegiatorum,* V, 33) was devoted to checking the abuses which had followed upon the granting of the privilege of exemption.

[21] *Conc. Trid.,* Sess. XXIV, *de ref.,* c. 11; Sess. XXV, *de regularibus,* cc. 8-14.

[22] Cf. Innocent X, const. *"Cum sicut,"* 14 maii 1648—*Fontes,* n. 232; Benedict XIV, const. *"Firmandis,"* 6 nov. 1744—*Fontes* n. 349; const., *"Apostolicum ministerium,"* 30 maii, 1753—*Fontes* n. 425; Leo XIII, const., *"Romanos Pontifices,"* 8 maii, 1881—*Fontes* n. 582.

[23] Bulla *"Immensa aeterni Dei,"* 21 ian. 1588—*Bull. Rom. Taur.,* VIII, 985.

[24] Const. "Sapienti Consilio"—*AAS,* I (1909) 7 ff.; *Fontes,* n. 682.

Chapter III

THIRTEENTH TO EIGHTEENTH CENTURY

Article I: IV General Lateran Council (1215) and II General Council of Lyons (1274)

With the rejuvenation of monasticism and the rise of the Mendicant Orders, Pope Innocent III (1198-1216) saw the concomitant danger inherent in an uncontrolled expansion. Especially unwise he considered the rise of too many distinct communities. Aside from the loss of dignity in the eyes of the faithful, the communities would likely suffer also from economic necessity arising from unnecessary competition. In the IV General Lateran Council (1215), therefore, the right of approbation and institution was taken from the local bishop and reserved directly to the Holy See.[1]

The foundation of the Mendicant Orders, however, continued notwithstanding this regulation of the Council. Consequently the II General Council of Lyons (1274) in its twenty-third canon reaffirmed the law of Pope Innocent III in more emphatic terms, making it applicable to all institutes founded since 1215 except those specifically approved by the Holy See.[2]

These two enactments abrogated the law of the Council of Chalcedon (451) and deprived the local bishop of the right of approbation. Henceforth the approbation of religious orders was

[1] Canon 13: "Ne nimia religionum diversitas gravem in Ecclesia Dei confusionem inducat, firmiter prohibemus ne quis de cetero novam religionem inveniat; sed quicumque voluerit ad religionem converti, unam de approbatis assumat. Similter qui voluerit religiosam domum fundare de novo, regulam et institutionem accipiat de religionibus approbatis."—C. 9, X, *de religiosis domibus,* III, 36.

[2] C. unic., *de religiosis domibus,* III, 17 in VI°. The Franciscans, Dominicans, Augustinians and Carmelites, who had been founded during this era, had obtained special approbation of the Holy See and were not included in the prohibition. Cf. Schaefer, *De Religiosis, n.* 64.

a *causa major* reserved to the Holy See.[3] These enactments, however, were not wholly observed in practice. The Council of Trent did not confirm them and the Holy See itself did not strive for constant enforcement of them.[4]

Custom, even when contrary to the written law, can obtain the force of law by the consent of competent ecclesiastical superiors, provided it is reasonable and juridcally entrenched by continued and uninterrupted usage. Thus the juridical necessity of pontifical approbation for all religious congregations soon began to yield to contrary custom. Many religious institutes were erected in fact, especially during the period that followed the Protestant Revolt, with the sole permission of the local bishop. To this various Popes gave their tacit consent.[5]

[3] "A comparison of can. 13 of the IV General Council of the Lateran with can. 23 of the II General Council of Lyons brings to evidence the fact that the latter repeats the former, but also goes farther. For in the Council of Lyons those orders which had been formed since the year 1215 without papal consent, even though approved by the bishop, were absolutely forbidden and the faithful were prohibited from leading a religious life in these same communities; and whatever effects may have followed their profession were expressly invalidated by the positive action of the Pope. The law was only for those living in a community, professing the same rule, and wearing a special garb distinctive of their calling."—Orth, *The Approbation of Religious Institutes,* p. 34. Bouix, (*Tractatus de Iure Regularium,* I, 291) extends this prohibition to establishment even of congregations.

[4] Cf. Bouix, *op. cit.,* I, 212.

[5] Bouix (*op. cit.,* I, 210) mentions in particular: a. Sisters of Annunciation founded by St. Joan of Valois with permission of the ordinary and later confirmed by Pope Alexander VI, Feb., 1501. b. Hospital Sisters of St. Joseph, founded in the diocese of Angers in 1642, approved by Pope Alexander VII, Jan. 8, 1666, with no mention of the permission of the Apostolic See for its foundation. c. The Sisters of St. Joseph, first approved by the Bishop of Annecy, Sept. 23, 1661, with no mention of the permission of the Holy See. d. The Christian Brothers, the Marists, the Sisters of the Holy Family, the Society of Mary Reparatrix. Cf. Schaaf, *The Cloister,* p. 54; Lucidi, *De Visitatione Sacrorum Liminum. Instructio S. Congr. Concilii* (3. ed., Romae, 1883), II, n. 260 ff.

ARTICLE II: THE COUNCIL OF TRENT; THE CONSTITUTION *"Circa Pastoralis"* OF POPE PIUS V

In treating of regulars and nuns, the twenty-fifth session of the Council of Trent (1545-1563) was concerned more with the reform of abuses of discipline rather than the prohibition against new foundations. For the orders of women the Council accorded to the bishop, or his representative, the right to preside at the elections of abbesses, prioresses and superioresses.[6] To him was ascribed the right and duty of canonical visitation of all religious houses of women; and in particular he was charged with the entire superintendence of the observance of the cloister.[7] At the time of the reception of the habit of the order, as also at the profession made by a candidate, the bishop was to investigate and assure the voluntary character of entrance on the part of the candidate.[8] The appointment or confirmation of ordinary and extraordinary confessors for religious houses of women was to be made by the local bishop.[9] Finally he was charged with supervision of the management of the property of the orders and the houses of women religious.[10]

In the matter of the cloister the Council of Trent renewed the legislation of Pope Boniface VIII (1294-1303) and declared that enclosure for nuns (women in solemn vows) must be enforced. Boniface VIII in the Constitution *"Periculoso"* had commanded that all women who have made religious profession should live in perpetual enclosure and had forbidden them to leave their monastery for any reason, except in the case of evident danger or if one had become a cause of scandal to others.[11]

Three years after the Council of Trent, Pope Pius V (1566-1572) decided to enforce the declaration of the Council concerning

[6] Sess. XXV, *de regularibus*, c. 7.

[7] *Ibid.*, c. 5.

[8] *Ibid.*, c. 17.

[9] *Ibid.*, c. 10.

[10] *Ibid.*, c. 17.

[11] C. un., *de statu regularium*, III, 16 in VI°; cf. Schaaf, *The Cloister*, p. 43 ff.

this matter of enclosure for women religious. Determined that the provisions of the Council should be properly enforced, he extended the cloister to *all* women religious, any custom to the contrary notwithstanding.[12]

The intention of Pope Pius V was clearly that of dissolving any congregation of women living in common without solemn vows and strict enclosure. There can be no doubt about his wish to eliminate from the Church all manner of community life except that which was approved by the long tradition of the Church, that is, such as was in accordance with the norms of strict regulars. As later events proved, the efforts of Pius V never fully achieved their purpose. But his enactments did serve, for the ensuing three hundred years, as a most formidable obstacle to the establishment and juridical recognition of institutes of women religious of simple vows. The circumstances of the foundation and change in the Order of the Visitation of St. Francis de Sales serves as an excellent illustration of the difficulties ensuing from this legislation of Pope Pius V.

During the first decade of the seventeenth century St. Francis de Sales had founded at Annecy the Congregation of the Visitation with simple vows and had placed Jane de Chantal at its head. The principal end of the institute was the visitation of the poor and the sick. When the Congregation extended into the Archdiocese of Lyons, Cardinal de Marquemont demanded that the institute adopt solemn vows and strict enclosure. St. Francis de Sales, realizing that solemn vows and strict enclosure were incompatible with the primary work of the institute, wrote to Cardinal Bellarmine at Rome to ask if strict enclosure must be adopted by all institutes of women. Cardinal Bellarmine replied that this strict enclosure was not absolutely necessary for every institute of women religious, since there had been women religious both in the East and in the West, before the time of Boniface VIII, who were not bound to the observance of the cloister. As an extant example in the city of Rome, he cited the convent of noble ladies

[12] Const. *"Circa pastoralis,"* 29 maii 1566—*Bull. Rom. Taur.*, VII, 447; cf. also bulla *"Lubricum vitae genus,"* 17 nov. 1568— *op. cit.* VII, 725; const. *"Ex incumbenti,"* 17 sept. 1569—*op. cit.* VII, 772.

founded by St. Francis of Rome, who were living at that very period without papal enclosure or solemn profession, contrary to the law of Pius V.

St. Francis de Sales "clung to his humble little Congregation, without cloister, without solemn vows, living in humility and prayer and pouring out its heart in works of charity. But, finally, the persistence of Cardinal de Marquemont, the species of threat that terminated his *"Memoire,"* and, on the other hand, the mild and condescending disposition of the Saint, joined to the little confidence he had in his own lights, determined him, after long discussions of which we have no record, to make whatever concessions the Archbishop of Lyons desired."[13] The Congregation of the Visitation with simple vows became the Order of the Visitation with solemn vows and enclosure.

Article III: Early Institutes of Simple Vows

The efforts of Pope Pius V, as has been stated, never fully achieved their purpose. Notwithstanding his unmistakable legislation, many houses of simple vows continued to exist without strict enclosure. Towards these institutes the Holy See evolved the policy of tacit permission, declaring them subject to the local ordinary, but lacking any positive pontifical approval as an institute. Thus the successors of Pope Pius V found themselves in the anomalous position of seeing and recognizing the utility of certain communities and the abundant fruits of their work, of permitting their existence and even in some cases of approving

[13] Bougaud, *St. Chantal and the Foundation of the Visitation* (translated from the 11th French edition by a Visitandine, New York, 1895), I, 396. It is interesting to note that the original constitution of the Sisters of the Visitation was accepted from the hands of St. Francis de Sales by Madame de Villeneuve, who used it in the foundation of her Institute of the Daughters of the Cross, which received the approbation of Msgr. Jean François de Condi, Archbishop of Paris, in 1640. The American Foundation of the Daughters of the Cross was made in Louisiana under Bishop Martin in 1855. Cf. *Across Three Centuries, A History of the Congregation of the Daughters of the Cross* 1625-1930, by Sister Saint Ignatius, D. C. (Benziger Bros.: New York, 1932), p. 24.

their manner of life, and at the same time of denying them official approbation.[14]

In 1572 St. Charles Borromeo, in order to further the work of reformation in his archdiocese, called a group of Ursulines to Milan and, under the authority of Pope Gregory XIII (1572-1585), instituted them as a community of simple vows. He placed them under the jurisdiction of the local bishop and, in the provincial Synod, declared that he knew of no better aid to the work of reform than these institutes.[15]

In fact, the great majority of communities of women religious founded during the seventeenth and eighteenth centuries became institutes of simple vows. Remarkable for the practical scope of their work, they devoted their lives to the nursing of the sick, the instruction of children, and to other charitable purposes. To carry on the charitable and educational work for which they were founded, it was necessary for such women religious to be free of the strict enclosure; yet without cloister they could not profess solemn vows or receive pontifical recognition.[16]

The Holy See consistently refused to recognize these women as true religious or to approve their institutes, and the whole problem was left to the jurisdiction and judgement of the local bishop. The

[14] Schaefer, *De Religiosis,* n. 67.

[15] Heimbucher, *Die Orden und Kongregationen,* I, 632.

[16] Cf. Lucidi, *De Visitatione Sacrorum Liminum,* II, n. 265. "Among the new congregations devoted to nursing the sick, to teaching children, and to care of the female sex were: (1) *The Sisters of Charity, Filles de la charité,* divided into two branches, the more numerous being that founded at Paris in 1633 by St. Vincent de Paul with the assistance of a pious widow Le Gras. The smaller branch is that of the Sisters of St. Charles Borromeo, established at Nancy in 1652. (2) *The English Ladies,* who arose out of the remains of a Society of Jesuitesses, founded by Mary Ward at St. Omer for the education of girls (1609). The Society was dissolved for certain irregularities (1631), but a few of its members, having obtained permission to fulfill their simple vows in the world under the supervision of the diocesan bishop, again united themselves into a community. (3) *The Sisters of Refuge,* founded by P. Eudes at Caen for the reclaiming of fallen women. (Through a union of houses, this community later became the community of the Good Shepherd)."—Funk, *A Manual of Church History* (St. Louis: Herder, 1910), II, 171.

only exception of attitude of the Holy See to the profession of simple vows may be noted here, though it had no direct infiuence on the juridical development under consideration. Pope Gregory XIII (1572-1585)[17] officially affirmed that those professing only simple vows in the Society of Jesus were to be recognized as religious in the true sense of the word. The majority of the members of the Society of Jesus did not advance to solemn profession, but by this disposition the Pope placed those who remained in simple profession on a par with those who were professed solemnly. This was a decided innovation in the traditional stand of the Church. That its novelty raised a controversy is evident from the wording of the Bull *"Ascendente Domino"*[18] in, which the previous declaration was reemphasized and vigorously defended. It is true that the words of the Pope has as their object a particular group, but they are sufficient to prove that simple profession itself was not inconsonant with the true religious state.[19] This is the only exception, until the present century, to the general practice of the Church and is referred to by the Congregation of Bishops and Regulars as a derogation of the general discipline.[20]

Even the communities of Tertiaries lost the privilege of exemtion which they had enjoyed under Pope Leo X (1513-1521), and were left entirely to the jurisdiction of the local bishops, as is evident from the instruction issued by the Congregation for the Propagration of the Faith on January 17, 1763.[21] Although they continued to exist as tolerated by the Holy See, they were in no way to be understood as approved, nor could their houses be considered as canonically erected houses, but rather as dwellings (*domicilia*) established contrary to the mind of the Holy See. In consequence, they were subject entirely to the jurisdiction of the local bishop

It is true that the Holy See occasionaly gave approval to the rule of a "conservatory" or institute of women during this period,

[17] Bulla *"Quanto fructuosius,"* 1 feb. 1583—Fontes, n. 150.

[18] Const. *"Ascendente Domino,"* 25 maii, 1584—*Fontes,* n. 153.

[19] Larraona, *"Commentarium"*—*CpRM,* I (1920), 45.

[20] Cf. *Coll. S. C. Ep. et Reg.,* p. 744.

[21] Cf. *Coll. S. C. P. F.,* n. 445.

though they lived without the cloister which had been demanded by the decretal of Pope Boniface VIII, the decrees of the Council of Trent, and the Constitution *"Circa Pastoralis"* of Pope Pius V. This approbation, however, extended only to the rule as such, and not to the institute itself. This was definitely stated when approbation was given to the rule, by the addition of the following clause: *"Ceterum non intendimus per praesentes ipsum conservatorium in aliquo approbare."*[22]

[22] Lucidi, *De Visitatione Sacrorum Liminum,* II, n. 266; cf. Benedict XIV const. *"Quamvis iusto,"* 30 apr. 1749, § 5—*Fontes,* n. 398.

Chapter IV

THE EIGHTEENTH CENTURY

The Constitution *"Quamvis iusto"* of Pope Benedict XIV.

In the face of such a definite dearth of juridical norms of guidance in the relations of jurisdiction between the local bishop and the communities of women of simple vows one can understand that conflict and controversy could easily arise, especially since such communities were increasing so rapidly in number. This conflict was brought to a focal point by the refusal of a house of the Congregation of English Ladies (Virgines Anglicanae), in Germany, to recognize the authority of the Bishop of Augsburg. It was fortunate that, at the time that the matter was brought before the Holy See, the reigning Pontiff was Pope Benedict XIV (1740-1758), one of the greatest canonists of all times.

Having discussed the matter thoroughly with a commission of Cardinals, Pope Benedict XIV issued the famous Constitution *"Quamvis iusto,"* wherein he discussed the history and background of the case and drew eight practical conclusions as norms of guidance and decision.[1] Though directed to one particular institute, this constitution served as a basis for all subsequent juridical decisions for similar institutes during the next century and a half, and can be considered as the first juridical outline of a constitution for congregations of women of simple vows.[2]

The constitution mentions that the English Ladies were sometimes confused with the Jesuitesses, whose institute they were thought to have renewed. In 1609, a society of Jesuitesses had been founded by Mary Ward (*Marie de Warth, or della Guardia*) for the education of youth. Houses had been established in dioceses without approval of the local bishops and the members of the

[1] Const. *"Quamvis iusto,"* 30 apr. 1749—*Fontes,* n. 398.

[2] Cf. Schaefer, *De Religiosis,* n. 13; Lucidi, *De Visitatione Sacrorum Liminum,* II, n. 267 ff; Larraona, "Commentarium in Partem Secundam Libri II Codicis," *CpRM,* I (1920), 138, note 20.

society had claimed to be subject to the general superior and not to the local ordinary The society had been suppressed by Pope Urban VIII (1623-1644) in 1631.

Pope Benedict XIV, in drawing sharp distinction between the English Ladies and the Jesuitesses, recounted the origin of the Institute of the English Ladies, tracing their history during the period of exile from England because of persecution and detailing their work in Germany until the time of their controversy with the Bishop of Augsburg. He also gave an account of the efforts of Mary Ward to reestablish her own Institute against the prohibitions of the bishops and the Holy See and, as stated above, he definitely classified the English Ladies as distinct and separate from the group that Mary Ward had founded and had attempted to reestablish.

In determining the juridical rights of the Bishop, the Pope declared that the constitutions of the English Ladies which had been approved by Pope Clement XI were to be observed, with the right of recourse to the Holy See for any changes that might be needed. Members of the institute, however, were not to be considered as true religious, since they had taken only simple vows, and they were to be subject to the jurisdiction and correction of the bishop in whose diocese they dwelt. Free choice of appointment of spiritual directors and confessors was left to the local bishop.

In the matter of internal government, it was determined that the superioress-general must be restricted, under the authority of the local bishop, to the visitation of houses, to the supervision of the education of the girls who were under the care of the Institute, and to the transfer of members of the Institute from house to house. Thus the superioress-general did not have supreme authority in internal government, but was subject to the local bishop; she could not claim the exemption of a general-superioress of an order or of an abbess. Her faculties pertained to matters of lesser importance, and were exercised subject to the local bishop under whose jurisdiction the institute existed.

The visitation of the houses by the superioress-general included the right to inquire into discipline, the observance of the constitution, and the local administration, with due subordination to the ordinary of the place to whom she was to submit her report, that he might profit by it for the better direction of his subjects in the institute. Transfer of the members of the institute, as has been stated, was to be made by the superioress-general, but with due consideration accorded to the needs and jurisdiction of the local bishops and the diocese concerned.[3]

This constitution formed the first stepping stone across the line that separated institutes of simple vows from recognition by

[3] Cf. *"Quamvis iusto"*: § 8. " . . . *Primo,* adhuc vigere Constitutionem editam a Summo Pontifice Urbano VIII super suppressione Iesuitissarum, nec ei unquam fuisse derogatum, nec subsistere assertum a nonnullis fundamentum Pontificiae tolerantiae dictae Constitutioni adversantis; *Secundo,* Institutum Virginum Anglicanarum non esse Institutum Iesuitissarum; *Tertio,* Virgines Anglicanas, reprobatis caeteris aliis Constitutionibus, teneri ad observantiam earum tantummodo Constitutionum, quae fuerunt confirmatae a sanctae memoriae Clemente XI. Posse tamen ad Sedem Apostolicam habere recursum, quatenus alias edendas censuerint. . . . § 11 . . . *Quarto,* non posse (Anglicanas Virgines) recognoscere in Matrem, seu Fundatricem Mariam Warth, seu *della Guardia;* multoque minus fas esse ipsis, et quibuscumque aliis, eam invocare, tamquam in Coelis regnantem, ipsique exhibere cultum publicum, vel alium quemcumque actum, per quem eius asserta Sanctitas approbari censeatur. . . . § 13 . . . *Quinto,* Virgines Anglicanas non esse vere Religiosas; promissiones, quae ab ipsis emittuntur, non esse ad summum, nisi Vota simplicia; et transmittendam esse formam, et notificanda verba, quibus dictae promissiones emittuntur. *Sexto,* Virgines Anglicanas, earumque coetus, esse iurisdictioni ordinariae Episcoporum subditos, in quorum Diocesibus sunt; et ad Ordinarios praedictos pertinere, deputare Directores spirituales, et Confessarios, qui sibi apti videantur, sive ex coetu Presbyterorum Saecularium, sive Regularium . . . § 16 . . . *Septimo,* nihil innovandum quoad Superiorissam: eius tamen auctoriatem coercendam esse ad visitationem, superintendentiam in materia educationis Puellarum, translationem Virginum de uno in alium locum; accedente debita subordinatione in praedictis ab Ordinariis Locorum; prout latius explicabitur a Sanctitate Sua in Constitutione suis tempore et loco edenda . . . § 24 . . . *Ultimo,* quod, facta a Virginibus Anglicanis Civitatis Mindelheimensis obligatione observandi contenta in hoc Decreto, restituantur in integrum; Missae in ipsarum Ecclesia celebrentur, uti prius; et Sanctissimum Eucharistiae Sacramentum in ea asservetur; pro qua asservatione Sanctitas Sua, cui id reservatum est, facultatem opportunam indulget Episcopo Augustano."—*Fontes,* n. 398.

the Holy See. Although Pope Benedict XIV repeatedly declared in the constitution that he did not intend to give pontifical approbation to an institute of simple vows,[4] and in consequence the English Ladies were not formally recognized as true religious, yet a formal permission and at least an implicit approbation *in fact* was attained. It is extremely significant, moreover, that after the Constitution *"Quamvis iusto"* the privative phrase *"citra approbationem conservatorii"* was omitted in the approbation of the constitutions of Congregations of women religious, even though the particular institute might not receive full approbation.[5]

[4] Cf. *ibidem,* §§ 13, 23..

[5] "Non nisi paulatim admodum et per gradus, sensim sine sensu ac furtim fere, Congregationes, mulierum praesertim, initio non una de causa aversatae, aegre tolleratae postea, dein permissae, laudatae paulo post ac demum plene approbatae, Religionibus proprie dictis aequiparatae quadantenus fuerunt ac religiosi iuris, exceptis semper privilegiis, participes effectae."—Larraona, "Commentarium in Partem Secundum libri II Codicis"—*CpRM,* I (1920) 46; Schaefer, *De Religiosis,* n. 13.

Chapter V

THE NINETEENTH CENTURY

Article I: The Effects of the French Revolution

Historical events have a powerful influence on the lives of men in their private concerns as in social aspects. And because the religious life of the Church enters into the lives thus affected, her institutions and laws feel the reaction of such events. The force of necessity produces its own results. The traditional attitude of the Church up to the end of the 18th century was almost exclusively in favor of the life of the regulars in religious orders in the strict sense of the word. In the 17th and 18th centuries it had at best exercised an attitude of toleration to the forming, by local bishops, of institutes which did not bind themselves to the strict forms of the life of regulars, in order the better to achieve their purposes of charity and teaching. In the closing years of the 18th century the French Revolution broke over one of the great Catholic lands of Europe and with its consequent political and social turmoil upset the traditions of the ages. The Church was forced to adapt herself to the change. For the effects of the upheaval were felt throughout Europe and disastrous indeed were the consequences to the regular orders.[1]

Monasteries and convents were uprooted, their means of support confiscated, many of their members forced into secularization, and laws adopted which made the life of regulars impossible in civil law or, at least, unstable to the extreme. Solemn vows and papal enclosure, which had long been the safeguard of institutes of women religious, became a menace to their civil rights, since monasteries were deprived of the recognition formerly accorded to their moral personality and were thus denied the capacity of holding title to property.[2]

[1] Cf. Funk, *Manual of Church History,* II, 208 ff.

[2] Larraona, "Commentarium in Partem Secundam libri II Codicis"—*CpRM,* I (1920), 133; Steiger, "De Propagatione et Diffusione Vitae Religiosae"—*Periodica,* XIII (1924), (174).

A general modification of the rule of life of religious orders of women was evolved in this exigency, a modification that was extended to other parts of the world. The Holy See ceased to demand solemn vows, or at least suspended their effects principally in the matter of personal ownership of property.[3]

Nuns who had been exempt from the jurisdiction of the local bishop, having been dependent rather on the jurisdiction of a regular superior, now were placed under the authority and protection of the bishop, as delegate of the Holy See, in those cases where they could continue their religious life. Though they still retained the right to solemn vows (solemn *de iure*), the Holy See declared their vows simple *in fact.*[4] However, their traditional juridical status was preserved either by custom or pontifical rescript, a status that was not identical with the conditions of institutes of simple vows, for the nuns had a right to solemn vows and the spiritual privileges attached thereto. Moreover, since in most cases each house of the order was an independent unit, there was no organization under a central government. Hence, the members of such a house were considered in law as nuns with solemn vows under the jurisdiction of the local bishop. As such they were not affected either by the development of law for institutes of simple vows during the 19th century or by the provisions of the Constitution *"Conditae a Christo"* issued by Pope Leo XIII on December 8, 1900.[5]

[3] *Coll. S. C. Ep. et Reg.*, pp. 72, 86, 412, 451, 454, 487, 723, 736-740; Vermeersch, *De Religiosis Institutis et Personis,* Suppl. p. (81); Lucidi, *De Visitatione Sacrorum Liminum,* II, 269.

[4] Bouix, *Tractatus de Iure Regularium,* I, 500 ff; Maroto, "Annotationes"—*CpRM,* I (1920), 258; Schaefer, *De Religiosis,* n. 47.

[5] This condition remained unchanged after the Code, as is evident from a reply of the Sacred Congregation of Religious on May 22, 1919, to a question proposed by various bishops and religious communities. Cf. *AAS,* XI (1919), 240. Again, a decree of the Congregation of Religious, June 23, 1923, established the status of members of such monasteries as true monastic nuns in the sense of Canon 488, 7°. They are, however, subject to regular superiors, but dependent on the jurisdiction of local ordinaries according to the prescriptions of the Code determining episcopal jurisdiction over monastic nuns. Cf. *AAS,* XV (1923), 357;

Article II: Problems of Centralized Government

The French upheaval effected a changed social status that made demands and presented opportunities for good that the cloistered nuns, in their obligatory seclusion of life, could not meet. Nobly and effectively, however, were the demands for the instruction of the youth, the care of the sick, and the aged and the poor, met by the increasing number of institutes of simple vows. And yet the juridical development of these institutes did not keep pace with the factual. The principal deterrent to their juridical recognition was the necessity of the adjustment of the problem of centralized government in its concurrence with the jurisdiction of the local bishop.

The preservation of unity and stability demanded a centralized government for institutes of simple vows, and yet a centralized government precluded the plenary jurisdiction of one local bishop over an institute extended into several dioceses. Perforce the rights and jurisdiction of the respective local ordinaries, which had been so steadfastly upheld in relation to communities with simple vows, had to be restricted in some measure. Yet, while this departure was reflected in the granting of particular exceptions in the interests of central government for any given institute, the tendency to maintain the traditional power of the ordinary continued manifest in the clause which was always added to the approbation granted to such an institute: *"salva ordinariorum iurisdictione ad praescriptum sacrorum canonum et Apostolicarum constitutionum."*[6]

And yet, in the very application of these canons and Apostolic Constitutions, a gradual development was to establish a new norm

Bastien, *Constitution "Conditae a Christo" de Leon XIII sur les Instituts à Voeux Simples et leurs Relations avec l'authorité Diocésaine* (Rome, 1902), p. 91 ff.

[6] A notable exception, the condition of the Daughters of Charity of St. Vincent de Paul, may not be used as a valid argument to the contrary, for their status was the result of special privilege. Cf. Bastien, *Constitution "Conditae a Christo,"* p. 94 ff.; Heimbucher, *Die Orden und Kongregationen,* II, 463.

for institutes of women of simple vows. An integral application of the law for regulars was impracticable, since so many of the enactments were irrelevant to institutes of simple vows. Thus the Holy See slowly departed from the exacting norms established for regulars with solemn vows, and evolved a new norm for these newly-established institutes of women of simple vows. As these new plans were evolving, the communities remained merely diocesan.

The hesitancy and vacillation of the policy of the Congregation of Bishops and Regulars is well illustrated in the determination of the governmental problem for the institute of the Sisters of St. Joseph. Founded at Le Puy-en-Velay in France in 1630, its constitutions were based on the original rule of the Visitation Sisters, which provided for simple vows. According to the prevailing practice, there was no provision for a general-superioress and each house was fully subject to the local bishop. The houses of the various diocese were associated only in so far as they were subject to the bishop, who could transfer the members from house to house within the diocese, or even to another diocese at the request of the other bishop. In 1826, however, Pope Leo XII (1823-1829) empowered the Bishop of Lyons to appoint a superioress-general to govern the entire community. The bishops of Savoy objected to this arrangement and proposed as a substitute measure that a superioress-general be appointed in each diocese who would govern dependently on the local ordinary.[7]

To promote the unity and stability of the institute, a possible provision, in imitation of the plan of the regular orders, could be the placing of an exempt general-superior, resembling the supreme moderator, over the whole institute.[8] In a second plan, the general-

[7] Cf. *Coll. S. C. Ep. et Reg.*, p. 499 ff.

[8] Pope Benedict XIV, in the const. *"Quamvis iusto,"* 26 Apr. 1749 *(Fontes* n. 398) mentioned incidentally the exempt power of two abbesses. D'Angelo *(La Esenzione dei Religiosi,* p. 20, note 3) adds that jurisdiction could be given to women, if the Church had not otherwise legislated.

superioress could be made directly subject to a clerical superior,[9] or to a Cardinal Protector.

It was the general policy of the Congregation of Bishops and Regulars to forbid the nomination of any bishop as superior general of an institute, lest he encroach upon the jurisdiction of the bishops of other diocese where houses were or could be established.[10] And the Sacred Congregation did not wish to exempt the general-superioress from the jurisdiction of the local bishop without subjecting her, by necessity, to some other source of authority and supervision.

The question concerning the Congregation of the Sisters of St. Joseph was deferred, therefore, until the various chapters could be polled regarding the type of government they desired. When it became clear, however, that the chapters were hopelessly divided in their opinions, the Congregation of Bishops and Regulars imposed the plan of a general-superioress in each diocese, this superioress being dependent upon the ordinary of the diocese. The extent, however, of this dependence on the ordinary of the diocese was not determined specifically and the question was left in midair.[11] Little was done, therefore, to clarify the problem of central government beyond maintaining the traditional authority of the local ordinary.

It may be remarked, in passing, that during two decades of the nineteenth century (1840-1860) the plan of appointing a Cardinal Protector to supervise the administration of the superioress-general and to aid her in her relations with the local bishops was generally adopted. The practice of assigning a Cardinal of the Curia to an institute as Protector seems to have begun in the thirteenth century. St Francis of Assisi in his Rule refers to the

[9] The plan of the Daughters of Charity of St. Vincent de Paul was similar to this. Cf. Bastien, *Directoire Canonique a l'usage des Congregations a Voeux Simples* (3 ed., Bruges: Beyaert, 1923) p. 348.

[10] *Coll. S. C. Ep. et Reg.*, pp. 779, IV, 1°; 779, V, 1°; 780, VI, 5°; 781, VII, 5°; 784, IX, 1°; 785, X 7°; 787, XI, 2°; 788, XIII, 1°; 789, XIV 2°; 792 XVI 1°.

[11] *Coll. S. C. Ep. et Reg.* p. 524.

Cardinal Protector as the governor, protector and corrector of the Order.[12]

The extent of the authority of the Cardinal Protector over the congregations of women of simple vows must be ascertained from the Constitution that gave him appointment. The superioress-general was subject to the Cardinal Protector in a general way and had to consult with him in matters of importance. The latter's office, too, served as a means of unification for the plans that the bishops of the various dioceses may have had concerning the institutes. From the various constitutions it can be seen that, in addition to the general supervision over the superioress-general to see that she performed her office diligently, the Cardinal Protector was endowed with the authority to act as mediator in any controversy between the superioress-general and the bishop.[13] At the election he had the right of presiding and of granting confirmation to the election.[14] He was to be consulted for the approval of the foundation or suppression of houses in the congregation.

In the Constitutions of the Institute of the Good Shepherd of Angers it was proposed that the authority of the Cardinal Protector be delegated to the confessor of the general house of the Institute, but the Congregation of Bishops and Regulars declared that it would not be expedient for a confessor to have such a power in affairs of the external forum.[15]

[12] "And this, moreover, I enjoin on the Ministers by obedience, that they ask of the Lord Pope one of the Cardinals of the Holy Roman Church to be governor, protector and corrector of this Fraternity, that always subject and submissive at the feet of the same Holy Church, firm in the Catholic faith, we may observe the poverty and humility and the holy Gospel of our Lord Jesus Christ, which we have firmly promised."—*The Rule and General Constitutions of the Friars Minor* (Paterson, N. J.: St. Anthony Guild Press, 1936), c. XII, p. xiv.

[13] Cf. *Monacen. et Frisingen.,* Super app. const. inst. nuncup., "Le povere Suore di Nostra Signora 1858"—*Coll. S. C. Ep. et. Reg.,* p. 776; Lucidi, *De Visitatione Sacrorum Liminum,* II, p. 305, n. 387; p. 314, n. 422.

[14] Lucidi, *op. cit.,* pp. 308-310, nn. 400, 405, 409, 410; *Coll. S. C. Ep. et Reg.* p. 775, I, 5°.

[15] Lucidi, *op. cit.,* p. 314, n. 427.

It is interesting to note how steadfastly the S. Congregation of Bishops and Regulars, during the period, defended the authority of the Cardinal Protector when it was assailed.[16] Yet the Code of Canon Law suppressed this same jurisdictional power of the Cardinal Protector, leaving him, except in particular cases, a mere counselor and patron for any institute of women of simple vows.[17]

Article III: The Method of Approbation

To trace, during the nineteenth century, the evolution of the attitude of the Holy See towards the approbation of institutes of women of simple vows, one's search must advance through a maze of decrees, *animadversiones,* responses to *dubia,* decrees by the S. Congregations, and *schemata* for the use of the S. Congregation of Bishops and Regulars.[18]

With the definite and marked increase in institutes of women of simple vows, founded with episcopal approbation but now spread beyond the diocese of their origin, and the increasing concomitant conflicts of jurisdiction inherent in such expansion, these communities soon appealed to Rome for definite pontifical approbation. Thus the S. Congregation of Bishops and Regulars, deluged with such petitions, was forced to evolve a definite norm of action. Consequently a *Method* to be used by the S. Congregation in approving new institutes of simple vows was established.[19]

The petition for approbation had to be accompanied by letters of commendation from the bishops of the diocese wherein the houses of the Institute were established. This petition was then remitted to the local bishop of the mother house of the Institute for verification of facts and frank counsel concerning the end or scope, the foundation, the number of houses and members, the

[16] Lucidi, *op. cit.,* p. 313, n. 418.

[17] Canon 499, § 2; Schaefer, *De Religiosis,* n. 98.

[18] The principal source-book for the *Animadversiones* is the *"Collectanea in usum Secretariae Sacrae Congregationis Episcoporum et Regularium (Coll. S. C. Ep. et. Reg.),* which was edited by Archbishop Bizzarri (Rome, 1885). It is to be regretted that the collection is not more complete.

[19] Cf. *Coll. S. C. Ep. et Reg.,* p. 772.

means of support, the utility, progress and morale of the Institute.[20] A copious list of questions was transmitted by the S. Congregation to the bishop and he was expected to answer these questions with all candour and sincerity.[21]

When this information had been received from the bishop, the case was assigned to one of the consultors of the S. Congregation for more detailed study. If the consultor's report was satisfactory, the S. Congregation usually granted a Decree of Praise (*Decretum Laudis*).[22] This Decree of Praise varied according to circumstances. At times, merely the scope and purpose of the society were praised;[23] at times the Institute together with its scope was accorded praise.[24] In some cases there was an approval of the institute, but nothing beyond a decree of praise for the constitutions.[25] But the general decree of praise included the scope as part of the institute.

[20] The Sacred Congregation was particularly vigilant about the means of support, since the spiritually ambitious so often, in the heat of their fervor, forget about the material aspects of a community. Cf. "Urbevet. sup. app. nov. inst. perp. adorat. SSmi. Cordis Iesu"—Lucidi, *De Visitatione Sacrorum Liminum,* II, p. 257, n. 285.

[21] S. Flori, Super. app. congr. inst. Infantis Iesu:—". . . quando et a quo dicta congregatio erecta fuerit; utrum aliquod laudis decretum a S. Sede obtinuerit; quot sint domus erectae; et quatenus congregatio in aliis etiam dioecesibus diffusa sit, exhibeat testimoniales litteras respectivorum Ordinariorum; quot mulieres professae; quando regulae et constitutiones elucubratae sint: etenim haec C. Congr. constitutiones (et idem de institutis dicendum est) approbare et confirmare minime solet, nisi prius per congruum temporis spatium experientia satis comprobentur, et plures domus instituti erectae sint."—Lucidi, *op. cit.,* p. 256, n. 283.

[22] Cf. Battandier, *Guide Canonique pour les Constitutions des Instituts a Voeux Simples* (6 ed., Paris: Lecoffre, 1923), p. xxvii ff.

[23] Particularly if the Institute had not expanded sufficiently or if some defect was found in the constitutions in that they were opposed to the approved discipline of the S. Congregation or did not properly correspond to the aim of the Institute. Cf. "S. Flori, Super app. const. congr. Infantis Iesu," Sept. 2, 1853; "Ferrarien., Super app. inst. et congr. sor. a B.M.V. sine labe concepta," May 10, 1844—Lucidi *op. cit.*, p. 258, n. 287.

[24] *"Monacen. et Frisingen.,"* Dec. 11, 1853—Lucidi, *loc. cit.*

[25] *Bergomen,* Super app. inst. filiar. Sacratissimi Cordis, May 15, 1841—Lucidi, *De Visitatione Sacrorum Liminum,* II, p. 258, n. 287.

From 1814 to 1862 one hundred and twenty-four societies of men and women religious applied to Rome for approbation. During a period of thirty six years of that time (1814-1850) only five Institutes of women of simple vows received approbation.[26] A detailed list of ensuing approbations may be found in the *Collectanea Sacrae Congregationis Episcoporum et Regularium.*[27]

Even though some institutes of women of simple vows did, indeed, achieve approbation from the S. Congregation of Bishops and Regulars during this period, it must be noted, however, that *formal juridical recognition* of institutes of women of simple vows was not accorded until Pope Leo XIII (1878-1903) published the celebrated Constitution *"Conditae a Christo."*[28]

Article 4: Changes in Constitutions

From this initial period of the concession of a decree of praise for institutes of simple vows by the S. Congregation of Bishops and Regulars stems the classification of Congregations of pontifical approval and of merely diocesan approval, a classification that was perfected in the Constitution *"Conditae a Christo."*

[26] "Filiae SS. Cordis Mariae, Andegavenses," 1821; "Sorores Misericordiae, Cadurcenses," 1824; "Sorores Instructionis Christianae Gandavenses," 1827; "Sorores a S. Theresia, Burdigalenses," 1835; "Congregatio Mulierum ab Infante Iesu, Lisbonenses," 1844—cf. Steiger, "De Propagatione et diffusione vitae religiosae"—*Periodica,* XIII (1924), (176).

[27] Cf. *Coll. S. C. Ep. et Reg.*, p. 808 ff.

[28] Const. *"Conditae a Christo,"* 8 dec. 1900—*Fontes,* n. 644. Regarding this period Archbishop Bizzari remarks: ". . . verum tractu temporis, et praesertim post Galliarum vicissitudines, et civiles leges circa proprietatem bonorum quoad Moniales, S. Sedes instituta votorum simplicium et sine papali clausura pro mulieribus non solum tolerare sed etiam laudare coepit, quin imo postremis hisce temporibus etiam peculiaribus decretis huius S. C. ea approbare non renuit. Haec autem approbatio minus solemnis est, nec confundi debet cum approbatione solemni, quae pro professione votorum solemnium impertiri solet, quando nempe conceditur erectio canonica alicuius Monasterii in quo aliqua ex antiquis regulis ab apostolica Sede approbatis cum votis solemnibus, et clausura papali, assumatur."—*Coll. S. C. Ep. et Reg.*, p. 412, note 1.

In the evolution of legislation for the constitutions of institutes of pontifical approval undoubtedly the provisions of the Constitution *"Quamvis iusto"* were used as a general norm. But many of the component parts of this Constitution were gradually deleted by various declarations and *animadversiones* of the S. Congregation of Bishops and Regulars. As a consequence, very little of the Constitution *"Quamvis iusto"* remained as a practical norm for such institutes at the period of the publication of the Constitution *"Conditae a Christo."* Changes in various constitutions illustrated this evolution.

The Daughters of the Sacred Heart of Jesus at Bergamo were directed by the S. Congregation of Bishops and Regulars to regulate the relations of their superioress-general with the local bishops according to the provisions of the Constitution *"Quamvis iusto."*[29] When their constitutions were approved, however, Pope Pius IX (1846-1878) revoked this declaration of the S. Congregation.[30]

From the changes advised in later constitutions, it is evident that the superioress-general could act independently of the ordinary in the visitation regarding internal matters, in the transfer of sisters from house to house, in some nominations and in all the confirmations of superioresses of houses, mistresses of novices and prefects, and in the reception of postulants.[31]

The permission of the local bishop was necessary for the admission to the reception of the habit and the making of the profession, though in one case mention is made only of the right of the bishop to explore the will of the novices.[32] The bishop was

[29] *S. C. Ep. et Reg.*, Resp. ad dubia, May 14, 1841—Lucidi, *De Visitatione Sacrorum Liminum,* II, p. 327, n. 463. "In approbatione data aliquibus institutis praescripta fuit relatio inter Episcopos dioecesaneos, et Moderatricem generalem iuxta Constitutionem Bened. XIV pro Virginibus Anglicanis incipien. *"Quamvis iusto."* "—*Coll. S. C. Ep. et Reg.*, p. 775 note 1.

[30] Pius IX, breve *"Cum maxima,"* 13 nov. 1847.

[31] *Monacen. et Frisingen.*, Super app. const. inst. nunc. "Le povere Suore di Nostra Signora, 1858"—*Coll. S. C. Ep. et Reg.*, p. 775.

[32] Animadversiones in "Constitutiones Pauperum Ancillarum Iesu" dioecesis Limburgensis, March 23, 1860—*Coll. S. C. Ep. et Reg.*, p. 778, ad 6°.

to preside over the general chapter as Apostolic Delegate and not as local ordinary.[33] His authority was limited in any event by the statutes and constitutions of the institutes, as approved by the Holy See.[34]

As the power of the superioress-general of institutes of women of pontifical approval slowly evolved from the scope of a merely economic administration with perpetual dependence on the local ordinary to that of a more ample controlling power (*potestas dominativa*), there was a consequent diminution of the visitational power of the local ordinary. Thenceforth his visitation extended to general matters, and not to those pertaining properly to the Institute as such, unless contrary provision was made in the approved constitutions.[35]

This was particularly emphasized in a controversy between the Bishop of Nancy and the Sisters of the Good Shepherd concerning the matter of temporal administration.[36] The Bishop of Nancy maintained that the provisions of the Council of Trent and the Bull *"Inscrutabili"* of Gregory XV (1621-1623) accorded to him full supervisory power over the temporal administration of all institutes in his diocese.[37] The Sisters of the Good Shepherd replied that, since the provisions of the Council of Trent and of the Bull *"Inscrutabili"* were intended for institutes of solemn vows, these provisions did not apply to their own institute of simple

[33] *Coll S. C. Ep et Reg.*, pp. 780, 785 ad 4°; 790 ad 15°. This provision was retained in the Const. *"Conditae a Christo" (Fontes* n. 644), but not in the Code (Canon 506, § 4).

statutes and constitutions of the institutes, as approved by the Holy

[34] ". . . *salvis statutis et constitutionibus ab Apostolica Sede approbatis*" was the phrase generally used by the S. Congregation in its declarations, Cf. *Coll. S. C. Ep. et Reg.*, p. 709, note 1.

[35] *Coll. S. C. Ep. et Reg.*, pp. 49, 155, 433, 709 note 1; Larraona, "Commentarium in Partem Secundam libri II Codicis"—*CpRM*, I (1920), 139, note.

[36] Cf. Decr.. *S. C. Ep. et Reg., in causa Nanceyen.*, 27 mar. 1896—*Analecta Ecclesiastica*, IV (1896), 146-156.

[37] Sess. III, *de ref.*, c. 3; Sess. VII, *de ref.*, c. 14; Sess. XIII, *de ref.*. cc. 4, 5; Sess. XXV, *de regularibus et monialibus*, c. 14; Gregorius XV, bulla *"Inscrutabili,"* 5 feb. 1622—*Bull. Rom. Taur.*, XII, 657.

vows. In an institue of simple vows, it was asserted, the administration of the affairs of the community belongs to the community itself, independently of the local bishop, and this administration is conferred on the person of the superioress-general by canonical election. Economic and controlling power, they continued, was essential to her very office as superioress-general. Furthermore, they said, the phrase *"salva iurisdictione Ordinariorum,"* contained in their Constitution, referred to jurisdiction alone and not to controlling power.

The S. Congregation of Bishops and Regulars decided that, even though an account of some part of the administration must necessarily be rendered to the local bishop, nevertheless the temporal administration belonged to the superioress-general and not to the bishop.[38]

Article 5. Conciliar Provisions

Before proceeding to a consideration of the Constitution *"Conditae a Christo"* of Pope Leo XIII, one may usefully complete the picture of this period of development by sketching the attitude of the hierarchy towards this problem of jurisdiction over the new institutes of simple vows. On the one hand, the I Provincial Council of Westminister (1852) and the Plenary Council of Cashel (1853) are offered as examples of particular legislation before the aforementioned *Method* of the S. Congregation of Bishops and Regulars was published; the Plenary Council of Latin America held in Rome in 1899, on the other hand demonstrated the influence of the discipline of the S. Congregation.

The I Provincial Council of Westminister in England maintained the traditional authority of the ordinary and expressly declared that all institutes, except those legitimately subject to a regular superior, were subject to the visitation of the ordinary, even though they were dependent on some other house (i. e., in

38 "An et quomodo Communitas Nanceyen. a Bono Pastore subiiciatur iurisdictioni Ordinarii Diocesani in casu? Resp.: Negative in omnibus." *S. C. Ep. et Reg.,* in causa Nanceyen., 27 mar., 1896—*Analecta Ecclesiastica,* IV (1896), p. 156.

institutes of central government). The economic administration of all non-exempt monasteries, even those of nuns subject to a regular superior in other matters, was subject to the approval of the ordinary and under his vigilance.[39]

The Plenary Council of Cashel refers in general to religious institutes of women with simple vows, declaring that in Ireland they are to be generally subject to the bishop, who is to see that the constitutions are observed.[40]

The Plenary Council of Latin America, on the other hand, demonstrated the influence of a more defined practice. It treated specifically of the houses of institutes of simple vows, declaring that these were under the jurisdiction of the ordinary, but within the limits established by the sacred canons, apostolic constitutions and the constitutions of the institute. It further reminded the ordinary that his authority was such that he could not interfere in those things fhich pertained to the general regime of the entire institute, even though the principal house of the institute was in his diocese.[41] This Council also legislated that not even the smallest change could be made in the constitutions of such institutes, once they were approved, without the consent of the S. Congregation of Bishops and Regulars.[42]

Finally, it is apparent from the *postulatum* prepared for the Vatican Council in 1869 that the attitude of the bishops of France and Belgium was adverse to any legislation that would diminish the power and authority of the bishop over the institutes under his jurisdiction.[43]

[39] *Collectio Lacensis,* III, 844, 945.
[40] *Ibidem,* III, 832.
[41] *Concilium Plenarium Americae Latinae* (Romae, 1902), n. 326.
[42] *Ibidem,* n. 324.
[43] *Collectio Lacensis,* VII, 837, 877.

CHAPTER VI

LEGISLATION WHICH IMMEDIATELY PRECEDED THE CODE

ARTICLE 1: THE CONSTITUTION *"Conditae a Christo"* OF LEO XIII

In the pre-code legislation the *"Magna Charta"* for institutes of simple vows was the Constitution *"Conditae a Christo"* of Pope Leo XIII, published on December 8, 1900.[1] Its salutary prescriptions were the fruit of a century of circumspect consideration and practical disposition of individual cases by the Holy See through the Sacred Congregations. This Constitution placed the institutes of simple vows on a definite juridical basis, established the categories of congregations of pontifical approval and those of merely diocesan approval, and in practical terms defined the relations between the local ordinaries and the institutes.[2]

The Constitution is divided into two chapters, the first treating of institutes of diocesan approval, the second dealing with those of pontifical approval. This classification of the institutes is made even more clear in the *Normae* published by the Holy See in the following year.[3] For the latter document recounts in detail the three steps generally employed by the Holy See in the procedure of granting approval to institutes of simple vows.

At the instance of a favorable report from the ordinary, the S. Congregation may commend the intention of the founder of the institute and the end or scope of the work undertaken.[4] This commendation (*laus intentionis et finis*) has no juridical effect on the status of the institute, since it yet remains a private and

[1] *Fontes,* n. 644.

[2] Cf. Larraona, "Commentarium in Partem Secundam libri II Codicis" —*CpRM* I (1920), 171, note 1.

[3] *Normae secundum quas S. Cong. Episcoporum et Regularium procedere solet in approbandis novis Institutis votorum simplicium* (Romae: Typis S. Cong. de Prop. Fide, 1901).

[4] *Normae,* Art. 1.

diocesan association.[5] If the institute has sufficiently expanded and shown its worth, the Sacred Congregation, at the further petition of the ordinaries, may issue a decree of praise (*decretum laudis*).[6] Once this decree of praise has been issued, the institute ceases to be diocesan and becomes pontifical. The third step is the concession of a decree of approbation (*decretum approbationis instituti*), wherein the Holy See approves and confirms the institute.[7] Though this is the ordinary method of procedure, there may be special instances in which one of these steps may be omitted.

The Constitution *"Conditae a Christo"* followed that of the *"Quamvis iusto"*, for the greater part, in the legislation for institutes of diocesan approval, leaving them subject to the local bishop in practically all matters, though a certain fixed outline was given to the juridical relationship between these institutes and the ordinary.[8] Though there appears in it no trace of strict exemption (i.e., in the external government) for institutes of pontifical approbation, the Constitution made clear provision for their withdrawal from the jurisdiction of the bishop in matters of internal government. Thus the best interests of a community with a central government were served by the assurance of unity in administration and discipline without undue interference. Consequently there was no longer place for any arbitrary disposition of those matters concerning which the Constitution legislated. Since the relationship of the Constitution *"Conditae a Christo"* to the legislation of the Code will be considered in the *Commentary* of this work, only a brief synopsis will be given here to complete the investigation into the historical development of this independence.

In the introductory paragraphs the Constitution *"Conditae a Christo"* refers to the customary verbal formula employed in the approbation of such an Institute as a "pious society of simple

[5] Vermeersch, *De Religiosis Institutis et Personis,* II, (1931).

[6] *Normae,* Arts. 2, 4.

[7] *Ibidem,* Art. 6.

[8] Cf. Gallik, *The Rights and Duties of Bishops Regarding Diocesan Sisterhoods,* p. 14 ff.

vows, under the rule of a general moderator, the jurisdiction of the Ordinaries being respected in conformity with the sacred canons and the apostolic constitutions". From this recognition of the internal government of a superior, Pope Leo XIII deduces that there must be limits placed on the authority of the bishops over such institutes, and that the extent of the superior's administration and rule must be authoritatively defined. It was precisely to determine the relative powers of the bishop and the superior, a question that had long been a source of misunderstanding and difficulty, that the Constitution was published. Hitherto the sacred canons and apostolic constitutions were too numerous and vague and were of little help in determining in detail the extent and limitation of episcopal jurisdiction over these institutes. By force of this Constitution, the administrative power (*potestas dominativa*) of the superior, concerning at least the more important phases of internal government, was determined and stabilized.[9]

The second chapter of the Constitution, in so far as it regards pontifical congregations of women religious and their relationship in law with the bishop, may be divided into four sections: I. The Government of the Institute (Arts. 1, 2, 3): II. The Spiritual Administration (Arts. 3, 5, 8, 10): III. The Temporal Administration (Arts. 9, 11): IV. The Religious Discipline (Arts. 4, 7, 11).[10]

I. The Rights of the Bishop in the Government of the Institute

1. FOUNDATION: The Bishop is accorded the right to consent to or to prohibit the foundation of new religious houses within the limits of his diocese. The law of the Council of Trent for regulars is here extended to congregations of pontifical approval,

[9] Bastien, *Constitution "Conditae a Christo de Leon XIII,* (Bruges: Beyaert, 1902), p. 69 ff.

[10] Article 6, concerning the reception of Sacred Orders, is irrelevant to the purpose of the present study.

in accordance with the constant practice of the S. Congregation of Bishops and Regulars.[11]

2. Reception and Dismissal: The right of the superiors of the institute to decide upon the admission of candidates to the reception of the habit and the making of the profession is confirmed (Art. 1). The bishop, however, retains his right and duty to examine these candidates, in institutes of women, before the reception of the habit and the making of the profession, in accordance with the prescription of the Council of Trent for women religious.[12] The right of the dismissal of members belongs to the religious community, as determined by the approved constitutions (Art. 1). Dispensation from temporary or perpetual vows of profession is reserved to the Holy See (Art. 2).[13]

3. Election: It is the right of the bishop of the diocese where the election takes place to preside, but only as delegate of the Holy See (Art. 1). It may be noted that this Constitution does not provide for any power of confirmation or rejection by the bishop of the religious elected.

4. Government: When the constitutions of an institute have been approved by the Holy See, no bishop has any right to change or modify them, since the jurisdictional power of the bishop is inferior to that of the Sovereign Pontiff.[14] Nor does a bishop have the right to change or modify the regime duly established, in virtue of the approved constitutions, by the general or local superiors of the institute (Art. 2). The rights of the bishop do not extend to the interior regime of the institute

[11] Sess. XXV, *de regularibus et monialibus,* c. 3. It is to be noted that the *beneplacitum apostolicum* had to be obtained for the opening of a novitiate house. Cf. *Coll. S. C. Ep. et Reg.,* pp. 779, 4°; 779, 7°; 787, 15°; 793, 11°.

[12] Sess. XXV, *de regularibus et monialibus,* c. 17.

[13] The basis for this reservation can be found in numerous *animadversiones* to constitutions presented for approbation. Cf. *Coll. S. C. Ep. et Reg., pp.* 777, 11°; 779, 8°; 780, 10°; 781, 7°; 782, 11°; 783, 15°; 788, 5°; 789, 4°, 8°.

[14] Cf. c. 16, X, *de maioritate et obedientia,* I, 33; c. 2, *de electione et electi potestate,* I, 3, in Clem.

which has pontifical approval. Thus, as long as the constitutions are duly observed, the bishop is not to interfere in the transfer of members, the replacing of superiors, or any other such matter that pertains to the internal governing power of the institute.[15]

II. The Rights of the Bishop in the Spiritual Administration

Members of pontifical institutes of women religious may be considered under a double aspect, in as much as they belong to the body of the faithful and in as far as they are also members of a pontifical religious institute. As members of the faithful, they are subject to the bishop in the internal forum (the forum of conscience) (Art. 5). And in the external forum the bishop has jurisdiction over them in matters of censures, in the reservation of cases, in the relaxation of vows not reserved to the Holy See, in the ordering of public prayers and in the granting of dispensations and privileges that can be given by the bishop to all the faithful of his territory.

Furthermore, they are subject to the bishop of the diocese in the following spiritual matters:

1. The erection of churches, as also of public or semi-public oratories, and the celebration of divine service in private oratories (Art. 3).
2. The public ceremonies in churches or chapels, particularly exposition of and benediction with the Blessed Sacrament (Art. 3).
3. The nomination of chaplains, confessors (extraordinary and ordinary), and preachers (Art. 8). This prescription, it may be added, definitely settled a controversy of long standing concerning chaplains.[16] The provision for the nomination of confessors was in accord with the Constitution *"Pastoralis Curae"* of Pope Benedict XIV (1740-1758) and the decree *"Quemadmodum"* of the S. Congregation of Bishops and Regulars.[17]

[15] Cf. Bastien, *Constitution "Conditae a Christo" de Leon XIII*, 67, 68.

[16] Bastien, *Constitution "Conditae a Christo" de Leon XIII*, p. 69; Ferraris *Prompta Bibliotheca*, s. v. "Capellanus monialium," II, 153.

[17] Const. *"Pastoralis Curae,"* 4 aug. 1748—*Fontes* n. 388; decr. *"Quemadomdum"* 17 dec. 1890—*Fontes* n. 2017.

4. The canonical vigilance regarding religious training and instruction, morals, the exercises of piety and the administration of the religious cult in all pensions, orphanages, hospitals, schools, asylums and other such establishments which are administered by institutes of pontifical approval, all privileges duly granted by the Holy See to colleges, schools or other institutions, and never revoked or lost in any other way, being duly honored and safeguarded in their continuance.[18]

III. The Rights of the Bishop in the Temporal Administration

The independence of these institutes in administering temporalities was maintained. However, funds which did not pertain directly to the institute, but which were given to a particular house for purposes of divine worship or public benefit in that place, came under the surveillance of the local bishop. The superioress of the house, indeed, administers them, but is responsible to the bishop in the accounting for the administration (Art. 9)[19].

IV. The Rights of the Bishop in Religious Discipline

1. Cloister: If a community had adopted the episcopal cloister, the bishop had the right of vigilance specified in law. In case of partial enclosure it was also the right of the bishop to see to its observance and to prevent abuses (Art. 4).[20]

[18] *Collectanea S. Congregationis de Propaganda Fide* (Romae: 1907), II, 1386.

[19] Though Pope Gregory XV (const. "*Inscrutabili,*" 5 feb, 1622—*Bull. Rom. Taur.,* XIII, 656) declared that the administrative accounts of the communities of women must be rendered to the bishop and reviewed by him, this enactment was often disregarded by the Holy See in approving the constitutions of many congregations, especially when there was a superior general. Cf. Bastien, *Constitution "Conditae a Christo" de Leon XIII,* 79; S. C. Ep. et Reg. *in causa Nanceyen.,* 27 mar. 1896—*Analecta Ecclesiastica,* IV (1896), 146-156.

[20] Conc. Trid., Sess. XXV, *de regularibus et monialibus,* c. 5; Cf. Schaaf, *The Cloister,* pp. 58, 101, 154.

2. Alms-gathering: When the constitutions of an institute permitted the collection of alms, the provisions of the Constitution *"Singulari quidem"*, of March 27, 1896, were to be followed[21], such collections being made under the vigilance and supervision of the local bishop and only with his express permission.[22] Norms for alms-gathering were later detailed in a Decree of the S. Congregation of Religious, Nov. 21, 1908.[23]

3. Canonical Visitation: As a general principle, in every congregation of simple vows the bishop had the right of canonical visitation in all that concerned his diocese relative to churches, chapels, public oratories, sacristies and confessionals. In congregations of women it was his duty to investigate the manner of discipline, the observance of the rule and of the cloister, the frequency and regularity in the reception of the sacraments and the proper maintenance of morals. The correction of breaches he had to leave to the superiors; only in cases of great import that demanded immediate attention could he act directly, and then he had to report his action to the S. Congregation of Bishops and Regulars (Art. 11).

In the conclusion of the Constitution the Supreme Pontiff stated that he did not intend by it to derogate from any special faculties or privileges granted previously by the Holy See or acquired through legitimate custom or contained in constitutions previously approved by the Holy See. Its provisions, therefore, rather looked to future discipline.

Article 2: The *"Normae"* of 1901; The Constitution *"Dei Providentis"* of Pope Pius X.

The juridical relations between the local bishop and the institutes of simple vows continued to be regulated, for the greater part, by the provisions of the Constitution *"Conditae a*

[21] Cf. *ASS,* XXVIII (1895-1896), 555-558.

[22] *S. C. Ep. et Reg.,* decr. 20 ian. 1769—Vermeersch, *De Religiosis Institutis et Personis, Suppplement,* p. 392, n. 191.

[23] *S. C. de Religiosis,* decr. *"De elesmosynis colligendis"—AAS,* I, (1909), 153-156.

Christo" until the Code. Its legislation, in fact, became the chief source for the Code legislation in this matter.

Six months after this Constitution had been issued, the S. Congregation of Bishops and Regulars published a list of rules, as mentioned above, detailing the procedure and requirements for pontifical approval, entitled: "*Normae secundum quas S. Cong. Episcoporum et Regularium procedere solet in approbandis Novis Institutis votorum simplicium*", 28 iun. 1901.[24]

The first section of these treated of the procedure required for the obtaining of the pontifical approval for institutes and for their constitutions. The second section presented an exemplar or outline for such constitutions. In an Appendix was added a list of the documents that had to be incorporated in a set of constitutions.[25] Rather than law, these rules were recommendations to be followed by an institute desiring pontifical approbation. They marked no substantial change from established legislation, but served to clarify some doubts and to provide a basis for a more definite knowledge of the "*stilus Curiae*".[26]

Even after the enactments of the Constitution "*Conditae a Christo*" and after the publication of the "*Normae*" the bishops still retained comparative freedom in the episcopal approbation of the foundation of new institutes. Fulfillment of the prescriptions of the Council of Trent and of the special rules of recent legislation was indeed necessary. With the startling increase of new diocesan institutes, however, the Holy See soon found that an excess of enthusiasm in approbation by local bishops was too often concomitant with a lack of sufficient diligence and prudence in preliminary investigation. When a petition for pontifical approval of such institutes was presented, in due course, to the S. Congregation of Bishops and Regulars, it was found impossible, on several occasions, to grant such an approval.[27]

[24] The *Normae* were issued in a separate print, Rome, 1901.

[25] Decr., "*Quemadmodum,*" 17 dec. 1890—*Fontes* 2017; decr. "*Auctis admodum,*" 4 nov. 1892; decr. "*Singulari,*" 27 mar. 1896—*ASS,* XXVIII (1895-1896) 555-558; decr. "*Romani pontifices,*" 25 ian. 1898.

[26] Vermeersch, *De Religiosis Institutis et Personis,* II, (128).

[27] Battandier, *Instituts a Voeux Simples,* p. 8 ff.

Pope Pius X, in the Constitution *"Dei Providentis"*, sought to remedy this situation by a more precise determination of the mode of procedure by the local bishop in the episcopal approval of institutes of simple vows.[28] Thenceforth, bishops were counselled not to permit the foundation of a religious institute within the diocese without written permission of the Holy See. In making application for this permission, the bishop submitted a report of the name and purpose of the institute, of its intended work, and of the form of habit to be worn by its members. Once the Holy See had granted this permission, the Bishop could make no changes in these matters on his own authority. As a natural consequence of this provision, the bishops no longer had the power of suppressing even a diocesan institute, once it had been erected in accordance with the provisions of the Holy See.[29]

[28] Pius X, const. *"Dei providentis,"* 16 iul, 1906—*Fontes* n. 675.
[29] Schaefer, *De Religiosis,* n. 77.

PART II COMMENTARY

CHAPTER VII. THE SUMMARY STATEMENT OF STATUS

In the second paragraph of canon 618 the juridical relationship between the local ordinary and the congregations as here treated is outlined in general terms. When the Holy See has placed its approval upon a congregation of women religious, three general limitations upon the jurisdiction of the local ordinary are thereby effected: 1. The local ordinary cannot change the constitutions of the congregation in any way on his own authority; 2. His right to enquire into the economic administration of the congregation is limited; 3. His intervention in the internal government and discipline is restrained.

The constitutions are the particular law of a religious congregation, determining in detail the norms of life within the institute and its government.[1] And to obtain the *decretum laudis* of pontifical approbation these constitutions of the congregation must be sent to the Holy See.[2] Frequently the congregation and the

[1] "The 'Rule' in ecclesiastical law means the group of principles regarding the religious life proposed to their disciples by the first organizers of this kind of life. (In the strict sense of the word there are but four rules, namely, that of St. Basil [d. 379], that of St. Augustine [d. 430], that of St. Benedict [d. 543] and that of St. Francis [d. 1226]). In contrast with the rule thus understood, the constitutions contain the laws which are characteristic of the different institutes which follow the same rule. But since the sixteenth century a great many institutes have arisen which do not follow the ancient rules; in their case the rules are called constitutions."—Creusen-Garesche-Ellis, *Religious Men and Women in the Code* (3 ed., Milwaukee: Bruce, 1940), n. 271; Geser, *The Canon Law Governing Communities of Sisters* (St. Louis: Herder. 1939), q. 81; Fanfani, *De Iure Religiosorum,* n. 31; Schaefer, *De Religiosis,* n. 54.

[2] Cf. *Normae secundum quas Sacra Congregatio de Religiosis in Novis Religiosis Congregationibus Approbandis procedere solet,* n. 8—*AAS,* XIII (1921), 312. (Hereafter these will be referred to as *Normae of 1921).*

constitutions are approved at the same time. But if there is need of many changes or corrections, the approbation may be deferred for a more opportune time (*Dilatio cum animadversionibus*), or again the constitutions may be approved by way of experiment for a certain period, usually seven years (*Approbatio ad experimentum*), and finally definite approbation (*Approbatio definitiva*) is given by the S. Congregation.[3] But it is clearly stipulated that, once the *"decretum laudis"* has been issued for the congregation, the congregation itself loses all proper power of changing the constitutions. And canon 618 extends this same restriction to the local ordinary.

A change in the constitutions would include any addition or subtraction therefrom. The S. Congregation intends that the unity of the congregation shall be preserved primarily through its constitutions and thus prohibits any change in these constitutions, even though such change might be more suitable or advantageous to the particular religious house or the particular territory over which the ordinary has jurisdiction.

Little need be said at this particular moment regarding the right and duty of the local ordinary concerning the temporal administration of the congregation of women religious of pontifical approval or regarding his rights and duties concerning the internal government and discipline of the congregation, since particular studies of these factors will be made in subsequent chapters.[4]

But it is quite useful to repeat the second section of paragraph two of canon 618; "As regards Institutes approved by the Holy See, however, the local ordinary may not: . . . . interfere in the internal government and discipline, except in the cases expressed in law; nevertheless, in regard to lay Institutes, the local or-

[3] Cf. *Normae of 1921*, nn. 20, 21.

[4] "Internal government, as the term is used in canon 618, § 2, has reference to the reception of candidates, their admission to the vows, their dismissal, the appointment of members to offices and duties, the placing of them in the various houses, the holding of chapters and elections, and the administration of the goods and properties of the institute."—Geser, *The Canon Law Governing Communities of Sisters*, c. 1001.

dinary can and must enquire: whether the discipline is maintained conformably to the constitutions, whether sound doctrine and good morals have suffered in any way, whether there have been breaches of the law of enclosure, whether the reception of the Sacraments is regular and frequent; and, if Superiors having been warned of the existence of grave abuses have failed to remedy them, the ordinary himself shall provide; if, however, something of greater importance, which will not suffer delay, occur, the ordinary shall decide immediately; but he must report his decision to the Holy See."

Our study will be primarily concerned with searching out those cases which attribute to the local ordinary a right and duty over the congregations of women religious of pontifical approval, as expressed in the law.

CHAPTER VIII. THE CONGREGATION, PROVINCE AND HOUSE

ARTICLE 1. FOUNDATION AND SUPPRESSION OF THE CONGREGATION

The establishment of a congregation of women religious of pontifical approval is exclusively reserved to the Holy See. While it is true that the Sovereign Pontiff, if he so desires, can directly establish such a congregation without any formality of positive law, the establishment of a congregation into pontifical status is customarily effected through the S. Congregation for Religious or, if the institute is designed principally for work in mission fields, through the S. Congregation for the Propagation of the Faith.[1]

The ordinary form of procedure entails various formalities determined by the *stylus curiae,* and at present time the S. Congregations usually require that the congregation of women religious should first attain canonical establishment as a diocesan congregation and undergo a period of probation in this juridical status.[2] And when the Holy See has decided that the congregation has sufficiently proved its worth, stability and possibility of growth, a petition for pontifical approval is willingly received.[3]

Since the consequent formalities required by the Holy See antecedently to the concession of pontifical approval are beyond the scope of this study, it will suffice to note that when the congregation of women religious receives at least a decree of praise (*decretum laudis*) from the Holy See, its juridical status is changed from diocesan to pontifical.[4]

[1] Cf. Coronata, *Institutiones,* I, n. 516.

[2] Cf. canon 492; Schaefer, *De Religiosis,* n. 74.

[3] Cf. *Normae of 1921,* n. 7—*AAS,* XIII (1921), 312.

[4] Coronata, *Institutiones,* I, n. 517; Fanfani, *De Iure Religiosorum,* n. 13; Schaefer, *De Religiosis,* n. 75. For a special study on the approbation of religious institutes cf. Orth, *The Approbation of Religious Institutes, The Catholic University of America Canon Law Studies, No. 71,* (Washington, D. C.: The Catholic University of America, 1931).

When a congregation has received pontifical approbation many phases of its subjection are withdrawn from the local ordinaries in whose territory the congregation exists, and this jurisdiction is supplanted by direct subjection to the Holy See. Thus, unfettered by the divergencies of the multiplicity of diocesan jurisdictions, the congregation achieves an extensive opportunity to exercise in a wider way the autonomy of moral personality, affording a unity of purpose throughout the various ramifications of its internal government to accomplish more effectively the work and purpose of its foundation.

A congregation of women religious of pontifical approval, like other moral persons, becomes extinct only when it has ceased to exist for the space of one hundred years,[5] or when it is suppressed, or when it is united to another religious institute by the Holy See, which alone is competent to suppress or unite any religious institute that has been legitimately established.[6]

Hence it is beyond the jurisdictional power of the local ordinary to establish or suppress any congregation of women religious of pontifical approval. Nor does the jurisdiction of the local ordinary extend to the disposition of the property of such congregations that have been suppressed or have become extinct. In all cases it belongs to the Holy See to determine this disposition of property, safeguarding, however, the intention of its donors.[7]

[5] Even if there are no members left in the institute, natural extinction does not take place until the hundred years have run their course. Thus the congregation would remain *in statu suspensivo.* But if a person wished to restore the institute by joining as a member, it is evident that some act of competent ecclesiastical authority must intervene, for there would be no religious superioress extant who could grant legitimate admission. Cf. Fanfani, *De Iure Religiosorum,* n. 15. This author likewise requires such intervention when the members become so dispersed that there remains no hierarchical constitution among them.

[6] Cf. canons 102, § 1; 493. Coronata, *Institutiones,* I, n. 515; Larraona, "Commentarium Codicis"—*CpRM,* V (1924), 256.

[7] Cf. canons 493; 1501.

ARTICLE 2. FOUNDATION, DIVISION AND SUPPRESSION OF THE PROVINCE

A religious province is the union under the same superior of several houses that form a part of the same religious institute.[8] The Holy See has reserved to itself the division into provinces of a congregation of women religious of pontifical approval, the union of existing provinces or the modification of their boundaries in any manner, and the establishment of new provinces or the suppression of provinces already existing.[9]

Thus even a religious house of the congregation cannot be detached from one province and adjoined to another without permission of the Holy See.[10]

Once legitimately established, a province of a congregation of women religious of pontifical approval becomes a juridical person with the rights of a moral personality, having its own religious superioresses and officials with the consequent right of administering its own property.[11] And, unless the constitutions make other provisions, a province of the congregations here treated becomes extinct or can be suppressed under the same provisions that obtain for the extinction or suppression of the religious congregation itself. Hence, neither in the act of suppression or in the disposition of the property of the province does the local ordinary have any jurisdiction.[12]

[8] Cf. canon 488, 6°.

[9] Cf. canon 491, §1. Normally the Holy See requires at least four houses of twelve religious for each province. Cf. Bastien, *Directoire Canonique,* n. 524; Coronata, *Institutiones,* I, n. 519.

[10] Coronata, *(Institutiones,* I, n. 519) says that it would seem possible to effect a temporary union of a house with another province if grave circumstances, for instance in time of war, would preclude the presentation of a petition to the Holy See.

[11] Its existence dates from the moment when the rescript of the Holy See is executed. Cf. Larraona, "Commentarium Codicis"—*CpRM,* XII (1931), 248.

[12] Cf. canon 494, § 2. Disposition of the property of the supressed province pertains to the general chapter or, outside the time of meeting of the general chapter, to the supreme moderator with her council. Blat, *De Religiosis,* n. 62; Vemeersch-Creusen, *Epitome,* I, n. 556.

Article 3. Foundation of the House

In the wide sense of the term, any house or residence that belongs to a religious congregation or is inhabited by religious may be called a religious house. Specifically in the canonical sense, by the term religious house is meant a permanent (*stabilis*)[13] and canonically established foundation endowed with collegiate moral personality. This implies that at least three religious of the same institute[14] are ordinarily assigned thereto for the practice of the common life in accordance with the constitutions and subject to their own superioress.[15]

Thus even a non-formal house, that is, one to which less than six members of a congregation of women religious of pontifical approval are assigned, may be a religious house with moral collegiate personality in the canonical sense.[16]

No religious house may be established unless it can be prudently estimated that it will be able to provide suitably for the habitation and maintenance of its members from its own resources, or from habitual alms, or otherwise.[17]

In the writers opinion, the obligation of this prudent judgment is common both to the local ordinary and to the religious superioress in their own properly authorized spheres.[18] Full provision for the proper housing and support of the religious community must be foreseen. Yet this assurance becomes properly war-

[13] Cf. canon 102, § 1.

[14] Cf. canon 100, § 2. Battandier, *Instituts a Voeux Simples*, n. 513. Veermeersch *(Periodica*, X, (1922), 34-35) advances the opinion that even two members can constitute a juridical house.

[15] Cf. Coronata, *Institutiones*, I, n. 504. Larraona ("Commentarium Codicis"—*CpRM*, III [1922], 48), adds that the superioress of the religious house must be endowed with a power that is at least vicarious. For a study of filial houses, cf. Maroto, "Annotationes"—*CpRM*, V (1924), 122 sq.

[16] Blat, *De Religiosis*, n. 69; Fanfani, *De Iure Religiosorum*, n. 20.

[17] Cf. canon 496. Coronata *(Institutiones*, I, n. 523) holds that this condition is a requirement presupposed for the licit, and not the valid. giving of consent for the house's establishment.

[18] Fanfani *(De Iure Religiosorum*, n. 21) holds that it belongs to the bishop alone.

ranted only then, as a rule, when a proper estimate has been made of the facilities offered amid local surroundings. In the very nature of things the furnishing of this prudent estimate will rest quite naturally with the local ordinary. The requisite common judgment will therefore concern: 1. The needs to be met and the opportunities afforded in the locality; 2. The amount of temporal aid that the house will require and the guaranteed possibility of the religious house to reap that required aid.[19] 3. The purpose and special work of the institute.

The judgment of the local ordinary should be objectively and subjectively inclined for the good of the diocese. In virtue of his position he is thoroughly competent to judge the needs, opportunities and possibilities of the locality. On the other hand, the religious superioress should be expected to be more competent to judge the needs of the religious community and, subjectively at least, whether these needs can be provided in the particular locality. But the burden of judgment should not be thrown upon one or the other person exclusively, since each is judging from a different angle, the agreement should be most prudent, and prudence must be the deciding factor concerning the establishment of the house.

It is true that only indirectly does one find in the common law an acknowledgment of the right of congregations of women religious of pontifical approval to establish religious houses.[20] But one may say that positive recognition of the right may well be considered as unnecessary, since religious institutes are naturally diffusive and their membership is not expected to remain static. Thus the right of expansion is a natural attribute inherent in the moral personality itself.

Commentators are in disagreement as to whether a formal decree is necessary for the legitimate establishment of a religious

[19] Thus a strictly contemplative order would not ordinarily need so much external support because of the dowries.

[20] The Code acknowledges this right for diocesan congregations in c. 495, § 1, and presupposes such a right for other institutes in canon 497, § 1, where it requires the consent of the Holy See and of the local

house or whether the mere fact of recognizing the house as part of the institute would suffice.[21] But the juridical act of recognition, whether by formal decree or by the mere fact of recognition, will issue from the major superioress of the congregation.[22]

But moral personality can be effected only indirectly through an act of a major superioress of a congregation of women religious, since the concession of moral personality is an act of jurisdiction, a power which no superioress possesses. Hence her act of recognition can be no more than an indirect concession of this personality. Direct concession of the personality comes from the law.[23]

Experience has taught that growth which is untrammeled and uncontrolled is often destructive of vitality. Hence, to establish a religious house in territory subject to the S. Congregation for the Propagation of the Faith, congregations of women religious of pontifical approval must have the *beneplacitum* of the Holy See and the written consent of the local ordinary.[24] In all other territory the permission of the local ordinary suffices.[25]

ordinary for the establishment of the various houses of such congregations. Cf. Coronata, *Institutiones,* I, n. 521.

[21] Larraona ("Commentarium Codicis"—*CpRM,* V [1924], 418) denies the absolute necessity of a formal decree. Coronata *(Institutiones,* I, n. 522) and Vromant *(De Bonis Ecclesiae Temporalibus ad usum praesertim Missionariorum et Religiosorum* [Louvain: Editions du Museum Lessianum, 1927], n. 19) base their contrary argument for that requirement on canon 100, § 1 and *S. C. de Religiosis,* decr. 20 nov. 1922—*ASS,* XIV (1922), 644.

[22] Cf. Blat, *De Religiosis,* n. 73; Coronata, *Institutiones,* I, n. 522; Larraona, "Commentarium Codicis"—*CpRM,* V (1924), 418. One may say that this is confirmed by the fact that in canon 498 the suppression of religious houses of the congregations here treated is reserved to the Supreme Moderator of the congregation. "Omnis res per quascumque causas nascitur, per easdem dissolvitur." Cf. Larraona, "Commentarium Codicis"—*CpRM,* VI (1925), note 423.

[23] Cf. Coronata, *Institutiones,* I, n. 522; Blat, *De Religiosis,* n. 73; Larraona, "Commentarium Codicis"—*CpRM,* V (1924), 418. Cf. canon 100, § 1.

[24] Cf. canon 497, § 1. It should be clearly understood that the question here is not concerned with the opening of the *first* house of a congregation. Such would be identical with the establishment of the congregation and would be governed by the same formalities as the establishment of the institute itself.

[25] Cf. canon 497, § 1. There is one exception to this rule. For the

It is disputed whether the Vicar Capitular can give permission for the establishment of a religious house, for some hold that the establishment of a religious house involves a notable change for the diocese.[26]

Can the Vicar General give permission for the establishment of a religious house of congregations of women religious of pontifical approval without a special mandate? Coronata[27] and Blat affirm that he can.[28] Chelodi feels that the possession of this right by the Vicar General can be conceded at most doubtfully.[29] And Goyeneche flatly denies such power to the Vicar General in the absence of a special mandate.[30]

The local ordinary whose consent is required in the establishment of a religious house of a congregation of women religious of pontifical pproval is the ordinary of the place where the house is to be located. The common law requires no consent from the ordinary of the diocese where the principal house of such congregations is located when there is a question of establishing houses in other diocese. But it must be remembered that the con-

establishment of a house of novitiate in a congregation of women religious of pontifical approval there is always required a permission of the Holy See (cf. canon 554, § 1).

"(Pro hac venia ordinarii) in codice scriptura expresse non postulatur, sed suadenda saltem videtur, cum eadem sit ratio pro consensu, in scriptis exprimendo, quando domus est exempta, ac pro venia, quando non est exempta, scilicet ut res etiam in posterum certe probari possit." —Fanfani, *De Iure Religiosorum,* n. 21; Blat, De Religiosis, n. 73; "Larraona, "Commentarium Codicis"—*CpRM,* V (1924), 426.

[26] Cf. Coronata, *Institutiones,* I, n. 523, who quotes Melo, *De Exemptione Regularium,* 1921, p. 122 in denying this right; cf. also Goyeneche, "Consultationes"—*CpRM,* I (1920), 115. On the other hand, Schaefer *(De Religiosis,* n. 88) holds that the Vicar Capitular may give the permission in some circumstances. Also Blat *(De Religiosis,* n. 76) holds that he has this right.

[27] *Ibidem.*

[28] *Ibidem.*

[29] *Ius de Personis* (2 ed. a Sac. Ernesto Bertagnoli recognita et aucta; Tridenti: Libr. Edit. Tridentum, 1927), 384, note 3.

[30] Goyeneche, "Consultationes"—*CpRM,* I (1920), 115. His opinion is quoted by Schaefer *(De Religiosis,* n. 88, 2°) and Larraona ("Commentarium Codicis"—*CpRM,* V [1924], 425).

sent required affects the validity of the establishment and, until duly obtained, the juridical effects of establishment and the privileges connected with habitation in a religious house of the congregation can not be claimed.[31]

By the fact of its legitimate establishment a religious house attains moral personality and, in congregations of women religious of pontifical approval, the right of exercising the pious works proper to the congregation, subject however to conditions attached by the local ordinary to the permission for the establishment of the religious house.[32] The local ordinary may attach any conditions or restrictions to his permission for the establishment of the house that are not contrary to the common law. Thus for the congregations here treated, he could stipulate that they have no church or public oratory joined to their religious house. And he may even restrict some of the work that is proper to the congregation. Thus, for a just reason, congregations whose work includes both teaching and nursing may be limited in this particular house to teaching alone, or their work may be restricted to a certain na-attached to the permission given for the establishment, otherwise the law will consider that the sisters are free to exercise any or all of the works proper to their congregations.[34]

[31] "Sanctio omissarum licentiarum est iuridica nullitas erectionis, ita ut in tali domo nec religiosi localibus suis privilegiis fruantur, immo nec legitime habitare pergant."—Vermeersch-Creusen, *Epitome,* I, n. 560; Blat, *De Religiosis,* n. 73; Schaefer, *De Religiosis,* n. 82; Fanfani, *De Iure Religiosorum,* n. 21; Wernz-Vidal, *De Religiosis,* n. 72.

[32] Cf. canon 497, § 2.

tionality, etc.[33] But these restrictions or conditions must be

[33] "Rationes ex quibus limitationes et conditiones rationabiles esse possunt, illae praecipue sunt quae ex desiderio proveniunt subveniendi ordinate parique modo singulis necessitatibus, et, e contrà, vitandi inter religiosos ipsos ac inter religiosos et clerum, contentiones et aemulationes."—Larraona, "Commentarium Codicis"—*CpRM,* V (1924), 430; Blat, *De Religiosis,* n. 73; Creusen-Garesche-Ellis, *Religious Men and Women in the Code,* n. 39.

[34] Cf. canon 497, § 2; Larraona, *ibidem;* Blat, *ibidem;* Creusen-Garesche-Ellis, *ibidem.*

ARTICLE 4: ALTERATION OF THE HOUSE

No change may be made in a legimately established religious house of a congregation of women religious of pontifical approval if it runs counter to the stipulations of the foundation, the contracts, or conditions legitimately incorporated in the permission as granted by the Holy See or the local ordinary.[35]

Prescinding from the stipulations of these foundations, contracts, and conditions, the common law attributes to the local ordinary no further jurisdiction concerning changes that pertain to the interior government or discipline of a legitimately established religious house.[36] Materially, the building may be enlarged, repaired or rebuilt; formally, the religious house can be changed to another use that pertained to the internal government or discipline. Thus a house of studies may be changed to a house of convalescence for infirm members of the congregation, the house may be changed from a non-formal to a formal house, etc.[37]

[34a] "*Salvis fundationis legibus*" (canon 497, § 4)—for if a religious house has been donated for a specific purpose, any conversion that would require a change from the original intention of the donor would likewise entail the obligation of obtaining consent for such action from the local ordinary and from the donor. While the permission of the legal heirs of the donors is not required, since they have nothing to say in the prescriptions of canon law, yet the intention of the donors is *per se* permanent and, unless the founder has expressly conceded to the local ordinary the right to moderate or change his last will, that right is reserved to the Holy See. Cf. canon 1517; Vromant, *De Bonis Ecclesiae Temporalibus,* n. 167.

[35] As intimated above, once a local ordinary grants an unrestricted permission for the establishment of a religious house, the religious can claim, by force of their *ius quaesitum,* that the local ordinary cannot change or restrict at will this permission at a later period. Cf. Larraona, "Commentarium Codicis"—*CpRM,* V, (1924), 430.

[36] Cf. canon 497, § 4; Vermeersch-Creusen, *Epitome,* I, n. 560, 3°; Coronata *Institutiones,* I, n. 525, 2°.

[37] As noted previously, one change in the use of the house must specifically be pointed out as not herein included. For the establishment of a house of novitiate, or for the conversion of an established religious house to such use in congregations of women religious of pontifical approval, the permission of the Holy See is always necessary, even

A formal external change is one in which the house is converted to a use which will have external influence on the public, be it the clergy or the faithful of the diocese. Such would be the change from an apostolic school to a school for extern boarders or day students.[38] And the formalities of § 1 of canon 497 (viz., those for the establishment of a new house) are required for such external formal changes which cannot be considered as included either implicitly or explicitly in the original permission of the local ordinary for the establishment of the religious house.[39]

ARTICLE 5. TRANSFER OF THE HOUSE

Just how far the site of a religious house can be moved or transferred before one must consider such a transfer as in itself equivalent to the establishment of a new religious house, thus necessitating a new consent of the local ordinary, is a question unsettled by canonists. Certainly before making any transfer one must recur to the articles of the foundation and to the

though this would be considered as an internal formal change. Cf. canon 554. Larraona ("Commentarium Codicis," *CpRM,* V [1924], 434) adds: "Sunt mutationes internae conversio domus formatae in non formatam et vice versa, elevatio domus ordinariae ad categoriam domus provincialis vel generalis, transformatio alicuius novitiatus in collegium pro internis scholasticis, etc."

38 "Mutationes externae illae sunt quae sese referunt ad domus religiosae ministeria exteriora ususque publicos, quae scilicet fidelium seu externorum in genere intersunt."—Larraona, "Commentarium Codicis" —*CpRM,* V (1924), 436; Coronata, *Institutiones,* I, 525, 3°.

39 Cf. canon 497, § 4. Coronata, *ibidem;* Schaefer, *De Religiosis,* n. 87, b. It should be noted, however, that it is possible for such changes to be included, at least implicitly, in the original permission. For, unless the admission of the religious to the diocese or the permission for the establishment of the house restricted the religious to a particular part of their work, no one should maintain that they have not the right to proceed to any or all of the work that is proper to their institute and that such work was not implicitly included and permitted in the general concession of the permission for the establishment of their house. Ordinarily this will not be difficult to deduce from the tenor of the permission and from the contract which is usually entered into between the local ordinary and the superioress. Cf. Larraona, "Commentarium Codicis"—*CpRM,* V, 434-435.

original permission for the establishment of the house to ascertain whether restrictions were particularly stipulated in the consent for this establishment as to its exact site. For there can be no question of a transfer beyond the strict limits of the restriction, either implicit or explicit, which is stipulated in the permission of the establishment.[40]

But even when the original permission of the establishment is not specifically limited to an exact site, Schaefer holds that a move to a place other than the place of the location of the house must be considered as a new establishment. Moreover, he is of the opinion that a transfer from one site to another within the same village or city would be possible only with permission of the local ordinary.[41]

Larraona[42] and Balmes[43] hold that a religious house can be moved anywhere within the limits of a village or city without permission of the local ordinary. Fanfani, however, does not justify such a transfer within the entire territory of a large metropolis, for he maintains that a transfer without the previous permission of the local ordinary may not be undertaken if there is involved a distance of more than two or three miles.[44] While the question remains a disputed one, it must surely be admitted that a transfer from one diocese to another, no matter how short the distance that is involved, does require a new permission, for the consent originally given by the local ordinary cannot be used for the establishment of a religious house outside of the limits of the diocese in which alone his consent can have a valid effect.[45]

[40] Cf. Larraona, "Commentarium Codicis"—*CpRM,* V (1924), 419.

[41] Schaefer, *De Religiosis,* n. 87, 3°.

[42] *Ibidem.*

[43] *Les Religieux à Voeux Simples d'aprés le Code* (Paray-le-Monial, 1921), p. 41.

[44] *De Iure Religiosorum,* n. 23.

[45] In such cities as Kansas City, Kansas-Missouri and Bristol, Virginia-Tennessee a transfer from one diocese to the other could be effected if the location of the religious house were moved merely across the street which marks the dividing line between the two dioceses.

If the religious house of the congregation of women religious of pontifical approval has a public oratory or church joined to it, then another factor must be taken into consideration in change of location. For the special permission required of the local ordinary in the establishment of a church or public oratory extends to the determination by him of the definite location of that church or public oratory.[46] And this definite specification of the site of the church or public oratory may be so very restrictive as to be an effective obstacle to almost any change of site of the religious house itself.

If an institute of pontifical approval were to consist of several independent houses, the union of such houses into a centralized government does not come within the jurisdiction of the local ordinary. For such an act would entail a substantial change of the institute, redounding to suppression and consequent establishment of a new institute. The granting of permission for such an innovation is of course reserved to the Holy See.[47]

Article 6. Establishment of Edifice Separated from the House

The third paragraph of canon 497 stipulates that "for the building or opening of a school, a hospice, or any other such edifice separated from the religious house, even if it be exempt, the special written permission of the ordinary is necessary and sufficient."

While this sentence is seemingly simple in construction and connotation, it is nevertheless felt that it can give rise to endless difficulties and disputes. It is remarkable indeed to find that most canonists have provided little aid in its interpretation; so

[46] Cf. canon 1162; Larraona, " Commentarium Codicis"—*CpRM*, V (1924), 420: Schaefer, *De Religiosis*, n. 87, 3°.

[47] Cf. Maroto, "De Unione Plurium Monasteriorum Muliebrium in Religiosam Congregationem Sub Communi Regime"—*CpRM*, III (1922), 305-317.

many, in fact, have done little more than quote the words of the canon, inserted mention of one or two exceptions, and then passed on.[48]

A few others, however, are agreed that in virtue of this paragraph relative to the edifices mentioned therein no permission of the Holy See is required for their construction or the act of opening them,[49] as long as proper permission for the establishment of a religious house itself has been duly obtained. Moreover, they agree that the canon here treats of a special permission of the local ordinary, which is distinct from the original permission for the establishment of the religious house.[50]

[48] Cf. Vermeersch-Creusen, *Epitome,* I, n. 560, 2°; Cocchi, *Commentarium,* IV, n. 16; Wernz-Vidal, *De Religiosis,* n. 72; Pruemmer, *Manuale Iuris Canonici,* q. 181.

[49] Permission of the Holy See for contracting debts, however, would be required, Cf. canon 534.

[50] Cf. Coronata, *Institutiones,* I, n. 524, c.; Schaefer, *De Religiosis,* n. 86; Larraona, "Commentarium Codicis"—*CpRM,* V (1924), 430.

In summary fashion, Beste *(Introductio in Codicen* [Collegeville, Minn.; St. John's Abbey, 1938], pp. 323-324) holds that an edifice is separated from a religious house when it is not materially joined, that is, when it is not under the same roof or so contiguous that it forms one group of buildings. Claeys Bouuaert-Simenon *(Manuale Iuris Canonici,* I [4 ed. Gandae et Leodii, 1934], n 604, III, 2°) agree that the edifice must not be a new house *sui iuris* but a dependent one. In their solution of the problem of separation they maintain that no special permission is required if, without changing the destination of the house, the religious would open a school, college, etc., in the *same* house. But, they continue, such institutions would be separate from the house if they were erected "*procul* a domo vel etiam juxta domum, modo tamen revera separata sint. De quo puncto moraliter judicandum erit, spectato etiam primo domus scopo."

Fanfani *(De Iure Religiosorum,* n. 27), in determining when permission is not needed, seems to say that as long as the edifice is *either* materially *or* morally joined, no permission of the local ordinary is required. But, in turning the phrase, he has confused the meaning.

Augustine *(Commentary,* III, 91) avers that "*separated* seems to imply that the buildings mentioned must be distinct from the religious house, so that they are not under one roof with the latter, but form a distinct and independent entity, for instance, for fire insurance and taxation."

Beyond this, however, there are two difficulties inherent in the legislation of the paragraph:—I. What is the connotation of the phrase "any other such edifice"? II. When is an edifice so separated from the religious house as to require the permission of the local ordinary, which permission is sufficient for the construction and opening of the edifice?

I. "Any other such edifice". Blat says that this phrase was added so as to include all edifices that have external influence on clergy or laity, for such was the connotation implied by the Constitution *"Romanos Pontifices"* of Pope Leo XIII, to which this paragraph refers.[51] Other canonists specifically include hospitals, orphanages, day-nurseries and other such ecclesiastical non-collegiate institutes. Generally such buildings are not considered as religious houses in the technical sense, for they have no collegiate personality and are governed by a delegate of a principal religious house that is duly established.[52]

Summer villas intended solely for the religious women of the congregation seem to be entirely excluded from the connotation of this paragraph by the common opinion of the canonists. For they hold that such buildings, even though separated and distant from the religious house, are only secular houses and can be opened without permission of the local ordinary.[53]

II. "Separate from the religious house". Coronata gives what is probably the best interpretation of this phrase in explaining that a school, hospice or other such edifice may be separate from the religious house either formally or materially. It is formally separate, even though possibly materially united, if the work therein is not proper to the purpose of the institute. It is materially separate, even though not formally, if the building is constructed or opened at a considerable distance (about a

[51] Blat, *De Religiosis,* n. 73, p. 88.

[52] Cf. Vermeersch-Creusen, *Epitome,* I, n. 560, 2°; Beste, *Introductio in Codicem,* p. 323 (nosocomia, xenodochia, orphanotrophia, valetudinaria, domus exercitiorum, etc.).

[53] Vermeersch-Creusen, *Epitome,* I, n. 560, 2°; Wernz-Vidal, *De Religiosis,* n. 72; Larraona, "Commentarium Codicis"—*CpRM,* V (1924), 431; Cocchi, *Commentarium,* IV, n. 16; Beste, *Introductio in Codicem,* p. 324; Claeys Bouuaert-Simenon *Manuale Iuris Canonici,* I, n. 604, III, 2°; Maroto, "Annotations"—*CpRM,* V (1924), 130, note 18.

half mile) from the house, for the local ordinary can easily have a grave reason for not permitting the opening of a school, hospice, etc., at such a distance from the house.

Hence, when such buildings are either formally or materially separate from the religious house, the specially written permission of the local ordinary is necessary and also suffices. On the other hand, when the school, hospice, etc., prosecutes work that is proper to the institute and is connected with the religious house materially—or so near to it that it must be considered morally united—then no special permission is necessary for the erection or opening of such an institute. For, in virtue of § 2 of this same canon, the permission to establish a religious house includes permission to conduct the work proper to the institute, provided the local ordinary has not attached to the original permission a clause that would restrict or prohibit this particular work.[54]

Though Coronata has thus clarified the distinction between formal and material separation, it appears that his interpretation of material separation is too broad and that the distinction of formal separation cannot be applied to congregations of women religious of pontifical approval. For in a formal separation, as explained by Coronata, the special permission of the local ordinary would not be entirely sufficient for the opening of an institute where work is not proper to the scope of a congregation of women religious of pontifical approval, if he means that this permission alone suffices. In undertaking a work that is beyond the scope of their constitutions, the religious would thus be making a change in the constitutions, and such a change requires permission of the Holy See, by whom their constitutions have been approved.[55] Moreover, if Coronata uses the term "religious

[54] Cf. Coronata, *Institutiones,* I, n. 524, c. Blat *(De Religiosis,* n. 73, p. 88), adhering to his original distinction of external influence, holds that any building that is outside the enclosure of the religious house and that has its separate entrance, even though it be attached to the house materially, must be considered as formally separate as long as the work undertaken is of external influence.

[55] Cf. canon 618, § 2, 1°.

house" in its proper technical sense, then his interpretation regarding the phrase "material separation" also seems too broad, when he implies that if a building is not as much as a half mile away from the religious property it may be opened without the special written permission of the ordinary. There is all the more reason for considering his interpretation too liberal in this case if alien property should lie between the two respective sites.

Though it is true that one cannot definitely determine a moral union by a surveyor's chain or a carpenter's rule, one can scarcely regard a building as materially joined to a religious house even when it is separated from the latter by a public thoroughfare. Such a public thoroughfare would seem to effect a definite and decided separation between the religious house and the building. It is difficult to find any juridical basis for allowing such a building to be constructed or opened without the special permission of the ordinary.

Again, if the distance admissible in the moral union of Coronata's interpretation is to be measured from the material building of the religious house (though there is nothing in canon law which requires that only one building and not a group or the whole of the property can be called materially the religious house), one must take into consideration that it is possible that the plot of land of some religious houses may cover a thousand acres or more. Thus it would be possible for a building, while still on the same religious property, to be constructed or opened at a distance of two or three miles from the main building of the religious house. Therefore, since such a building is erected on the same property, one may consider it to be morally joined to the principal religious house.

Larraona, basing his distinctions on the dependency of the edifice on the religious house, immediately excludes the general statement that the legislation of this paragraph can be applied to all filial houses (*domus filiales*) in general. For the concept of affiliation is too broad, and many affiliated houses are in verity religious houses in the proper sense and for their establishment there are required the formalities of § 1 of this same canon.[56]

[56] Thus he explains that a house that is governed by a superioress

The only houses that can be considered in this paragraph, he continues, are those that are governed directly by the superioress of a principal religious house or by her simple delegate in the strict sense.[57]

While this distinction relative to dependency is of value, yet Larraona's explanation concerning the elements or factors which imply a separation of the edifice from the principal religious house appears altogether too vague.[58] He does not draw any distinction between houses that are properly part of the internal work of the congregation and those that have external influence, which, Blat says, was the basis of this legislation.

In conclusion, therefore, one may draw upon all three of these last explanations for a practical rule of application to congregations of women religious of pontifical approval. One may justifiably assume that all edifices that have an external influence (Blat), that are governed directly by the superioress of the religious house or by her simple delegate (Larraona), and that are not within the confines of the property of the religious house (modified material separation of Coronata) may be erected and opened only with the special written permission of the local ordinary. The permission thus obtained from the local ordinary will suffice of itself for the construction and opening of such an edifice.

with governing power *ex officio,* even though exercised vicariously in the name of the superioress of the principal house, must be considered as a religious house in the proper sense and the formalities of § 1 are required for its establishment. Cf. Larraona, "Commentarium Codicis" —*CpRM,* V (1924), 432.

[57] The term "simple delegate" implies that the one in charge of the edifice derives her power not *ex munere,* that is by exercising it as a vicaress of the superioress of the religious house, but *ex commissione a persona* (personal commission), that is, by exercising it as a delegate of the superioress. Cf. Larraona, "Commentarium Codicis,"—*CpRM,* V (1924), 432, note 386.

[58] ". . . satis constat hic agi de domo separata quae *parum* distat a domo principali et in eadem civitate, vel *dioecesi* saltem, invenitur."—Larraona, Commentarium Codicis"—*CpRM,* V (1924), 432.

Article 7. Suppression of the House

The moral personality of a religious house can be lost in two ways: by natural extinction and by legitimate suppression.[59] Canon 498 attributes the right of the legitimate suppression of a house of a congregation of women religious of pontifical approval to the supreme moderator of the congregation, and not to the local ordinary. However, the supreme moderator can exercise this power of suppression only after she has obtained the consent of the local ordinary. Otherwise the act of suppression is invalid and without effect.[60]

The consent of the local ordinary is here provided as a legal safeguard to the rights of the diocese. It is true that an unjust refusal of consent by the local ordinary for the suppression can be overruled by the Holy See.[61] But if the local ordinary has entered into a contract with the religious concerning the religious house, then the rights and obligations of this contract must be respected and he can effectively prevent the suppression of the house if he judges that this is necessary in order to safeguard these rights.[62]

But this right of suppression enjoyed by the supreme moderator does not extend to the suppression of the last house of the congregation, since this would be almost necessarily equivalent to the suppression of the congregation itself, an act which is reserved to the Holy See.[63]

[59] Cf. canon 102, § 1.

[60] Cf. canon 105, § 1; Blat, *De Religiosis,* n. 78; Larraona, "Commentarium Codicis"—*CpRM,* VI (1925), 19. It may well be noted that the permission of the Holy See is not required by the common law for the suppression of any house of the congregations treated in this study.

[61] Vermeersch-Creusen, *Epitome,* I, n. 562; Larraona, "Commentarium Codicis"—*CpRM,* VI (1925), 19.

[62] Cf. Coronata, *Institutiones,* I, n. 526, p. 619, note 4; Creusen-Garesche-Ellis, *Religious Men and Women in the Code,* n. 40, 2°; Vermeersch-Creusen, *Epitome,* I, n. 562; Larraona, "Commentarium Codicis," *CpRM,* VI (1925), 18.

[63] It is true that juridically the suppression of the last religious house would not be the same as the suppression of the institute itself. For juridically the moral person of the institute could survive,

Since the Code makes no special provisions for the disposition of the property of a religious house of congregations of women religious of pontifical approval that has been legitimately suppressed by the supreme moderator, or that loses personality through natural extinction, the constitutions of the congregation should contain due provision. If the constitutions contain no special provisions, then the general norms of canon law regulating the property of an extinct ecclesiastical moral person will determine the disposition.[64]

In canon 1501 the general legislation provides that if a legal person ceases to exist, its goods shall belong to the immediately superior legal person. However, in the application of this special norm the due fulfillment of the expressed will and intentions of the founders and benefactors must be procured, and the lawfully acquired rights as well as the special laws which goverened the extinct moral personality must be duly safeguarded and respected. The immediately superior legal person in the congregation is the province. If the congregation is not divided into provinces, then the congregation itself is the legal person to whom the property will cede.[65]

Desertion of the material building or of the property of a religious house must not be considered as synonymous with the legitimate suppression of the house itself. For as long as the religious house subsists juridically, even though, in the material sense, the house has been destroyed or deserted, then the formalities of canon 497, § 1, namely, the requirements for the establishment of a new house, are not necessary for the restoration or the taking possession again of the material property.[66]

at least for a time, the suppression of the last religious house. But religious life cannot long subsist without a religious house in which proper provision can be made for the continuance of this mode of life. Hence extinction of the congregation would naturally follow, in due course of time, the suppression of the last religious house. Cf. Larraona, "Commentarium Codicis"—*CpRM,* VI (1925), 20, note 434.

[64] Cf. Blat, *De Religiosis,* n. 80.

[65] Schaefer, *De Religiosis,* n. 88, note 2.

[66] Larraona, "Commentarium Codicis"—*CpRM,* V (1924), 419; Coronata, *Institutiones,* I, p. 618, note 1.

Moreover, it is evident that the entire personnel of the religious house could be removed by the competent superioress of a congregation of women religious of pontifical approval and other religious substituted, with no consequent loss of the moral personality of the religious house, for, as Goyeneche says,[67] the moral personality of a religious house is incorporated not by the individual religious of the house, but by the province or the congregation that is efficient cause of that personality.

Canonists agree that religious have a right to return to a house from which they have been unjustly expelled.[68] And Coronata definitely asserts that in case of an unjust expulsion the extinction of the religious house does not take effect even after the lapse of a hundred years. But Larraona simply acknowledges that the religious will have the right of regaining their house without the formalities of a new establishment of it as long as its juridical suppression or natural extinction have not intervened. He thus leaves unanswered the question whether a continued unjust expulsion for a period of time longer than one hundred years automatically effects either the juridical suppression or the natural extinction of the relinquished religious house. Goyeneche observes that the ultimate juridical disposition of such a case will depend in great part on the particular attendant circumstances, in as far as the *praxis curiae* usually resolves the case in view of such telling factors as 1) the length of time during which the unjustly enforced expulsion was continued and a) the degree of effort with which a reestablishment of the house was sought in the meanwhile.[69]

When the religious congregation has voluntarily deserted a religious house, it seems difficult to prove that a legitimate suppression is not implied by such an abandonment. It is hardly to

[67] "Consultationes"—*CpRM,* VII (1926), 394.

[68] Goyeneche, *ibidem;* Larraona, *ibidem;* Coronata, *ibidem;* Fanfani, *De Iure Religiosorum,* n. 520; Balmes, *Les Religieux a Voeux Simples d'apres le Code,* p. 42.

[69] Coronata, *Institutiones,* I, p. 618, note 1; Larraona, "Commentarium Codicis"—*CpRM,* V (1924), 419; Goyeneche, "Consultationes"—*CpRM,* VII (1926), 395.

be assumed that the *praxis curiae* will favor the congregation in any claim to reestablish its voluntarily deserted house apart from a new permission of the ordinary. This assumption appears all the more tenable relative to a case in which this voluntary desertion of the religious house has continued for a considerable interval of time.[70]

[70] Cf. Goyeneche, *ibidem.* One may readily agree with Coronata *(ibidem)* that a voluntary desertion of the religious house is in itself not destructive of the moral personality of that house, but in the circumstance of a voluntary desertion which continues over a long interval of time it is difficult to see how such moral personality is still maintained.

Chapter IX

THE GOVERNMENT

Article 1. The Elections

The legislation of the Council of Trent stipulated that the local ordinary should preside at the election of the Abbess or Prioress of monasteries of nuns.[1] With the growth of congregations of simple vows, this practice of attributing to the local ordinary the right of presiding at the election of the superioress-general was adopted into the majority of the religious constitutions.

When the Constitution *"Conditae a Christo"* was published, the chairmanship of the local ordinary at elections in all congregations of women religious was made obligatory, and his right of presiding thereat was extended to the election of all the religious superioresses.[2] While with reference to the elections in congregations of women religious of pontifical approval the local ordinary was to preside as a delegate of the Holy See, special provision was made for the possible subdelegation of this right and duty. But the subsequent jurisprudence of the S. Congregation tended to a partial modification of this plan by restricting the chairmanship of the local ordinary at elections to the case of the election of the superioress-general alone, and this restriction was inserted in sereval constitutions that were subsequently presented for approval.[3]

The Code has confirmed this jurisprudence of the S. Congregation and the common law attributes to the local ordinary the right to preside at the election of the superioress-general alone to the exclusion of the elections of all other religious supe-

[1] Cf. Conc. Trid., Sess. XXV, *de regularibus et monialibus,* c. 7.

[2] Leo XIII, const. *"Conditae a Christo,"* 8 dec. 1900, § II, n. 1—*Fontes,* n. 644.

[3] Cf. Bastien, *Directoire Canonique,* n. 303.

rioresses in a congregation of pontifical approval.[4] Moreover, the local ordinary no longer acts as delegate of the Holy See, but his right of presiding at this election in the congregations here treated is now definitely attributed to him by law (*ex iure*).[5]

While the delegation of this right of the local ordinary is frequent, especially when the place chosen for the chapter of election is at a great distance from the cathedral city, Larraona observes that it would seem that the ordinary confessor of the sisters should not be delegated to preside. Since express provision is made in canon 506, § 3, that an ordinary confessor be not chosen as teller when the chapter of election is conducted by nuns, he concludes that *a fortiori* the ordinary confessor should never be chosen to preside at any election.[6]

This right of presiding is not reserved to the ordinary of the place of the mother-house of the congregation. The provisions of canon 506, § 4, expressly state that the ordinary of the place where the election is held will preside. If the constitutions of the congregation do not determine the place where the election is to take place, then this matter of location is freely chosen by the superioress-general presently in office, who thus indirectly determines also the ordinary who shall be thus designated to preside over the election.[7]

The presidency of the local ordinary is one of jurisdiction that is effective and immediate. Not only does he occupy the place of honor and direction, but he has the duty to make due provisions (even before and subsequent to the election) for the

[4] Cf. canon 508, § 4.

[5] Vermeersch-Creusen, *Epitome,* I, n. 579, a; Pruemmer, *Manuale Iuris Canonici,* q. 185; Schaefer, *De Religiosis,* 131, e.

[6] "Sane Praeses est scrutator natus, imo magis quam ipsi simplices scrutatores in electione ipsa intervenire debet. Si ergo confessarii ordinarii non possunt scrutatores esse, nec etiam in Praesides eligi valebunt."—Larraona, "Commentarium Codicis"—*CpRM,* VIII (1927), 24, note 334.

[7] Leo XII, const. *"Conditae a Christo,"* 8 dec. 1900, § II, n. 1—*Fontes,* n. 644; *S. C. de Religiosis,* resp. 2 iul. 1921—*AAS, XIII* (1921), 481; Schaefer, *De Religiosis,* n. 131, e; Creusen-Garesche-Ellis, *Religious Men and Women in the Code,* 51.

government of all the acts prescribed by law or made necessary by the nature of the election. In general, he may exercise all discretionary power. Hence he may impose precepts, settle practical questions within the limits of the law, and even impose penances, if necessary, in keeping with this jurisdictional power.[8]

The Code makes explicit provision that in elections which are made by chapters[9] the prescriptions of canons 160-182 shall be observed.[10] Although the superioress-general is not elected to an ecclesiastical office in the strict sense,[11] and though it is true that the Code uses the term "assembly" (*comitia*) in the preceding canon,[12] the process of election of the superioress-general must be regulated by the provisions of canon 507.[13]

Moreover, the constitutions of the congregation, supplementary to the common law, are to be observed in so far as they are not contrary to this universal law. For the constitutions form a body of particular law which, if examined and approved by the S. Congregation for Religious, derive authority from the Apostolic See.

[8] Larraona, "Commentarium Codicis"—*CpRM,* VIII (1927), 22-23; Parsons, *Canonical Elections, The Catholic University of America Canon Law Studies No. 118,* (Washington, D. C.: 'The Catholic University of America, 1939), p. 135. *P. C. I.,* 30 iul. 1934—*AAS,* XXVI (1934), 494.

[9] It may be noted that appointments by the council are not included in this regulation of the common law, though the constitutions may, indeed, extend this prescription to such appointments. Cf. Toso, *Commentaria Minora,* II-II, p. 41.

[10] Canon 507, § 1: In elections which are made by chapters, the universal law as set forth in canons 160-182 shall be observed, as well as the constitutions of the Institute which are not contrary to this universal law.

[11] Cf. canon 145, § 1; Blat, *De Religiosis,* n. 135.

[12] Cf. canon 506, § 2.

[13] "Disputari quidem posset, si quis insistere voluerit in verbo *Capitulis* ('in electionibus quae *a Capitulis* fiunt') allegando Codicem non Capitula sed *Comitia* vel *Congregationes* (c. 506, §§ 2, 4) conventus Religiosarum appellare. Tamen ex doctrina recepta iurique anteriori conformi, Capitulis sub hoc respectu aequiparari debent Comitia in quibus Antistitae Monialium et Superiorissae Congregationum nominantur."—Larraona, "Commentarium Codicis"—*CpRM,* VIII (1927), 108.

It is possible that a congregation of women religious of pontifical approval has obtained an apostolic indult regulating the election or, perhaps, permitting a postulation.[14] Any indults granted by the Holy See and any privileges acquired by the congregation remain intact and must be respected, provided they are still in use and not otherwise revoked, since there is no general reprobation of such grants in the common law for elections.[15]

Again, customs which are contrary to the common law but of century-long duration or immemorial may in the prudent judgment of the ordinary be retained under certain restricted conditions. Such customs, unless they are expressly reprobated by the Code, may be tolerated if the ordinary judges that they cannot be prudently abolished because of circumstances of places and persons. All other customs contrary to the law of the Code are suppressed, unless the Code makes an express provision that permits them to be retained.[16]

Since, then, there are so many factors to be taken into account in the regulation of an election in a congregation of women religious of pontifical approval, it will prove beneficial for all who have a part in the election proceedings that every such congregation deposit with the diocesan chancery a copy of its constitutions together with a full notation of its indults and privileges along with a clear indication of the legitimate customs which form part of the norms by which the institute is governed.

14 Pruemmer, *Manuale Iuris Canonici,* q. 185, 1°

15 Cf. canon 4. "Privileges granted by Ordinaries *contrary* to the Code cease to exist, but not those which were given *outside the law.*" —Cicognani, *Canon Law,* 477.

16 Cf. canon 5. Special customs are explicitly safeguarded by three canons of the article on elections, viz., canons 162, § 1; 168; 171, § 2. The S. Congregation for Religious, in a decree of March 29, 1919 *(AAS,* XI (1919), 239) directed that all congregations of women religious of pontifical approval should, within the year, transmit their custom books, directories, etc., to the S. Congregation for examination. However, they could continue to use these books until the S. Congregation ruled otherwise.

When the Code, in the general law on elections, says that the voters shall be convoked for the election by the president of the electorial college,[17] in congregations of women religious of pontificial approval the right and duty of convoking the electors devolves on the superioress-general presently in office, or on the person who by law is designated to exercise her powers, as in the case of her demise, her absence, her serious illness, etc.[18] Hence it must be clearly noted that, although the local ordinary presides at the election of the superioress-general of a congregation of women religious of pontifical approval, he is only the presiding officer at the *voting* and not the president of the *voters*. For the superioress-general presently in office is competent to convoke the electors as well as to determine the place of election. However, it is the duty of the local ordinary to see that the superioress who convokes the electors fulfills all that the constitutions, the common law, and the particular customs require for the convocation.

In the election of a superioress-general for a congregation of women religious of pontifical approval priests are not allowed to act as tellers at the election, for the tellers who will count the votes and tabulate the result are to be selected from the members of the assembly.[19] But it may prove helpful for the local ordinary to be accompanied by a canonist, since the prescriptions for the election are so exacting in detail. This is fully permissible, for canon 165 forbids the admission of externs only to suffrage, so that there is nothing in the common law prohibiting a canonist from accompanying a local ordinary to the election. It is acknowledged of course that he enjoys no

[17] Cf. canon 162, § 1.

[18] "Superiorissa est collegii praeses, perinde pertinet ad ipsam electrices convocare et locum capituli definire."—Schaefer, *De Religiosis*, n. 127; S. C. de Rel., decr., 2 iul. 1921—*AAS*, XIII (1921), 481; Parsons, *Canonical Elections*, 99; Coronata, *Institutiones*, I, n. 538, p. 640.

[19] Cf. canon 171, § 1, Schaefer, *De Religiosis*, n. 132, a; Coronata, *Institutiones*, I, n. 538, p. 641; "Scrutatores si non sint iure designati debent per veram electionem nominari."—Larraona "De Electionibus Religiosorum,"—*CpRM*, VIII (1927), 183, note 22.

right to cast a vote. The tellers chosen from the assembly must take the oath to discharge their office faithfully and to keep secret the transactions in the assembly even after the completion of the election.[20]

Probably to forestall any danger of scruples, women religious are not required to take an oath at the election that they will cast their vote for the most worthy candidate.[21]

Though the constitutions of the congregation, in conformity with the norms of the Code, will usually determine the method by which the superioress-general will be chosen, there are two possible methods: compromise and scrutiny.[22]

In the method of compromise the election may be entrusted, with the unanimous consent of the electors, to one or several specified persons (*compromissarii*), even to persons who are not members of the electoral college. This act of delegation may be absolute or conditional, with or without reservations.[23] Though this is indeed an exceptional method, custom may endow it with the force of a particular law, and thus it must always be

[20] Canon 171, § 1; Larraona, "Consultationes"—*CpRM,* II (1921), 363. "This obligation to secrecy has to do only with acts which are secret by their nature. Thus, for example, the counters of the votes are not allowed to reveal the names of those who have voted for or against anyone; nor to discuss the votes obtained by a candidate who has not been elected; nor to say who has cast an invalid vote, etc."—Creusen-Garesche-Ellis, *Religious Men and Women in the Code,* p. 55.

[21] In canon 506, § 1, this oath is required only for men religious. Cf. Larraona, "Consultationes"—*CpRM,* II (1921), 363; Coronata, *Institutiones,* I, n. 538, p. 639.

[22] Most canonists agree that in religious congregations the method of election by acclamation has been abolished by the Code. Cf. Parsons, *Canonical Elections,* p. 142; Cappello, *Summa Iuris Canonici,* I (Romae: Universitas Gregoriana, 1932), 347; Chelodi, *Ius de Personis* (2 ed., Tridenti: Libr. Edit. Tridentum, 1927), p. 238, note 6; Coronata, *Institutiones,* I, n. 232; Maroto, *Institutiones Iuris Canonici* (3 ed. Romae: Apud Commentarium Pro Religiosis, 1921), n. 626, note 1; Fanfani, *De Iure Religiosorum,* n. 95.

[23] Cf. canons 172; 173.

regarded as a possible method of election, unless it is explicitly excluded by the provision of law.[24]

In the method of election by scrutiny, the tellers receive the votes (either written or otherwise communicated in secrecy).[25] If the number of votes, after being counted, is found to be no greater than the number of voters,[26] then the votes are opened, read in the presence of the local ordinary as the presiding officer at the voting, tabulated, and the result announced to the assembly.[27] Goyeneche holds that the reading and the announcing of the votes are essential to the validity of the form of scrutiny and that any custom of not announcing how many votes each candidate received should be suppressed as contrary to canon 171, § 2.[28]

[24] Cf. Coronata, *Institutiones,* I, n. 538, d.

[25] "A written ballot, though it is not ordered, is the most common form, the most convenient one and, it seems, the only one that is contemplated by the Code. Nevertheless, if one of the members of the chapter cannot write, she may declare before the president and the counters of the votes which candidate she chooses. Members of the chapter who are sick and who dwell in the same house will secretly write their vote and give it, in a sealed envelope, to the counters of the votes, who are delegated by law to come and take it (c. 168)."—Creusen-Garesche-Ellis, *Religious Men and Women in the Code,* p. 56. Voting by letter or by proxy is excluded by the Code (cf. canon 163) unless it be permitted by particular law or by privilege granted by the Holy See.

[26] If the number of votes is less than the number of voters, it may be presumed that some voters have renounced their right of voting, a fact that need not hinder the proceedings in any way.

[27] "Although no particular method of reading and announcing the votes is essential, probably the most satisfactory method is had in the following procedure. The president opens the individual votes before he hands them to the tellers. The first teller will read them one by one and mark down for whom the vote is cast. As she proceeds with this she will pass the individual votes to the second teller who will duplicate the action of the first. The president and tellers will then compare notes and finally announce the result to the assembly."—Parsons, *Canonical Elections,* 151.

[28] Cf. Goyeneche, "Consultationes"—*CpRM,* XI (1930), 354.

"One may not deny that this prescription does at times encounter a

In determining an election result, the local ordinary must clearly distinguish between an absolute majority (i. e., more than half of the total valid vote) and a relative majority (i. e., a plurality or a larger vote than is given to any of the remaining candidates). In the first and second ballots, the Code requires an absolute majority for an election. A relative majority, however, will suffice in the third ballot.[29]

This is a change from the *Normae of* 1901, which required an absolute majority for the election of a superioress-general even in the third ballot. If no candidate attained an absolute majority even in the third ballot, the choice was left to the S. Congregation, provided the electoral body was assembled in Europe. Otherwise a fourth ballot could be taken, in which only those two religious were eligible candidates who received the greater number of votes in the third ballot. If the fourth ballot resulted in a tie vote, the choice was determined by seniority in profession and as a further alternative by seniority in age.[30]

At present time the constitutions of several religious institutes allow, in case of a tie vote in the third ballot, a fourth ballot in the election of the superioress-general.[31] But, when such provision is not made in the constitution of a congregation of women religious of pontifical approval at whose election the local ordinary is presiding, a real dispute among canonists exists concerning the right of the local ordinary in the determination of such a tie vote. Specifically the question is: does the local ordinary have the right to break a tie vote in the third ballot for the

serious difficulty: when a superior-general is elected unanimously, with his own vote excepted, his vote by the very nature of things becomes public, a thing absolutely prohibited by the Code. Seemingly, the only way to avoid this inconvenience would be not to announce the votes as soon as they are opened, but only after having examined the entire scrutiny, and not to announce the single vote, the author of which would thus be betrayed."—Creusen-Garesche-Ellis, *Religious Men and Women in the Code*, p. 57.

[29] Cf. canon 101, § 1, 1°; Coronata, *Institutiones*, I, n. 145; Maroto, *Institutiones*, I, n. 467.

[30] Cf. *Normae of 1901*, nn. 232; 234.

[31] Cf. Parsons, *Canonical Elections*, p. 155.

election of a superioress-general in the congregations here treated?

In canon 101, § 1, 1°, where the Code treats of the juridical acts of a collegiate moral person, there is express provision whereby, after a third ballot without an election result, the president may break a tie *voto suo* (by his vote or his decision), if he so wishes; or, when the president is unwilling to break a tie in the election, then the senior in orders, or, if there be a parity in the time of ordination, then the senior by the initial religious profession, or, if here too a parity exists, then the senior in age will be declared elected. Basing themselves upon this ruling, Larraona,[32] Vermeersch-Creusen[33] and Coronata[34] hold that the local ordinary has the right to break a tie vote in the third ballot of an election for the superioress-general in congregations of women religious of pontifical approval.

Larraona, in delineating the arguments for his opinion, says that since the presidency accorded to the local ordinary at elections of congregations of women religious of pontifical approval is not merely one of honor but also one of direction and jurisdiction *ad normam iuris,* and since he presides as sole chairman at such elections, the local ordinary has every right attributed by law to the presiding officer at an election, including the duty of receiving the votes, of making due annotation of these votes, and, unless particular law states otherwise, of deciding a tie vote in the final ballot. Moreover, he advances the theory that the term *"suo voto"*, as used in canon 101, does not presuppose that the presiding officer must be endowed with active voice in the electoral college, but that the term was used precisely to exclude such a supposition. For the Code, when treating of the exercise of the active voice ordinarily designates this act by the word *"suffragium"*, and not by *"votum"*. Hence the singular expression *"suo voto"* is deliberately used to extend to the

[32] "Commentarium Codicis"—*CpRM,* VIII (1927), 22; 104, note 361.

[33] *Epitome,* I, n. 579.

[34] *Institutiones,* I, n. 538, p. 640.

local ordinary, even though he has no active voice in the electoral college, the right to break a tie vote.[35]

Michiels[36] supports this opinion in his interpretation of canon 101, declaring that the term *"suo voto"* means "his decision" and that the legislator thereby attributes to the presiding officer the right of final decision, even if he is not a voting member of the chapter.

On the other side, Chelodi,[37] Schaefer[38] and Parsons[39] hold the opinion that the local ordinary cannot break a tie vote in the election for the superioress-general in congregations of women religious of pontifical approval. To the present writer this opinion seems much more consonant with the juridical principles that must guide the local ordinary in his jurisdictional claims over congregations of women religious of pontifical approval.

Before the Code, the local ordinary was not permitted to cast the decisive vote in the event of a tie. It would seem, then, that the interpretation of the present law should recur to the interpretation of the old law for its proper elucidation.[40] It is true that the singular expression *"suo voto"* is used in canon 101 when one might expect *"suo suffragio."* But one can find many instances in the pre-code legislation where the terms *"suffragium"* and *"votum"* were used indiscriminately and interchangeably to denote an identical meaning.[41] Nonetheless it does seem that the term

[35] Larraona, "Commentarium Codicis," *CpRM,* VIII (1927), 104, note 361.

[36] *Principia Generalia de Personis in Ecclesia* (Lublin in Polonia; 1932), p. 390.

[37] *Ius de Personis,* n. 253, d, note 4.

[38] *De Religiosis,* n. 131, h.

[39] *Canonical Elections,* p. 155.

[40] Cf. canon 6, 4°; Cf. Ferraris, *Bibliotheca,* s. v. "Abbatissa," and the decisions of the Sacred Congregations there cited; Larraona, "Commentarium Codicis"—*CpRM,* VIII (1927), 109.

[41] Cf. Conc. Trid., sess. XXV *"de regularibus et monialibus,"* c. 6: ". . . in electione quorumcumque Superiorum . . . omnes supra dictos eligi debere per vota secreta . . ."; *ibid.,* c. 7: "vota singulorum audiat, vel accipiat."; *S. C. de Religiosis,* decr. 27 aug. 1910: "singula vota Monialium in urna clausa colligantur . . ." *Fontes,* n. 4405.

"suo voto" was used in canon 101 to express a specific connotation. Instead of attributing an active voice to an extern who is presiding at a collegiate election, one is inclined to believe that this expression was used specifically to warn any member of the electoral college when presiding that he must not vote unless there is a tie The phrase *"suo voto,"* therefore, may be regarded, not as connoting an endowment of active voice on the part of an extern who presides, but a restriction and limitation of the presiding officer who is member of the college, for one of the basic principles of the general legislation on election is that no one may vote twice, no matter how many titles to a vote he may have.[42] If a member of the college who presides were to vote during the balloting, he would be an effective, though only partial, cause in the tie vote which later he is called on to break. His vote, then, should rather be restricted in its use for the breaking of a vote. This is in full consonance with general parliamentary procedure, where the very concent of the presiding officer's position restricts his use of a vote to the case in which a final determination must be made in the event of a tie vote. Moreover, since the local ordinary is not the president of the collegiate body but only the presiding officer at the voting, one may rightly consider that he too is included under the ruling of canon 165, which forbids all those who are extraneous to the electoral college to cast a vote.

Though it is true that we cannot apodictically state what was the mind of the legislator in using that term *"suo voto,"* could it not be possible that the term was used precisely for the purpose of indicating the initially restricted but eventually decisive capacity which one from the electoral college possesses when he presides, namely that he may not participate in the balloting of the electors, but that he may ultimately be called on by law to determine the entire election result when the balloting of the electoral body for a given candidate has ended in a stalemate?

In summation, it is evident that the question remains unsolved, though, as Parsons observes, "since the local ordinary, before the Code, was forbidden to cast the decisive vote in the event of

[42] Cf. canon 164.

a tie, it would seem that canon 101 should be interpreted in the light of the former law."[43]

In the absence of the local ordinary or his delegate, any attempted election of a superioress-general by the chapter of congregations of women religious of pontifical approval would be not merely rescindible but *ipso facto* null and void. For the act of presiding is essential to the validity of the election.[44] It would seem, therefore, that the provisions of canon 506, § 2, for the election of nuns, regarding the notice that should be given to the local ordinary concerning the time and place of the election, could serve as a norm for the religious congregations treated in this study.

While indeed it is merely stated that the local ordinary must be informed of the day and hour of the election on the part of nuns subject to a regular superior, and no definite period for the giving of this previous notice has been set by the common law, it need scarcely be remarked that the courtesy of a sufficiently timely notice is to the advantage not only of the local ordinary but also of the religious themselves, since they *cannot* proceed to the election without their duly authorized presiding officer.

At the completion of each balloting, or at the close of the session, the votes are to burned.[45] All the proceedings of the election shall be accurately recorded by one who acts as secretary, and these acts, signed by the president, the tellers and the secretary, shall be placed in the archives of the assembly.[46]

The religious who has been elected as superioress-general must be notified at once, and within eight days she must decide whether or not she will accept the office.[47] If she is permitted to refuse and

[43] Parsons, *Canonical Elections,* 155.

[44] Cf. Vermeersch-Creusen, *Epitome,* I, n. 579; Larraona, "Commentarium Codicis"—*CpRM,* VIII (1927), 105.

[45] Cf. canon 171 § 4; Schaefer, *De Religiosis,* n. 134.

[46] Cf. canon 171, § 5. Coronata, *Institutiones,* I, n. 538, p. 641. Schaefer, *(De Religiosis,* n. 134) notes that the secretary can be assumed from outside the electoral college, but as an extern has no vote.

[47] Pruemmer *(Manuale Iuris Canonici,* q. 185) notes that it is still disputed whether a religious can refuse to accept an office to which she has been elected. Cf. Vermeersch, *Periodica,* XI (1923), (153).

does so, the assembly must proceed to a new election within one month from the time that knowledge is had of her non-acceptance.[48]

Upon the completion of the election of the superioress-general the local ordinary shall retire from the assembly. For his right of presidency does not extend to the election of other officers of the congregation.[49]

In the election of a superioress-general of a congregation of women religious of pontifical approval the election is ordinarily ratified by the consent of the one elected, for confirmation of this election is not required by the common law.[50] The particular law of the congregation, however, may require such confirmation. But when it is so required, the right of confirmation pertains to the S. Congregation for Religious and not to the local ordinary in the case of the congregations here considered.[51] Judicial redress against the election will be transmitted to and heard by the court of the local ordinary in first instance. But extrajudicial redress against the election will be lodged with the S. Congregation for Religious.[52]

From these observations on the method of election it can be seen that, throughout the whole process of the election of a superioress-general in congregations of women religious of pontifical approval, the local ordinary may well be called, in his right and duty of presiding, the guardian of the law. For it is his duty to oversee and declare that the election has taken place according to the norms of law. But any right of confirmation of the election for the superioress-general in the congregations here

[48] Cf. canon 176, § 1; Schaefer, *De Religiosis*, n. 136. If the one who has been elected does not manifest her consent within the time limit, all right to the office is automatically lost. Cf. canon 175.

[49] Cf. Goyeneche, "Consultationes"—*CpRM*, XI (1930), 437.

[50] Cf. Schaefer, *De Religiosis*, n. 131; Pruemmer, *Manuale Iuris Canonici*, q. 185; Parsons, *Canonical Elections*, p. 182.

[51] Cf. *Normae of 1901*, nn. 231-238; Pruemmer, *loc. cit.;* Parsons, *loc. cit.*

[52] Cf. canon 1579, § 3; Larraona, "De Electionibus Religiosorum"—*CpRM*, IX (1928), 339, note 111.

treated and the right of appointment in case of devolution[53] belongs to the S. Congregation for Religious.[54]

ARTICLE 2. THE QUINQUENNIAL REPORT

When during the nineteenth century the S. Congregation of Bishops and Regulars conceded approbation to a constitution of women religious, there was usually inserted a clause providing that a report be made by the superioress-general concerning the status of the congregation and that this report be sent to the S. Congregation at Rome every three years.[55]

The Constitution *"Conditae a Christo"* made no mention of this report, but the *Normae of* 1901 gave some general details concerning it, requiring a report concerning the disciplinary, material, personal and economic status of the institute.[56] But the decree *"In approbandis"* contained a detailed list of questions to be answered and suggested a specific form for making the report. This decree, however, made no provision for the signature of the local ordinary to the report.[57]

In the Code, the time interval for this report was changed from three years to five, and the signature of the local ordinary of the diocese in which the superioress-general resides must be attached to the report.[58] Subsequently the decree *"Sancitum est"*

[53] Cf. canon 178.

[54] Cf. Larraona, "Commentarium Codicis"—*CpRM,* VIII (1927), 294; Parsons, *Canonical Elections,* 212; Pruemmer, *Manuale Iuris Canonici,* q. 185.

[55] Cf. *Coll. S. C. Ep. et Reg.,* nn. 793, 794; Battandier, *Guide Canonique,* nn. 404, 405.

[56] Leo XIII, const. *"Conditae a Christo,"* 8 dec. 1900—*Fontes,* n. 644; *Normae of 1901,* art. 262.

[57] *S. C. Ep. et Reg.,* decr. *"In approbandis,"* 16 iul. 1906—*Fontes,* n. 2052.

[58] Canon 510: "The superior-general of every institute approved by the Holy See must, every five years, or oftener if the constitutions prescribe it, send to the Holy See a written account of the state of the institute, signed by himself, and the members of his council, and, in the case of congregations of women religious, also by the ordinary of the place in which the superioress-general and her council reside."

detailed the order in which this report was to be made by the institutes from various parts of the world.[59]

This report of the status of the congregation is to be made in writing and must be signed by the superioress-general, by the members of her council, and by the ordinary of the place in which the superioress-general resides with her council. What, then, is the relation of the local ordinary to this report? Does the requirement of his signature give him any added jurisdictional power over the congregation or even over the report? Not at all. For the signature of the local ordinary is but an authentication of the genuinity of the document, testifying that the report was drawn up and signed by the superioress-general with her council, as required by law.[60]

By common law the local ordinary has no right or duty to check or investigate the quinquennial report of the congregation. He may indeed extend his aid for the details of form, but it must be clear that his signature affirms the authenticity but not the verity of the financial, economical, personal, or disciplinary details of the report. For it should be remembered that the *praxis curiae* requires that congregations of women religious should always transmit documents to the Holy See through some ecclesiastic. In other affairs it is possible for the superioress-general to use the good graces of the Cardinal Protector, if she so desires. Here, however, the Code expressly requires the service of the ordinary of the place in which the superioress-general resides with her council.

[59] Cf. *S. C. de Rel.*, decr. *"Sancitum est,"* 8 mar. 1922—*ASS,* XIV (1922), 161. According to the provisions of this decree the different institutes of women are to send their quinquennial report to the Holy See in the following order, reckoning the years from January 1, 1923: first year, the institutes in Italy, Spain and Portugal; second year, those in France, Belgium, Holland, England and Ireland; third year, those in the other countries of Europe; fourth year, those of North and South America; fifth year, those in the remaining parts of the world. Thus American institutes are to make their report in the first and sixth years of each decade, i.e., 1941, 1946, etc.

[60] Cf. Larraona, "Commentarium Codicis"—*CpRM,* VIII (1927), 282.

CHAPTER X. ADMISSION AND DEPARTURE

ARTICLE 1. POSTULANCY

Postulancy in the religious life is the time intervening between the moment when a candidate for membership in a congregation of women religious of pontifical approval takes her abode in the religious house of the congregation or in the house of postulants with due permission of the competent superioress and the moment of her admission to the novitiate.[1]

There is no special formality specified in the common law for the beginning of the postulancy. Nor does the Code determine to whom belongs the right of admiting candidates to the postulancy. However, custom or special law usually attribute this right of admitting a postulant to the major superioress.[2] Definitely, in congregations of women religious of pontifical approval this right of admitting candidates to the postulancy does not pertain to the local ordinary, since such an act is part of the interior government of the institute, which, save for cases of abuse, is by canon 618 ruled to be beyond his realm.[3]

Postulants are subject to the local ordinary, of course, as members of the faithful. However, though postulants cannot be considered in the proper sense as religious, it will pertain to the religious superioress and the constitutions of the congregation to determine and arrange the specific exercises, requirements, and order of the term of their postulancy. However, since the local ordinary has the right of vigilance over the discipline of congregations of women religious of pontifical approval, he definitely has the right to ascertain that the discipline of the religious

[1] Fanfani, *De Iure Religiosorum,* n. 188.

[2] Coronata, *Institutiones,* I, n. 567, b; Schaefer, *De Religiosis,* n. 215; Battandier, *Instituts a Voeux Simples,* n. 126.

[3] Cf. Schaefer, *De Religiosis,* n. 423; Battandier, *Instituts a Voeux Simples,* N. 126. Moreover, in the congregations here treated the local ordinary can claim no right to be notified when a woman has been admitted to the postulancy. Cf. Coronata, *Institutiones,* I, n. 578, note 9.

houses, where postulants are placed, is observed with particular care. For the Code specifically stipulates that postulants be placed only in houses where the discipline prescribed by the constitutions is faithfully observed and that they be placed under the special care of an experienced religious.[4]

Since his rights are thus restricted, the local ordinary will guard against undue interference with the postulancy as an act of interior government and discipline. In accordance with prudent vigilance it will be found in ordinary circumstances that tactful warning to the superioress by the local ordinary regarding any abuse that comes to his attention will most generally be effective. His action in a grave abuse will be in accordance with the norms of canon 618, § 2, 2°.[5]

ARTICLE 2. THE NOVITIATE

The Novitiate is the time of probation spent by a candidate for the religious life in a house of the novitiate of the congregation of women religious of pontifical approval, under the direction of a specially appointed mistress of novices. This probation is required of all candidates before their admission to religious profession.[6]

A novice belongs to the religious family of the congregation, but juridically cannot be considered a fully incorporated member of the moral person. By common law, however, the novices of congregations of women religious of pontifical approval enjoy the privileges and spiritual favors granted to the congregation

[5] Canon 618, § 2, 2°: ". . . if superioresses upon being warned of the existence of grave abuses have failed to duly remedy them, the ordinary himself shall provide; if, however, something of graver consequence needs settlement without delay, the ordinary shall decide immediately; but he must then report his decision to the Holy See."

[6] Cf. Geser, *The Canon Law of Sisters*, q. 607; Schaefer, *De Religiosis*, n. 219; Fanfani, *De Iure Religiosorum*, n. 191. As noted above in the chapter on the establishment of religious houses, the special permission of the Holy See is always required for the establishment of a novitiate house in congregations of pontifical approval. Cf. canon 554, § 1.

[4] Cf. canon 540, § 1, in conjunction with canon 618, § 2, 2°.

and the privileges of clerics that are compatible with their religious state.[7]

As members of the faithful they are subject to the local ordinary in all obligations that are common to membership in the Church of Christ.[8] As novices they are subject to the regular observance of the obligations of the religious life, to the vigilance of the local ordinary in the observance of discipline, and to the authority of the mistress of novices and the religious superioresses of the congregation.[9]

Nowhere in the Code will one find that the right of admitting candidates to the novitiate or novices to profession is attributed to the local ordinary in the case of congregations of women religious of pontifical approval. This act is part of the interior government of the institute, and belongs to the religious superioresses. From the Code it is clear that the local ordinary is never acknowledged by the common law as a religious superior of the congregations treated in this study.[10]

However, at least two months before the religious superioress exercises her right of admitting a candidate to the novitiate, official notification of the fact must be made to the local ordinary.[11] And the local ordinary, or, if he be absent or otherwise impeded, then a priest delegated by him, must, at least thirty days before her admission to the novitiate, gratuitously and carefully examine the dispositions of the candidate.[12] Since this

[7] Cf. canon 614; Wernz-Vidal, *De Religiosis,* nn. 288, 290; Fanfani, *De Iure Religiosorum,* n. 201; Schaefer, *De Religiosis,* nn. 390-415.

[8] Wernz-Vidal, *De Religiosis,* n. 289.

[9] Cf. canons 561, § 2; 618, § 2, 2°. Cf. Fanfani, *De Iure Religiosorum,* n. 199; Wernz-Vidal, *De Religiosis,* n. 289; Geser, *The Canon Law of Sisters,* q. 735.

[10] Cf. canon 543. Wernz-Vidal, *De Reliogiosis,* n. 261; Fanfani, *De Iure Religiosorum,* n. 197; Battandier, *Instituts a Voeux Simples,* n. 136.

[11] Canon 552, § 1. Particular law will determine whether a major or minor superioress will make this notification. If the constitutions do not make this determination, then the duty of notification will devolve on the supreme moderator. Cf. Coronata, *Institutiones,* I, n. 578.

[12] Canon 552, § 2. It should be noted that even an immemorial custom, whereby a fee for this examination could be demanded, has been

same official notification by the superioress and the subsequent examination by the local ordinary or his delegate is required before the profession of temporary vows and before the perpetual profession, all three examinations may here be treated simultaneously.[13]

The purpose of the examination is outlined in the canon requiring it, namely, to carefully examine the dispositions of the candidate. Thus the examiner must inform himself as to whether the candidate has been constrained or beguiled,[14] and if she understands the import of the step that she is about to take.[15] Even though the full knowledge and perfect freedom of the candidate in petitioning admission to the religious state is patent, this notification by the superioress and the subsequent examination by the local ordinary is of grave obligation.[16] For the Church is gravely solicitous that definite assurance be provided concerning the freedom of the will and the sufficient knowledge of the candidate relative to the new form of life contemplated by her, for

expressly reprobated. Cf. *S. C. de Religiosis,* resp. 20 mart. 1922—*AAS.*, XIV (1922), 352; Fanfani, *De Iure Religiosorum,* n. 193, b. The examination should take place outside the cloister, unless the examiner is admitted by the superioress for a just and reasonable cause. Cf. canon 552, § 3; Schaefer, *De Religiosis,* n. 234, b.

[13] Cf. canon 552. This examination is required both for the first profession of temporary vows and for the profession of perpetual vows. It need not be repeated upon renewal of the profession of temporary vows, for only two examinations are required by the common law for candidates who do not make perpetual profession. Cf. Fanfani, *De Iure Religiosorum,* n. 246, dubium, II.

[14] "A vow made under the influence of grave and unjust fear is by that very fact invalid."—Canon 1307, § 3. "For the validity of the religious profession it is required . . . that the profession be free from violence, grave fear, or fraud."—Canon 572, § 1, 4°.

[15] Canon 552.

[16] The omission of the examination, however, would not in itself render the profession invalid, for there is no invalidating clause or equivalent stipulation in the canon. But the superioress who culpably omits due notification to the local ordinary can be punished by him according to the gravity of the fault, even to the point of being deprived of her office. Cf. canon 2412, 2°.

these two conditions are essential to happiness and spiritual advancement in the religious life.[17]

While no restriction is placed by the common law on the local ordinary concerning the priest whom he may delegate for this examination, it would seem indicated that he should refrain from appointing to this duty the pastor, confessor, or any other priest who may have had some influence in the determination of the candidate's decision to follow this vocation.

If the local ordinary or his priest delegate is fully satisfied regarding the pious intention and freedom of action, then the candidate may be conceded or denied admission by the superioress to the novitiate or, if already a novice, to profession. The result of this examination, however, will determine only whether the candidate could take the next step in religious life with the proper freedom and knowledge. One may deem it a *"nihil obstat"* to admission. But the ultimate right of granting the candidate admission to the novitiate or to profession still belongs to the major superioresses of the congregation, and in no way does the common law, by virtue of this examination, deprive the superioresses of their right to concede or deny this admission, provided the candidate's knowledge and freedom of action are deemed satisfactory by the examiner.[18]

Dispensation from the impediments of the common law to a valid or licit novitiate in a congregation of women religious of pontifical approval is of itself reserved to the Holy See.[19] Hence, a local ordinary cannot dispense from these impediments unless this power has been explicitly or implicitly conceded to him, or unless it be a case of emergency in which recourse to the Holy See proves difficult and any delay would occasion the danger of serious harm or detriment, provided, also, that there be a question

[17] Conc. Trid., sess. XXV, *de regularibus et monialibus*, c. 17; Wernz-Vidal, *De Religiosis*, n. 273; Battandier, *Instituts a Voeux Simples*, n. 166, § 1.

[18] Cf. canon 543; Wernz-Vidal, *De Religiosis*, n. 273; Blat, *De Religiosis*, n. 428.

[19] Cf. Wernz-Vidal, *De Religiosis*, n. 260.

of such a dispensation as the Holy See is wont to grant.[20] Dispensation from impediments that arise exclusively from the constitutions of the congregation can be granted by the Holy See or by the superioress of the congregation whom the constitutions empower with that faculty.[21]

The training of novices is definitely a part of the internal government of the congregation, being reserved primarily to the Mistress of novices.[22] Hence the local ordinary has no right to interfere with that regime, excepting the right of vigilance accorded to him by canon 618, § 2, 2° and his part in the correction of abuses, as noted in this same canon.[23] In his provision of confessors for the novices the local ordinary will be guided by the same prescriptions which are to be followed in providing confessors for the professed members of the congregation.[24]

When a second year of novitiate is required by the constitutions of congregations of women religious of pontifical approval, due attention must be paid to the Instruction issued by the S. Congregation for Religious concerning some details of the regime of this second year.[25] Even during the second year of novitiate,

[20] Cf. canon 81; Reilly, *The General Norms of Dispensation, The Catholic University of America Canon Law Studies No. 119,* (Washington, D. C.: The Catholic University of America, 1939), p. 64 ff. Woywod *(A Practical Commentary,* II, Appendix V) notes that in their quinquennial faculties the Bishops of the United States usually enjoy the concession to dispense from partial or entire lack of dowry under certain conditions or provisions.

[21] Wernz-Vidal, *De Religiosis,* n. 260.

[22] Canon 561.

[23] But it must be noted that the ordinary of the place of the novitiate house has the same right and duty of making a canonical visitation of the novitiate house that he enjoys with relation to other religious houses within his territory that belong to the congregations of women religious of pontifical approval, for no religious house of such congregations is excluded from the ruling of Canon 512, § 2, 3°, which regulates the local ordinary's visitational rights and duties.

[24] Cf. canons 556, 520-577; Fanfani, *De Iure Religiosorum,* n. 212.

[25] Cf. *S. C. de Religiosis,* instr., 3 nov. 1921—*AAS,* XIII (1921), 539.

the Instruction declares, the discipline of the spiritual life must be attended to above all else. With prudence and moderation, and purely for the sake of instruction, the novices of the second year may be employed in the works of the institute, if the constitutions allow it. But they should be engaged in this work under the direction and supervision of an older religious and should never be so employed that they perform these works alone (for example, taking the place of absent teachers or instructors in schools, or ministering to the sick in hospitals). Moreover, two months before their profession of vows these novices must be withdrawn from all exterior works, and if they have been out of the novitiate they must be recalled to it, so that they may prepare for profession by strengthening themselves in the spirit of their vocation.

Practice teaching or practice nursing, therefore, would be permitted to the novices of the second year, provided they are under the direction and supervision of an older religious. But for a novice to act as regular or even substitute teacher, as head of hospital wards, etc., is strictly forbidden. When novices of the second year are employed in these exterior works, the vigilance of the local ordinary would seem to extend to the curbing of such abuses. Even when they are legitimately employed, these novices must be recalled to the house of novitiate at least two months before their profession.

Article 3. Profession

For the validity of any religious profession in congregations of women religious of pontifical approval it is required that the profession be received by the legitimate superior according to the constitutions, either personally or by delegate.[26] Reception of the profession of vows is not an act of jurisdiction but an act of dominative power, and is ordinarily reserved to the major superioress of the congregations here treated.[27]

[26] Cf. canon 572, § 1, 6°.

[27] Schaefer, *De Religiosis,* n. 266, 6°; Blat, *De Religiosis,* n. 428; Battandier, *Instituts a Voeux Simples,* n. 183.

At times, however, the formula of profession, in accordance with the constitutions, may make no mention of the superioress but only of the bishop or his delegate. In such a case the bishop or his delegate is considered as acting in the name of the superioress with the special mandate to receive the profession.[28] But, if the constitutions have not thus attributed this power to the local ordinary, he is not to be considered as acting in the name of the superioress of the congregations here treated, and he or his delegate would thus act only as ministers of cult or as qualified witnesses at a profession which is made in the hands of the religious superioress.[29]

[28] *P. C. I.*, 1 mart. 1921—*AAS*, XIII (1921), 177.

[29] Schaefer, *De Religiosis*, n. 266, 6°. If the ordinary of the place acts as delegate of the superioress, this fact should be noted in the register of professions so as to preclude any grounds of attack *de nullitate professionis*. Cf. Battandier, *Instituts a Voeux Simples*, n. 183.

CHAPTER XI. CANONICAL VISITATION

Article 1. The Local House

Canonical visitation of a religious house is a general inquisition made by a legitimate ecclesiastical visitor and concerns itself with the state of the house, its government, and the life of the religious membership.[1] Two general types of visitation are provided for with reference to congregations of women religious of pontifical approval—the extraordinary and the ordinary visitation. In the extraordinary visitation the procedure is in keeping with the judicial process, since the visitor acts as a duly authorized judge concerning some specific delict or against some certain and determined person.[2] In the ordinary visitation a general inquiry is made concerning the religious house, an inquiry which concerns itself with the state of the house, its government, and the life of the religious membership therein.[3]

Canon 512 attributes to the local ordinary the right and duty of making an ordinary visitation of each religious house of congregations of women religious of pontifical approval within his diocese. The general purpose of this visitation may be delineated in the light of the scope of the general visitation which a local ordinary must make of his diocese as stated in the Code, *viz,* the preservation of sound doctrine, the protection of good morals, the correction of evils, the promotion of peace, innocence, piety and discipline among the faithful, and the ordering of all other affairs that affect the welfare of religion.[4]

[1] Blat, *De Religiosis,* n. 153; Fanfani, *De Iure Religiosorum,* n. 69.

[2] When the ordinary of the place is making an extraordinary visitation to congregations of women religious of pontifical approval, he shall be guided by the instructions and particular purpose of the visitation as outlined in the mandate given by the Holy See. Cf. Fanfani, *De Iure Religiosorum,* n. 71.

[3] Blat, *De Religiosis,* n. 153; Fanfani, *De Iure Religiosorum,* n. 69.

[4] Cf. canon 343, § 1; Conc. Trid., sess. XXIV, *de ref.,* c. 3.

As members of the faithful, the members of the religious house of the congregations here treated are subject to the local ordinary in the same manner as other members of Christ's Church. As religious, they are not subject to him in matters of internal government or discipline except in the cases expressed by the law.[5] But in the internal discipline of religious houses of congregations of women religious of pontifical approval the Code instructs the local ordinary that he has the right and duty of inquiring: a) whether the discipline is maintained conformably to the constitutions; b) whether sound doctrine and good morals have suffered in any way; c) whether there are breaches of the law of enclosure; d) whether the reception of the sacraments is regular and frequent.[6] Inquiry into the temporal administration of the religious congregation in the case of the congregations here treated is strictly limited, being restricted to the matters treated in canons 532-535.[7] Thus one sees, that the visitation will concern places, persons, and things.[8]

In the prescriptions concerning the general visitation of the diocese, the local ordinary is not permitted to delegate that duty unless he is legitimately impeded.[9] But this restriction is not found in canon 512, for the canon merely states: "The local ordinary must visit . . . either in person or by delegate." It would appear, therefore, that the local ordinary is left free to delegate this duty.[10]

But he is certainly under grave obligation to see that the visitation is made. And so grave is this obligation that if the local ordiary neglects it, the duty will devolve upon the metropolitan, who, however, must first inform the Holy See of this neglect and receive

[5] Cf. canon 618, § 2, 2°.

[6] Cf. canons 512, § 2, 3° and 618, § 2, 2°.

[7] Cf. canon 512, § 3.

[8] Pruemmer, *Manuale Iuris Canonici,* q. 122; Coronata, *Institutiones.* I, n. 400.

[9] Cf. canon 343, § 1; Vermeersch-Creusen, *Epitome,* I, n. 413; Coronata, *Institutiones,* I, n. 400; Larraona, "Commentarium Codicis"—*CpRM,* VIII (1927), 358.

[10] Coronata, *Institutiones, I,* p. 647, note 5; Larraona, "Commentarium Codicis"—*CpRM,* VIII (1927), 440.

approval.[11] In the writer's opinion it would seem more in keeping with the spirit and purpose of the visitation that the local ordinary, when this is possible, make a personal visitation even of the religious houses, for thus he may acquire a direct knowledge and insight into those matters over which he has jurisdiction.[12]

In the norms for the general visitation of the diocese the local ordinary is directed to make this visitation at least (*saltem*) once every five years.[13] But, in expressing the time period for the visitation of religious houses, the Code has omitted the use of the phrase "at least" (*saltem*).[14] It may safely be stated, then that the local ordinary is not obligated to an ordinary visitation of the houses of these congregations more frequently than once every five years.

Larraona and Toso are the only commentators who, in the knowledge of the writer, press the question still farther. Is the local ordinary free to make an ordinary visitation of the houses of congregations of women religious of pontifical approval more frequently, if he so desires? Both Larraona and Toso agree that, if a faculty for more frequent visitation is necessary, such faculty cannot be found in canon 512.[15] The writer is of the opinion that the local ordinary must restrict his *ordinary* visitation of the houses

[11] Cf. canon 274, 5°; Pruemmer, *Manuale Iuris Canonici,* q. 122; Rèilly, *The Visitation of Religious, The Catholic University of America Canon Law Studies No. 112,* (Washington, D. C.: The Catholic University of America, 1938), 87; Larraona, "Commentarium Codicis"—*CpRM,* VIII (1927), 441.

[12] It may be observed in passing that in some dioceses one will find that the care of the affairs of women religious in their relations with the diocese has been entrusted by the local ordinary to certain officials (clerics). Such officials receive no mention in the Code. And whether they may make the visitation of the religious house depends on the faculties which they receive from the local ordinary. Cf. Goyeneche, "Quaenam sunt attributiones Directoris Congregationis dioecesanae?" —*CpRM,* XIV (1933), 357.

[13] Cf. canon 343, § 1.

[14] Cf. canon 512, § 1.

[15] Larraona, "Commentarium Codicis"—*CpRM,* III (1927), 444; Toso, Ad Codicem Iuris Canonici Commentaria Minora (Romae: Marietti, 1920-1934), II-II, 49.

of congregations of women religious of pontifical approval to once every five years. Definitely, unlike the diocesan congregations concerning which even the religious life is subject to the jurisdiction of the local ordinary,[16] the interior regime of congregations of women religious of pontifical approval is subject to the jurisdiction of the local ordinary only in the cases expressed by the law.[17] A visitation by the local ordinary is often disturbing to the general order of the religious house, as experience proves, and suspends the right of major superioresses to freedom of transfer of subjects.[18] Moreover, frequency of visitation might easily destroy that very freedom in interior government and in the exercise of the juridical acts of the institute which the congregation has received in achieving its pontifical approval.

One must concede that, if the superioresses fail to remedy the abuses brought to their attention by the local ordinary in his ordinary visitation, he may return and make due provision, but in that instance the second visit must rather be construed as morally forming a part of one and the same canonical visitation. Moreover, there is hardly any danger of abuse or laxity in this restriction of the visitation, for the local ordinary habitually has the right and duty of vigilance (a vigilance that can be exercised through other means than the detailed and thorough investigation of an ordinary visitation) over congregations of women religious of pontifical approval.[19] By way of correlative argument, it may here be in place to mention that in the preparatory edition of the Code there was a provision for repeated visitations of the monasteries of nuns subject

[16] Schaefer, *De Religiosis,* n. 148; Fanfani, *De Iure Religiosorum,* n. 45; Gallik, *The Rights and Duties of Bishops Regarding Diocesan Sisterhoods,* p. 83.

[17] Cf. canon 618, § 2, 2°.

[18] "Tempore quo Visitator visitationem incipit, Superioris ordinarii auctoritas, in iis ad quae manus apponit Visitator, impeditur, licet non cesset."—Coronata, *Institutiones,* I, n. 540, e.

[19] Thus, if he has reason to feel that there is some abuse or laxity that needs correction, he could telephone or write the superioress, or even make a personal visit, without all the fomalities of an ordinary visitation.

to a regular superior, but this was deleted in the promulgated edition of the Code.[20]

In matters pertaining to the Christian life and sacerdotal ministry, canon 512 enumerates as subject to visitation by the local ordinary the church, the public oratory, the sacristy, and the places where confessions are heard.[21] In this country, churches or even public oratories are rarely found in connection with the religious houses of women religious of pontifical approval.[22] For the chapels of these religious communities are most generally semi-public oratories, to which the religious superioress is usually free to admit the faithful, but has no obligation to do so. Chapels in the country house or summer villa, the secondary chapels in which a distinct group of religious assist at Holy Mass, and even the chapel in the infirmary of a religious house are generally classed as semi-public oratories.[23]

Though the norms for the general visitation of the diocese stipulate that the jurisdiction of the local ordinary in his visitation extends to all persons, things, and places within his diocese which have not been granted a special exemption from visitation by the Holy See,[24] it must be noted that, in the enumeration of sacred places to be visited in religious houses, canon 512, § 2, 2°, has

[20] Cf. canon 512, § 2, 1°; Larraona, "Commentarium Codicis"—*CpRM*, VIII (1927), 444, note 485.

[21] Common law places the public oratory on the same legal basis as the church. Cf. can. 1191.

[22] Churches and oratories are places designed for divine worship; the church for the worship of all the faithful, the oratory for the convenience of a particular group. Three kinds of oratories are listed by the Code: a) Public—if established in such a manner that all the faithful have a legitimately established right to enter, at least during the hours of divine service; b) Semi-public—if admission is not free to all the faithful; c) Private—if established in a private house for the benefit only of some family or private individual. Cf. canons 1161; 1188.

It may be added that the common law expressly stipulates that no church belonging to women religious may be made a parochial church. Cf. canon 609, § 2.

[23] Creusen-Garesché-Ellis. *Religious Men and Women in the Code*, n. 135.

[24] Cf. canon 344, § 1.

omitted mention of the semi-public oratories. Are then the semi-public oratories of congregations of women religious of pontifical approval excluded from visitation by the local ordinary?

Goyeneche,[25] and Schaefer[26] are of the opinion that the local ordinary is empowered to visit only the public oratories and church of religious and not their semi-public oratories, since semi-public oratories have been omitted from the specific enumeration of canon 512, § 2,2°, and may be considered as forming part of the elements that pertain to the inner life of the religious house.[27]

While the local ordinary may be justly excluded from the visitation of semi-public oratories of clerical congregations, since his visitation does not extend to their internal government or discipline, yet the chapels of women religious of pontifical approval, even though such chapels are connected with the inner life of the community, are subject to the visitation of the local ordinary. For, in the congregations here treated, some elements of the interior life of the community are subject to the visitation of the local ordinary. And the very center of religious life, of its discipline, its doctrine, its morals, as well as the place for the reception of the most frequently utilized of the Sacraments, is the chapel. Moreover, such chapels cannot be established without the permission of the local ordinary, who must first ascertain by inspection that the place of location is properly situated and equipped.[28] The local ordinary may even limit the services of divine worship performed within such semi-public oratories.[29] If, then, one were to exclude such semi-public oratories from the visitation of the local ordinary, these sacred places would be subject to the visitation of no ecclesiastical superior, which seems inconsonant with the exacting details and prescriptions of the law regarding such places.[30]

[25] Cf. "Consultationes"—*CpRM,* III (1922), 335.
[26] *De Religiosis,* n. 97 b.
[27] Cf. also Wernz-Vidal, *De Religiosis,* n. 146, note 91.
[28] Cf. canon 1192, §§ 1, 2, 3.
[29] Cf. canon 1193.
[30] Cf. Coronata, *Institutiones,* p. 648, note 2.

The local ordinary is not a religious superior to the congregations of women religious of pontifical approval. Hence he must carefully restrict his visitation concerning the affairs of internal government to the cases expressed in the law.[31] Nevertheless there are several matters pertaining to internal discipline and government concerning which he must inquire. Thus, in the congregations here treated, he must inquire: a) whether the discipline is maintained conformably to the constitutions; b) whether sound doctrine and good morals have suffered in any way; c) whether there are breaches of the law of enclosure; d) whether the reception of sacraments is regular and frequent.[32]

In the matter of discipline, it should be noted that the Code emphasizes that the regular observance of the religious house must be conformable to the constitutions of that particular institute.[33] With the divergency of scope and purpose that is manifest in the many congregations of women religious that have attained pontifical approval, it is to be expected that the rigor of discipline exacted by the particular constitutions will vary in its demands. Hence, previous to the visitation, an adequate study of the constitutions of the particular congregation is requisite for a due apperception and insight into what constitutes conformity to the required discipline, and for any ready advertence to what betokens a non-conformity to or a breach of the constiutional requirements in the discipline of the religious house.

Moreover, when one considers the weakness and frailty of human nature, it is only to be expected that, at times, the visitor will find some conditions or trends that are conducive to laxity or even abuse. The visitation, in fact, is specifically designed to disclose and to remedy such proclivities.[34] While it is true that the local ordinary must use tact and prudence, lest he interfere

[31] Schaefer, *De Religiosis*, n. 96; Wernz-Vidal, *De Religiosis*, n. 87 Coronata, *Institutiones*, I, n. 530; Vermeersch-Cruesen, *Epitome*, I, n. 568.

[32] Cf. canon 618, § 2, 2°.

[33] Coronata, *Institutiones*, I, n. 606; Schaefer, *De Religiosis*, n. 319; Fanfani, *De Iure Religiosorum*, n. 31.

[34] Blat, *De Religiosis*, n. 153.

unduly with the internal government of the religious congregation, yet, as a duly empowered inquirer, he is designated to seek out the facts, and therefore can never be satisfied with an investigation that is perfunctory or superficial, or with an inquiry which foils, rather than it promotes, any certified knowledge that due conformity to the required religious discipline obtains.

The investigation of the doctrine and morals of the religious house is a task whose exercise constitutes the unique right of the local ordinary, for he is the appointed teacher and guardian of faith and morals in the diocese.[35] With reference to the local ordinary's visitational rights and duties as touching upon the observance of the enclosure by congregations of women religious of pontifical approval a special study will be made in a later portion of the present chapter.[36]

Regarding the frequentation of the Sacraments, the Code prescribes that superioresses should promote the frequent, even daily, reception of Holy Communion; and liberty must be given to every properly disposed religious to approach frequently, even daily, the most Holy Eucharist.[37] Generally it is beyond the power of any superioress to proscribe or forbid the reception of Holy Communion to any member of the congregation, for the determination of the frequency in the reception of Holy Communion is part of the duty of the confessor.[38] If, however, a religious has since her last sacramental confession given grave scandal to the community, or committed a serious external fault, the superioress can forbid her to receive Holy Communion until she has

[35] Cf. canon 1326; Vermeersch-Creusen, *Epitome,* II, n. 662; Coronata, *Institutiones,* II, n. 908, b; Wernz-Vidal, *De Rebus,* n. 617, II, III,

[36] Cf. *infra.* Art. 2, p. 112.

[37] Cf. canon 595, § 2; *S. C. de Sacramentis:* Instructio reservata. De Communione habituali et pene generali in Seminariis, Collegiis, Communitatibus etiam religiosis et de abusibus in eadem praecavendis,—Larraona, "Adnotationes"—*CpRM,* XXI (1940), 133.

[38] Vermeersch-Creusen, *Epitome,* I, n. 698; Blat, *De Religiosis,* n. 517; Fanfani, *De Iure Religiosorum,* n. 323; S. C. Ep. et Reg., decr. *"Quemadmodum,"* '17 dec. 1890, n. 6—*Fontes,* n. 2017.

previously appproached the sacrament of penance.[39] Moreover, it should be noted that when the constitutions or the calendar of the congregation prescribe certain fixed days for the reception of Holy Communion, these have only a directive force.[40]

In the common law the religious are obliged to approach the Sacrament of Penance at least once a week. Since this is an *actus externus,* or at least an *actus mixtus,* the local ordinary has the right to ascertain that the precept is observed.[41] And the visitation to the religious house should provide the local ordinary with an excellent opportunity to ascertain whether the confessors appointed for the house are satisfactory and if there be need of any special provision for the spiritual needs of the members of the community.

The visitation of the local ordinary as it affects the administration of temporalities in congregations of women religious of pontifical approval is very definitely restricted. Canon 512, § 3, stipulates that the procedure in such a visitation will be guided by the norms of canons 532-535. In a subsequent chapter it will be shown that only the dowries, the funds that have been donated or bequeathed to the house for expenditure locally on divine worship or for works of charity, and the funds given to religious for the benefit of the parish or mission are comprised in the temporalities specifically mentioned as subject to the visitational inquiry and control of the local ordinary. All inquiry into and control of the other funds of the house, of the province, or of the congregation, used for the purpose of the institute's internal economic administration is beyond the realm of the local ordinary's visitational or jurisdictional rights.[42]

[39] Canon 595. § 3; Coronata, *Institutiones,* I, n. 608, note 6; Vermeersch-Creusen, *Epitome,* I, n. 698; Claeys Bouuaert-Simeon, *Manuale Iuris Canonici ad Usum Seminariorum,* I (4. ed. Gandae et Leodii, 1934), n. 664; Augustine, *Commentary,* III, 308.

[40] Canon 595, § 4; *S. C. C.,* decr. "*Sacra Tridentina Synodus,*" 20 dec. 1905, n. 8—*Fontes,* n. 4326; Vermeersch-Creusen, *Epitome,* I, n. 698; Coronata, *Institutiones,* I, n. 608.

[41] Fanfani, *De Iure Religiosorum,* n. 322; cf. canon 595, § 1, 3°.

[42] Fanfani, *De Iure Religiosorum,* n. 70; Reilly, *The Visitation of*

All schools, orphanages, asylums, recreational centers, and other similar institutes conducted by congregations of women religious of pontifical approval may and should be visited by the local ordinary, either personally or through a delegate, and investigation should be made of all matters connected with religious and moral instruction.[43] A detailed study of the subjection of schools, hospitals, ecclesiastical non-collegiate institutes and pious foundations will follow in subsequent chapters.

Since the local ordinary is visiting the religious house and not the province or the congregation, his visitation will not extend even to the provincial curia, for the provinces of congregations of women religious of pontifical approval are regarded by canonical legislation as transcending diocesan limits.[44] Nor does his visitation extend to the major superioresses as such, since they are representatives of the general government of the congregation. But it must be remembered that when these representatives are also members of the community of the local house that is visited, they can be interrogated by the local ordinary.[45]

In the matters that pertain to the visitation the local ordinary has the right and duty of interrogating all or any of the religious who are subject to the visitation and who he feels will be

Religious, 114. It may be noted, however, that the pious dispositions, trusts and endowments entrusted to religious are subject to the local ordinary's control by virtue of the general legislation. Cf. *infra,* p. 153.

[43] Canon 1382. The only schools excepted in this canon are the internal schools for professed religious of exempt institutes. In as far as this study is confined to non-exempt religious, one must conclude that even such schools of the congregations here treated are subject to the visitation of the local ordinary. Cf. Goyeneche, "Consultationes"—*CpRM,* IV (1923), 224.

[44] The right of examination of the general funds of the congregation as well as of the administration of them is reserved to the S. Congregation for Religious and is ordinarily executed through the quinquennial report. Cf. Reilly, *The Visitation of Religious,* 114.

[45] "Si superior generalis, qua talis, esset subditus Ordinarii, impossible esset regimen universale."—Larraona, "Studia Canonica"—*CpRM,* X (1929), 376, note 29.

of aid to him in executing this duty.[46] It is not required that the local ordinary should always question all the members of the religious house, or interrogate each in all the matters that are subject to the visitation, but it is left to his prudent judgment to subject to interrogation as many members of the house as it is necessary to interview for an adequate information in the matters that concern his visitation.[47] Indeed the local ordinary could well apportion his questioning among the various religious in such a manner as to obtain information concerning the entire scope of his visitation.

The species of questions to be asked is not stipulated in the common law, for circumstances and conditions will generally determine the form of questions to be asked. It would seem properly indicated, however, that at least one question that is more or less general in content should be proposed. This would give the individual religious an opportunity to supply information useful to the visitation and such information would in all probability throw light on matters that would otherwise either remain obscure or demand more specific investigation. Generally an oath will not be required for the ascertainment of truth in an ordinary visitation and, in usual circumstances, it is considered doubtful by some canonists whether such an oath should be imposed.[48]

There is no mention in the Code of any right on the part of the visitor to inquire into matters of conscience, although it is clear that voluntary confidences regarding the state of the individual's conscience may be made to the local ordinary at will. Ordinarily, however, these matters are better left to the spiritual director, or to the confessor, and the religious should confine her statements to the externals of religious discipline.[49] Secrecy con-

[46] Canon 513; Blat, *De Religiosis,* n. 161; Vermeersch-Creusen; *Epitome,* n. 581.

[47] Blat, *Loc. cit.*

[48] Cf. Geser, *The Canon Law Governing Communities of Sisters* (St. Louis: Herder, 1939), q. 375; Fanfani, *De Iure Religiosorum,* n. 71. In a judicial visitation, however, the oath is used. Cf. can. 1944, § 1.

[49] Cf. Reilly, *The Visitation of Religious,* p. 154, quoting Jombart,

cerning the interrogation may be imposed by the local ordinary if in his prudent judgment he feels that the gravity of the matter of the interrogation requires it.[50]

The obligation of furnishing a truthful reply to the interrogation embraces both the superioress and the members of the house.[51] But the secret faults or crimes of another member of the community should not be revealed by a religious in the ordinary visitation unless circumstances are such that the great harm to the community cannot otherwise be prevented or, at least, unless the imputation of the transgression had already been revealed. For justice demands that a religious retain the right to her good name and the local ordinary in this visitation is concerned primarily with the common good and is not acting as particular judge of secret faults and crimes. But when judicial denunciation is necessary, the local ordinary may command such denunciation by precept.[52]

As a general rule, however, the local ordinary should proceed in a paternal manner, and only when circumstances are of exceptional gravity should he have recourse to judicial forms.[53] The latter could take place if, for example, there were question of a crime committed by a religious, or if the transgression were of a serious or gravely scandalous nature.[54] But when the local ordinary has recourse to judicial forms, his decisions, like those of any

"Visite des monasteres et ouverture de conscience"—*NRT,* LI (1924), 624, 625

[50] Geser, *The Canon Law Governing Communities of Sisters,* q. 376; Fanfani, *De Iure Religiosorum,* n. 71.

[51] Canon 513; Blat, *De Religiosis,* n. 161; Larraona, "Commentarium Codicis"—*CpRM,* IX (1928), 27.

[52] Cf. canon 1935, § 2. Reilly, *The Visitation of Religious,* 155; Fanfani (*De Iure Religiosorum,* n. 72): In some institutes the religious have renounced their rights against the denunciation of their secret faults.

[53] Canon 345; Coronata, *Institutiones,* I, n. 540, e; Augustine, *Commentary,* III, p. 139; Creusen-Garesche-Ellis, *Religious Men and Women in the Code,* n. 93; Gallik, *The Rights and Duties of Bishops Concerning Diocesan* Sisterhoods, p. 87.

[54] Cf. canons 2220—2225.

other judge, will be subject to appeal which suspends their execution.[55]

The procedure for the correction of abuses is outlined in canon 618, § 2, 2°, instructing the local ordinary that, when he discovers abuses in houses of women religious of congregations of pontifical approval, he is to advise the superioresses of the fact. While the canon does not specify what superioresses are to be advised, one may rightfully conclude that this has been left to the prudent judgment of the local ordinary and will depend on the gravity of the abuse and its origin.[56] The local ordinary, therefore, will refrain from needless interference with internal matters of the house. But when the religious superioresses have not effected the necessary improvements or remedies within a reasonable time, the local ordinary may take action as the case demands.

A more direct procedure, however, is prescribed for affairs of greater importance which admit of no delay. At such times the local ordinary is to settle the matter immediately. A copy of his decree, containing the facts of the case and the course pursued, is then to be forwarded to the Holy See.[57]

Recourse against any ordinances, precepts or changes that the local ordinary imposes during visitation may be made to the Holy See. But such a recourse does not suspend the obligation of observing the decree, unless the local ordinary has proceeded in judiciary form.[58]

[55] Cf. canon 1889, § 2.

[56] "In cases, however, in which the local superioress is incapable of restoring good order or is herself the cause of discord and abuses, it will be necessary to acquaint the provincial or general superioress with the state of affairs."—Reilly, *The Visitation of Religious*, p. 113. It is reasonable to suppose that in most cases it will suffice to place the facts before the local superioress, as the latter in ordinary circumstances will have enough power and good will to effect a remedy.

[57] "The visitor seems to be obliged to send a copy of his decree to the Holy See, not only when he has immediately acted in grave matters, but also when he intervenes upon the failure of the superiores to remedy the abuses he has pointed out."—Reilly, *The Visitation of Religious*, p. 114.

[58] Canon 513, § 2. Blat, *De Religiosis*, n. 161; Vermeersch-Creusen, *Epitome*, I, n. 581.

Canon 513, § 1, clearly stipulates that it is not lawful for superioresses to divert the religious in any way from their obligation of replying to the interrogation of the local ordinary according to the truth, or otherwise to impede the scope of the visitation. As Blat remarks, this obligation extends not only to the local superioress but also to the major superioresses as well.[59] Moreover, all religious, whether superioresses or subjects, who personally or through others, directly or indirectly, have induced any religious not to reply to the questions of the visitor, or to dissimulate or not sincerely to expose the truth, and, finally, those who under any pretext whatsoever have molested any religious on account of the replies which she has given to the visitor, shall be declared by the visitor as incapable of obtaining any office which bears with it the government of other religious, and the superioresses, if found guilty in this respect, shall be deposed from office.[60]

It should also be remembered that once the approaching visitation has been announced to the religious house, the right of superioresses to move their subjects is suspended, unless consent of the visitor is obtained. And the same penalties as those above indicated are to be applied to any superioress who, after the visitation has been announced, transfers a religious to another house without the consent of the visitor.[61]

Article 2: The Enclosure

"Cloister" or "Enclosure" in the formal sense is that law by which religious are prohibited from going beyond the limits of their religious house except as permitted by law; and externs are denied free ingress into definitely determined portions of the religious house of the material cloister, i. e., of those portions of the religious house which are reserved for the exclusive use of the religious.[62]

[59] Blat, *De Religiosis,* n. 161.

[60] Canon 2413, § 1.

[61] Canon 2413, § 1. Coronata, *Institutiones,* I, 540, e; Blat, *De Delictis et Poenis,* n. 259.

[62] Fanfani, *De Iure Religiosorum,* n. 303; Wernz-Vidal, *De Religiosis,* n. 374; Coronata, *Institutiones,* I, n. 610.

The enclosure for regulars with solemn vows is known as the papal enclosure. Its provisions are minutely detailed in the Code. For the violation of this enclosure there are enacted severe penalties in the law of the Code.[63]

The legislation of the Code concerning enclosure as obligatory for congregations of women religious of pontifical approval is, indeed meager in detail. While it is not intended that the enclosure for these congregations be as severe as is that for nuns with solemn vows, one may conclude, from the various references to the enclosure of nuns, that this enclosure of nuns should serve as a norm, in a mitigated form, for the establishment of the enclosure of the congregations here treated.[64]

The Code expressly stipulates that enclosure must be observed in congregations of women religious of pontifical approval.[65] While it is true that this enclosure is of a modified type, yet its establishment is not a matter of judgment, choice, or discretion, but an obligation of the common law.[66]

In the law regarding enclosure for regulars all canonically established houses destined for the residence of these religious were embraced by the obligation of enclosure.[67] Even non-formal houses that are canonically established for the habitual residence of religious should have this enclosure.[68] Since enclosure is a safeguard against the distractions and cares of the world and therefore constitutes an integral aid to advancement in religious perfection, the opinion appears justified that all established houses of congregations of women religious of pontifical approval are obligated to partial enclosure.

[63] Cf. canons 597-603; 2342.

[64] In the canon that treats of the establishment of enclosure for congregations of women religious of pontifical or diocesan approval (c. 604) reference is made to canons 598, § 2, 599, and 600.

[65] Cf. canon 604.

[66] Cf. Coronata, *Institutiones*, I, n. 610, note 6.

[67] Cf. canon 597, § 1.

[68] This does not include summer villas or hospices where there is no established religious life. Cf. Coronata, *Institutiones*, I, n. 611; Pruemmer, *Manuale Iuris Canonici*, q. 227; Schaaf, *The Cloister*, 59.

While admittance of persons of the male sex to the enclosure of congregations of women religious of pontifical approval is in general regulated by the same provisions as those which obtain for the papal enclosure of nuns,[69] extern women are not prohibited by the common law from entering the enclosure of the congregations here treated.[70] But, as Pruemmer remarks, the admission of extern women should not be allowed to become an occasion for the decline of the religious spirit of the house.[71] Moreover, a superioress, if not restricted by the constitutions, may make exceptions, even for the admission of the male sex, for a just and reasonable cause; and no authorization of the local ordinary is necessary for the exercise of this faculty.[72]

The specific determination and clear indication of the exact limits of the particular area embraced by the enclosure of congregations of women religious of pontifical approval is not treated in the Code. While one realizes that the constitutions will generally determine what parts of the house should be considered as being within the enclosure, the common law seems to leave undetermined the question: whose right and duty is it to establish the limits of the enclosure in a particular house?

In orders of men this act is entrusted to the major superiors or to the general chapter in accordance with the constitutions of the institute.[73] In monasteries of nuns, however, this right and duty of exactly determining the limits of the enclosure in the religious house and of modifying these limits for a lawful reason is reserved to the local ordinary.[74] Since the enclosure of sisters is to be fashioned after that of nuns,[75] one may conclude by

[69] Cf. canons 598, § 2; 600; 604.

[77] Cf. *Normae of 1901,* n. 170.

[71] Pruemmer, *Manuale Iuris Canonici,* q. 228.

[72] But the jurisdiction of the local ordinary will certainly extend to the correction of any abuse in the exercise of the faculty.' Cf. canons 618, § 2, 2°, 605; Schaefer, *De Religiosis,* n. 363, 2°; Coronata, *Institutiones,* I, n. 613, e.

[73] Canon 597, § 3.

[74] Canon 597, § 3.

[75] Cf. Wernz-Vidal, *De Religiosis,* n. 381.

analogy that such a right and duty is reserved to the local ordinary in the case of establishing the limits of the enclosure in the congregations of women religious of pontifical approval.[76] It appears, therefore, that it is the duty and obligation of the local ordinary to establish the limits of the enclosure in the particular houses of the congregations here treated that are within his diocese. This could be done by consultation, by the marking of the architectural plans, or by visit to the house; and the parts of the house enclosed must be in accordance with the constitutions of the congregation.[77]

The penalties for the violation of the enclosure that are enacted in canon 2343 are inflicted only for the violation of the papal cloister in a house of religious with solemn vows and do not affect those who violate the enclosure in congregations with simple vows.[78] But in particular circumstances and for grave reasons the bishop may safeguard the enclosure of a congregation of women religious of pontifical approval with censures.[79] The local ordinary must be vigilant in the due enforcement of the regulations governing the enclosure and in the efficacious correction of abuses that may arise in this respect.

But the mind of the Church is adverse to the facile multiplication of penalties, and the local ordinary should be sparing in employing censures in this duty, particularly if other means will

[76] The limits of the enclosure must be clearly indicated. Cf. canon 597, § 3. It is suggested that some such sign as: CLOISTER—NO ADMITANCE should be placed at the entrance to the enclosure. Cf. Schaaf, *The Cloister,* 70; Fanfani, *De Iure Religiosorum,* n. 304.

[77] Cf. *Normae of 1901,* n. 170.

[78] Cf. Schaaf, *The Cloister,* p. 158.

[79] Cf. canon 604, § 3. Coronata (*Institutiones,* I. n. 614, b) notes that a remote occasion for sinning against chastity, since such occasion can be found anywhere, would not be a sufficient reason for the enacting of such censure, while frequent transgressions against the law of enclosure, if these are a source of scandal or talk among the faithful and canot be obviated by simple reproof or admonition, would suffice.

accomplish the purpose, for ordinarily such extreme measures are reserved only for serious abuses.[80]

The egress of sisters from the enclosure and their relations with externs will be governed by the judgment of the religious superioresses, who must take full care that the constitutions are faithfully observed.[81] Together with the local ordinary, the religious superioresses shall see that the sisters, except in cases of necessity, do not go out singly from the house.[82] Except for the regulations that concern alms-gathering, superioresses must not allow any of their subjects to remain outside a religious house of their own institute without a grave and just cause, and even then the absence must be most severely restricted in accordance with the constitutions. Save when the sister is absent for the purpose of study, the permission of the Holy See is required for any absence of more than six moths.[83]

In his visitation to the local houses of the congregations here studied the local ordinary will make a thorough inspection of the enclosure and search out any transgressions or breaches of the law.[84] But, in accordance with the norms for the enclosure of

[80] Cf. Fanfani, *De Iure Religiosorum*, n. 317, b; Schaaf, *The Cloister*, p. 158.

[81] Cf. canons 605, 606.

[82] Cf. canon 607. Under ordinary circumstances they should be accompanied by another member of their own congregation or at least by a respectable lay-woman, Cf. Blat, *De Religiosis*, n. 594; Schaefer, *De Religiosis*, n. 364, 2°.

[83] Cf. canon 606, § 2. The privilege of alms-gathering is proper to the Mendicant Orders and will be found rarely amongst congregations of women religious of pontifical approval. These congregations, in fact, are expressly forbidden to undertake such work unless they have obtained a special privilege from the Holy See and, most generally, written permission of the local ordinary. And the local ordinary is not to grant this permission, particularly in places where convents of mendicants already exist, unless it is clear that the needs of the house or the work undertaken by the sisters cannot be provided for in any other manner. The territory included in this permission must be strictly limited in accordance with the needs of the house or work. Cf. Canons 621-624.

[84] Cf. canon 618, § 2, 2°.

nuns, it would seem more proper that he should be accompanied by at least one cleric during this inspection, and that the personal visitation of the sisters as well as his examination of the funds and their administration in as far as this rests within his competency should be made in the visitors' parlor which is outside the enclosure.

CHAPTER XII. NON-COLLEGIATE INSTITUTIONS

Article 1. Non-Collegiate Institutions in General

Enucleation of the rights and duties of the local ordinary regarding hospitals, orphanages, day nurseries, homes for the aged, schools and other such institutions, is intricate and involved and depends on the particular status of the institution that is studied. For, while the Code classifies all of these as institutions, yet it provides no definition of the constitutive elements of an institution in general, and the canonists do not agree among themselves concerning it.[1]

However, for the purpose of this study, one may classify all such institutions into the following divisions of status: secular institutions and pious institutions; a pious institution may be lay or ecclesiastical; an ecclesiastical institution may have been established into a non-collegiate personality or again it may merely have been approved and conjoined with some ecclesiastical personality.[2]

A. *Secular Institutions.* These are such as have been established merely out of non-religious human motives, from the viewpoint of natural philanthropy or for sake of temporal profit and gain. As such, they can be considered as mere natural or commercial enterprises with no supernatural motive, and will have no concern with our study, since the work of the congregations here treated must be undertaken primarily and, one may even admit, solely for supernatural motives.[3]

[1] Romani, *Summa Iuris Canonici Lineamenta* (Romae, 1939), n. 418.

[2] Institutions
- Secular
- Pious
  - Lay
  - Ecclesiastical
    - Non-collegiate moral person
    - Approved with no proper personality

[3] Cf. Claeys Bouuaert-Simenon, *Manuale Iuris Canonici,* III, n. 245; Coronata, *Institutiones,* II, n. 1024; Vermeersch-Creusen, *Epitome,* II, n. 812.

B. *Pious Lay Institutions.* Institutions that have been established out of supernatural motives (such as religion, charity, or the spiritual or corporal works of mercy) but have received no recognized constitutional existence or official approval from ecclesiastical authority and are not endowed with ecclesiastical moral personality, are indeed to be considered as pious institutions, but must be classified as lay institutions. A well-known example of such an institution is the Confraternity of St. Vincent de Paul, which is a lay institution in the proper sense of the term.[4]

The property of a pious lay institution is not considered by the common law as ecclesiastical property, nor is it subject to the regulations of the Code that concern ecclesiastical property.[5]

Hence a knowledge of the extent of the rights and duties of the local ordinary over such pious lay institutions must be sought from canons 336, 344 and 1515: 1. The local ordinary must watch over the integrity of the faith and morals, and must see that the faithful (especially the children and the illiterate) are properly instructed in Christian doctrine, and that schools for children and institutions for youth are conducted according to the principles of the Catholic religion (c. 336). 2. Unless special exemption is proved to have been granted to such institutions by the Holy See, the local ordinary can make a visitation of these pious lay institutions concerning these matters, just as he has the right and duty of making a visitation of the other members of the faithful (c. 344).[6] 3. Moreover, as the naturally constituted

[4] ". . . sed laicum hic tantummodo dicitur per oppositionem ad ecclesiasticum."—*S. C. C., Corrienten.* 13 nov. 1920—*AAS;* XIII (1921), 139.

[5] Cf. S. C. C.—*AAS., ibidem,* p. 141.

[6] Vermeersch-Creusen, *Epitome,* II, n. 815. ". . . quandocumque incidit quaestio fidei et morum, evidens est subiectio cuisvis associationis auctoritati Ecclesiae; ex quo tamen non sequitur quod ipsa associatio necessario debeat quoad omnia subiici Ordinario, quoad existentiam, constitutionem seu organizationem, statuta, activitatem et internum regimen . . . sed sicut singuli fideles iurisdictioni Episcopi subsunt, ita manent huius iurisdictioni subiecti, quando in Societates uniuntur. Quamquam enim Episcopus ex hoc solo facto societatem vi suae iurisdictionis dirigere nequit, quemadmodum societates proprie ecclesiasticas et confraternitates dirigit, ius tamen habet et obligationem invigilandi, ne

executor of pious dispositions in consequence of his office, the local ordinary has the right of vigilance and supervision, even through visitation, to ascertain that all pious dispositions are faithfully fulfilled, and to him as constituted in this capacity all delegated executors of such donations and bequests must render an account at the completion of their duty.[7]

C. *Pious Ecclesiastical Institutions.* Such institutions as have been approved by the local ordinary or that have been approved and endowed with moral personality by him are distinct from lay institutions and are given the added title of ecclesiastical institutions. But the Code expressly stipulates that the local ordinary may concede such approbation only on two conditions: 1. That the purpose of the establishment is useful; 2. That the funds are sufficient, or that sufficient means will be obtainable for the purpose of the institution.[8]

D. *Non-Collegiate Ecclesiastical Pious Institutions.* Institutions that have been approved and that have been endowed with juridical personality by the local ordinary are classified as non-collegiate ecclesiastical pious institutions, and as such are capable of acquiring, administering and disposing of property. To such institutions can be entrusted pious foundations, and the property acquired by these institutions is considered as ecclesiastical property and as such becomes subject to the regulations especially stipulated by the Code.[9] The Code stipulates that the charter of such institutions should accurately define the entire constitution and government of the institution, its purpose, its endowment, its administration, the use of its revenue and the successor to the property in case of extinction or suppression of the institution.[10]

abusus irrepant neve fideles occasione societatum ruinam salutis incurrant."—*S. C. C., Corrienten,* 13 nov. 1920—*AAS,* XIII (1921), 140.

[7] Cf. canons 1515; 1493.

[8] Augustine *(Commentary,* VI, p. 547) adds that if the local ordinary neglects this duty, the blame falls on him, together with such undesirable consequences as debts, etc. Coronata *(Institutiones,* II, n. 1028) quotes this statement, but neither he nor Augustine provides any source of proof to substantiate the claim inherent in the statement.

[9] Cf. canons 100, § 1; 1495, § 2.

[10] Cf. canon 1490, § 1. In the articles of foundation the founder can

At least two copies of the charter must be drawn up, one to be deposited in the archives of the institution and the other in the archives of the doicesan curia.[11]

The rector of the institution is assigned the duty of administering the property of the institution.[12] Hence the general government, administration and use of the revenue of such institutions will be subject to or exempt from the jurisdiction of the local ordinary in accordance with the provisions of the charter. But the charter can never exclude his rights in his capacity as native executor of pious dispositions (which includes supervision, even by visitation, and the right to demand an accounting in respect to the disposition),[13] his rights over trusts (including the items of notification, inventory and vigilance over the investment and execution of the trusts),[14] and foundations.[15]

Moreover, the local ordinary has the right and duty to ascertain that the institution adheres to its established purpose,[16] (for sometimes he may find that a charitable institution has practically abandoned its purpose and is being run on a strictly commercial basis), and the local ordinary should give particular attention to the matter of social justice in the employment of workingmen connected with the institution.[17] And if such institutions are

determine all these matters as he wishes, even though the determination be contrary to the norms of canon law, with one exception only, namely that the founder cannot exclude the vigilance and surveillance of ecclesiastical authority altogether. Cf. Coronata, *Institutiones,* II, n. 1030.

[11] Cf. canon 1490, §§ 1, 2. "Necessitas accurate conficiendi tabulas fundationis ex eo apparet, quod instituta haec in omnibus, quae canon memorat, a voluntate fundatoris pendeant."—Beste, *Introductio in Codicem,* p. 720.

[12] Cf. canon 1489, § 3.

[13] Cf. canon 1515.

[14] Cf. canon 1516.

[15] Cf. canons 1545—1551.

[16] Cf. S. C. C., *Corrienten.,—AAS., ibidem,* p. 139.

[17] Cf. canon 1524: "All who employ workingmen must pay them just and decent wages, which rule applies especially to clerics, religious and administrators of ecclesiastical property. They must see that the workingmen are free to perform their religious duties at a convenient hour;

operated by congregations of women religious of pontifical approval, the local ordinary is charged with the right and duty of particular vigilance in all matters pertaining to the teaching of religion, to moral conduct, to the exercises of piety, and to the administration of the sacraments.[18]

E. *Approved Ecclesiastical Institutions.* Such ecclesiastical institutions that have received only approbation of the local ordinary or some other ecclesiastical authority and have not been endowed with moral personality are called Approved Ecclesiastical Institutions.[19] Since these institutions are devoid of juridic personality, one finds them generally conjoined with an ecclesiastical moral person, such as a religious house, province, or congregation, a cannonically established parish, a cathedral chapter or a diocese.[20] The general subjection of the institution to the jurisdiction of the local ordinary will be determined by the subjection of the moral person to which the institution is joined. Thus the local ordinary will have full control over a hospital or school that is conjoined with the personality of the diocese, and any power of administration that he wishes to delegate to the sisters employed therein will depend on his own articles of foundation.

Regarding ecclesiastically approved institutions which lack the status of a proper juridic personality and which are adjoined to a congregation of women religious of pontifical approval, Coronata holds that they are subject to the local ordinary only in his right of vigilance concerning the matters pertaining to the teaching of religion, to moral conduct, to the exercises of piety, and to

they shall make no arrangement that will interfere with the workers' duties to their families or the practice of thrift, and shall not impose on them work which is heavier than their strength can bear, or which is not suited to their age or sex." Need it be added that this canon is either unknown or ignored in many ecclesiastical institutions!!

[18] Cf. Canon 1491, §2; Leo XIII, const. *"Conditae a Christo,"* 8 dec. 1900, §2, n. X—*Fontes,* n. 644; Cocchi, *Commentarium,* VI, n. 163; Blat, *Commentarium Codicis,* Lib. III, pars V, n. 400.

[19] "Si de instituto alii personae morali unito agatur, subiectum cui bona inhaerent instituti est ipsa persona moralis cui institutum adnectitur."—Coronata, *Institutiones,* II, n. 1028.

[20] Cf. Claeys Bouuaert-Simenon, *Manuale Iuris Canonici,* III, n. 245.

the administration of the sacraments. But the two paragraphs of canon 1491 should be taken as being conjunctive rather than disjunctive in their structure and import.[21] Hence the local ordinary has the right and duty of visitation relative to all ecclesiastical institutions, and in approved ecclesiastical institutions which are adjoined to the congregations here studied he has the added obligation of particular vigilance concerning the matters just detailed. For it would be strange indeed that the local ordinary should possess the right of visitation to exempt institutions and be denied such right to institutions adjoined to the congregations of pontifical approval.

But there is no definite statement in canon 1491 which defines the limitations of this visitation. Hence one must discern the extent of the visitation from the general principles that concern the congregations here studied, and derive the degree of subjection of the institution to the local ordinary from the articles of agreement that were drawn up when the institution was established. If the articles of agreement and establishment were not accurately drawn up, so as to define the purpose, the endowment, the administration of the institution, the use of revenue and the successor to the property in case of the extinction of the institution,[22] then one must admit that the local ordinary must discern his rights and duties from the general principles that are developed in this entire study. For certainly the Code does not attribute to him any particular rights over the general financial administration of the institution excepting his rights over pious dispositions, trusts and foundations. Nor does the Code itself give him the

[21] Coronata, *Instutitiones,* II, n. 1031. It may be possible that, in disjoining the two paragraphs of canon 1491, Coronata has overlooked the force of the connecting term *"imo"* in the second paragraph of the canon. It is true that the term *"imo,"* when used in interrogation, may be an expression of a meaning contrary to what precedes. But in assertions, as used in this canon, *"imo"* has the force of *"maxime,"* i.e., especially. The text of the canon, therefore, would seem to indicate clearly that such institutions are subject to visitation *and especially* to the right of vigilance. Cf. Leverett, *Latin Lexicon* (Philadelphia: Lippincott), p. 399, s.v. *"imo."*

[22] Cf. canon 1490, § 1.

right of determining what patients shall be received in a hospital, what orphans are to be admitted to a home, what students may be enrolled in a school, etc. [23] Hence, as long as a group of women religious of pontifical approval adheres to the purpose of the approved ecclesiastical institutions operated by these religious, and unless a contrary agreement has been made in the establishment of the institution, the local ordinary cannot interfere in the internal affairs of government or in the temporal administration except in accordance with the general norms of the law.

Having thus detailed the prescriptions for pious and ecclesiastical institutions, the Code then stipulates that the local ordinary has the right of exacting an accounting from all pious institutions, lay or ecclesiastical, non-collegiate or merely approved (including those connected with the congregations here studied), notwithstanding any custom to the contrary, and even though the institution was erected as exempt from the jurisdiction and visitation of the local ordinary by virtue of its foundation, in view of prescription or by apostolic privilege. Hence all institutions that are founded through supernatural motive, even though without any authorization from the Church, are subject to this rendering of an account to the local ordinary. Though no definite stipulation is contained in the Code as to the time of this accounting, one may take as a norm the legislation of the Council of Trent, on which this prescription is based, and state that a maximum of one accounting each year can be demanded.[24]

It may finally be noted that none of these pious institutions can be suppressed, united to another benefice or diverted to uses foreign to the intentions of the founders, without permission of the Holy See, unless the agreement or charter drawn up at the time of their foundation stipulates otherwise. [25]

[23] Schaefer, *De Religiosis,* n. 86.

[24] Conc. Trid., Sess. XII, *de ref.,* c. 9; Blat, *Commentarium Codicis,* Lib. III, pars V, n. 409. Cf. canon 1492, § 1.

[25] Cf. canon 1494.

Article 2: Schools

The religious training of youth pertains by divine ordinance to the teaching office of the Church.[26] Since the bishops are the teachers of faith and judges of morals, ruling by divine authority the dioceses committed to their care, it is their right to see that nothing against faith or Christian morality be taught within their territory.[27]

Canon 1381 thus asserts that, since the religious teaching of youth in schools is subject to the authority and inspection of the Church, the local ordinaries have the right and duty to see that nothing is taught or done contrary to faith or good morals in any school of their territory.[28] In so far as there may be likelihood of danger or a probable obstacle to the faith or morals of youth, this right of supervision will extend to the entire school curriculum.[29] And by virtue of this personal obligation of office, the local ordinary must ascertain that the training of youth in schools be in conformity to the principles of the Catholic religion.[30]

In view of this official obligation the Code attributes to the local ordinary the right of approbation of the textbooks to be used in classes of religion, of the pedagogical methods to be employed in teaching, and of the teachers to be engaged in carrying on this work in the schools.[31] Likewise the local ordinary has the right of demanding that teachers or textbooks inimical to the

[26] Leo XIII, const. *"Immortale Dei,"* 1 nov. 1885, n. 6—*Fontes*, n. 592.

[27] Conc. Trid., sess XXIII, *de sacr. ord.*, c. 4.

[28] Fanfani, *De Iure Religiosorum*, n. 444; Vermeersch-Creusen, *Epitome*, II, n. 718. It should be noted that the word "school" is used throughout this article in the general sense and will include *oratoria, recreatoria, patronatus*, i.e., all such institutions wherein youth are admitted for the purpose of obtaining an intellectual as well as a moral and religious training.

[29] Leo XIII, epist. *"Officio sanctissimo,"* 22 dec. 1887, n. 9—*Fontes*, n. 596.

[30] Cf. canon 336, § 2; *S. C. C., Conimbricen.*, 18 aug.—1 sept. 1888—*ASS*, XXI (1888), 686; Vermeersch-Creusen, *Epitome*, II, n. 717.

[31] Cf. canon 1381, § 3; Fanfani, *De Iure Religiosorum*, n. 444; Vermeersch-Creusen, *Epitome*, n. 718.

interests of religion or morals be removed.[32] As was noted in a previous chapter, to build and open a school or any other such edifice separated from the religious house, the special written permission of the ordinary is necessary and of itself also sufficient.[33] Those schools which essentially come directly under the jurisdiction of the local ordinary, either because they were founded by him, or because, after their foundation by others, they were incorporated into the diocesan school system, are subject to the local ordinary as their chief superior. Hence the entire scholastic administration and pedagogical system will be subject to his jurisdiction.[34]

But also those schools for youth which have been founded and are conducted by the religious congregations here treated, and which, moreover, are independent of the diocesan school system are subject to the right of visitation by the local ordinary. For canon 1382 makes an exception only with regard to the internal schools for the professed members of exempt institutes. Thus schools for aspirants or postulants to the congregation, as well as all elementary, secondary, academic and collegiate schools, even though not directly under the jurisdiction of the local ordinary, are subject to his visitation in matters of teaching in which there can arise a danger to faith and morals.[35]

Canon 1382, however, does not bar the continued use of such privileges which in their acquisition before the promulgation of the Code granted an exemption from the visitation by the local ordinary. It is possible that some congregations of women religious of pontifical approval may have obtained a privilege of exemption from this visitation similar to that which was extended

[32] Pruemmer, *Manuale Iuris Canonici,* q. 412; Coronata, *Institutiones,* II, n. 948; Boffa, *Canonical Provisions for Catholic Schools, The Catholic University of America Canon Law Studies No. 117,* (Washington, D. C.: The Catholic University of America, 1939), p. 165.

[33] Canon 497, § 3.

[34] Boffa, *Canonical Provisions for Catholic Schools,* 181.

[35] Coronata, *Institutiones,* II, n. 950, 3°; Augustine, *Commentary,* VI, n. 426; Blat, *Commentarium Codicis,* Lib. III, pars IV, n. 275.

by Pope Leo XIII to the regulars in England for schools in which the conducted grades ranged above the elementary curriculum.[36] Such an exemption from the visitation of their schools on the part of the congregations here treated must, however, be regarded as unusual and altogether extraordinary. Express proof of the privilege must be furnished, since an exemption of this nature is contrary to the right attributed to the local ordinary by law.

In general, therefore, all schools within the diocese are subject to the supervision and visitation of the local ordinary in matters pertaining to the teaching of religion, to moral conduct, to the exercises of piety and to the administration of the sacraments.[37]

Moreover, if a school be viewed from the aspect of a charitable work, then the administration of pious dispositions, trusts and foundations will be regulated by the general legislation in such matters. The approval, establishment, endowment with moral personality, and government will be regulated by the general principles regarding institutions, as detailed in the preceding article of this chapter.

Since the schools of the present day are considered as of public character, teachers of religion must be regarded as acting in a public capacity and sharing in the magisterium of the Church. Consequently, in the case of the congregations here studied, a canonical mission must be obtained for the teaching of religion, whether the teaching of religion be the sole duty or whether it be shared with the teaching of other subjects.[38] This canonical mission is obtained from the local ordinary through designation or approbation. Correspondingly the local ordinary has the previous right and duty to ascertain that the candidate for the teaching office is endowed with proper qualifications.[39]

[36] Leo XIII, const. *"Romanos Pontifices,"* 8 maii 1881, §§ 18-20—*Fontes,* n. 582. By decree of the S. Congregation for the Propagation of the Faith (Sept 25, 1885) the provisions of this Constitution were extended to the United States. Cf. *Acta et Decreta Concilii Plenarii Baltimorensis Tertii (1884),* (Baltimore, 1886), p. cv.

[37] Coronata, *Institutiones,* II, n. 950, 3°.

[38] Coronata, *Institutiones,* II, n. 914, note 8.

[39] Cf. *S. C. C.,* decr. *"Provido sane,"* 12 ian. 1935—*AAS,* XXVII (1935). 148.

It should also be noted that the Third Plenary Council of Baltimore prescribed that all teachers in parochial schools, whether religious of a diocesan congregation or seculars, were to submit to an examination before the Diocesan Board of Examiners, and receive a testimonial or diploma of fitness.[40]

But in the customary arrangement of the present day, when schools are entrusted by the local ordinary to congregations of pontifical approval, he ordinarily places the general management of the school and the designation of its teachers in the hands of the religious superioress. Through this designation by the religious superioress, the teachers receive the indirect approval of the local ordinary. But the Third Plenary Council of Baltimore expressly stipulated that if the bishop found that a teacher in this group was incompetent, he was to notify the superioresses at once of the fact, in order that due provision could be made. If the superioresses neglected to take due action in the matter, then the Sacred Congregation was to be notified by the ordinary in order that an opportune remedy could be provided.[41]

[40] Cf. *Acta et Decreta Conc. Plen. Baltim. Tertii (1884),* n. 203. This Board of Examiners was to consist of one or more members, representing the Bishop. In the following decree (n. 204), in addition to the Board of Examiners, there is provision for diocesan "School Commissioners," whose duty was to consist in visiting and examining the schools. It may be noted that, since both these decrees are *praeter legem Codicis,* they are still binding in this country. Cf. Barrett, *A Comparative Study of the Third Plenary Council of Baltimore and the Code of Canon Law, The Catholic University of America Canon Law Studies No. 83,* (Washington, D. C.: The Catholic University of America, 1932), p. 182; Boffa, *Canonical Provisions for Catholic Schools,* p. 171.

[41] Cf. *Acta et Decreta Conc. Plen. Baltim. Tertii (1884),* n. 203.

Chapter XIII

DIVINE SERVICE

Article 1: Divine Worship

Sacred places are those which are set apart for divine worship or the burial of the faithful by consecration or blessing as prescribed by approved liturgical books.[1] Consecration or blessing of any sacred place belonging or entrusted to a congregation of women religious of pontifical approval, even though it be exempt, is reserved to the local ordinary.[2]

Rarely does one find, at least in this country, a church or even a public oratory belonging to sisters of a religious congregation of pontifical approval. For, from a practical viewpoint, it has been found that attendance by the faithful in general at divine services is apt to be a disturbing impediment to the daily devotions and interior life of the sisters. Moreover, the common law expressly forbids the establishment of a church of women religious as a parish church.[3]

Before a church or public oratory can be built, the written permission of the local ordinary must be obtained, a permission which the Vicar General cannot give without a special mandate.[4] Women religious of congregations of pontifical approval, even though they have obtained permission to establish a house, must in addition

[1] Cf. canon 1154; Vermeersch-Creusen, *Epitome,* II, n. 470; Coronata, *Institutiones,* II, n. 721.

[2] Cf. canon 1156. The Vicar General, even though a titular Bishop, could bless but not consecrate a sacred place unless he were endowed with a special mandate. It may be noted, however, that the ordinary may delegate even a priest, either secular or religious, to bless a place, but not to consecrate it. Vermeersch-Creusen, *Epitome,* II, n. 471; Coronata, *Institutiones,* II, n. 726.

[3] Cf. canon 609, § 2.

[4] Cf. canon 1162, § 1.

obtain the special permission of the local ordinary to open a church or public oratory in a certain and determined place.[5]

Moreover, there is a strict obligation to have the church or public oratory consecrated or blessed before any divine service is held therein.[6]

Once a church or public oratory has been consecrated or blessed, it may not be used for profane or secular purposes.[7] Again, definite provisions for the repair of the church or public oratory are prescribed by the Code,[8] and all sacred functions may be celebrated therein that are in accord with the prescripts of the rubrics.[9] Finally, neither a church nor a public oratory that has been blessed or consecrated may be returned or reduced to profane use without permission of the ordinary, who must first ascertain that the church or public oratory cannot in any way be used for divine worship and that there is no hope for its restoration.[10]

Semi-public oratories cannot be established without the permission of the local ordinary. Before this permission is given an inspection must be made by the local ordinary or his delegate to ascertain that the proposed place is decently constructed and furnished.[11]

[5] Cf. canon 1162, § 4.

[6] This means that Mass may not be said, the sacraments may not be administered, and there is to be no preaching, for it is these functions which mainly constitute "divine worship." Cf. Augustine, *Liturgical Law*, 434. The local ordinary, however, could permit services to be held there *per modum actus*. Cf. canons 822; 1194; Vermeersch-Creusen, *Epitome*, II, n. 482.

[7] Cf. canon 1178.

[8] Cf. canon 1186.

[9] Cf. canon 1191, § 2. In the churches or oratories of the women religious here treated, this will not, of course, include parochial functions. Cf. Coronata, *Institutiones*, II, n. 765, b.

[10] Cf. canon 1187.

[11] Cf. canon 1192. "Before permission is given, an inspection must be held concerning: (a) the building, which should represent a sacred edifice and be constructed of solid materials, or at least plastered; (b) the furniture and utensils which are required for the sacred functions, also the neatness and cleanliness of the place; (c) the surroundings of the oratory and its destination."—Augustine, *Liturgical Law*, 25. Coronata

In a congregation of women religious of pontifical approval the semi-public oratory may not be converted into profane use without the authority of the local ordinary.[12]

It is fitting, indeed, that the dedication of a semi-public oratory to divine worship should be perpetual, but Vermeersch-Creusen say that the law is not as strict for the conversion of semi-public oratories to some other use as the proscriptive conditions that concern churches and public oratories. Hence they conclude that the local ordinary may permit this conversion for a just cause.[13] Moreover, the blessing or consecration, as prescribed for churches, is not of obligation in the case of semi-public oratories. However, if the sisters wish this blessing or consecration, it may be imparted by the local ordinary, since the law excludes only private oratories from this consecration or blessing.[14]

The common law expressly stipulates that in colleges, schools, orphanages, prisons, etc., the local ordinary should not permit subsidiary oratories in addition to the principal oratory, except for reasons of necessity or because of great utility.[15] Vermeersch-Creusen are of the opinion that, since religious houses are not specifically enumerated in this list, the local ordinary could more easily permit subsidiary chapels in religious houses.[16]

In legitimately established semi-public oratories of the congregation here treated, the divine offices and ecclesiastical functions that are not contrary to the rubrics may be celebrated, unless the local ordinary has made some exception.[17]

(*Institutiones,* II, n. 767) is of the opinion that since written permission is not required in canon 1192 for the establishment of semi-public oratories, oral permission will suffice.

[12] Cf. canon 1192, § 3.

[13] *Epitome,* II, n. 501, 2.

[14] Cf. canon 1196; Vermeersch-Creusen, *Epitome,* II, n. 501, 3.

[15] Cf. canon 1192, § 4.

[16] Cf. Vermeersch-Creusen, *Epitome,* II, n. 501, 5.

[17] Cf. canon 1193. Generaly the rubrics prohibit the blessing of ashes, candles and palms, and also the Holy Week services when sufficient ministers cannot be had. But, where the *Memoriale Rituum of Benedict XIII* can be used through indult, such services can be held. It should further be noted that the local ordinary can make what exceptions he chooses,

With the permission of the local ordinary the Blessed Sacrament can be reserved in the principal public or semi-public oratory of a pious or religious house, provided: 1) that there is someone who is bound to care for it; 2) that at least once a week a priest should regularly celebrate Mass in the sacred place.[18] But the local ordinary can grant this permission only for the principal oratory, whether it be public or semi-public. And the Blessed Sacrament can be reserved habitually by permission of the local ordinary in other subordinate oratories only after an apostolic indult has been obtained.[19]

The Commission for the Interpretation of the Code has declared that the meaning of canon 1267 is this: if a house of religion or piety is connected with a public church and makes use of it for its ordinary daily exercises of piety, the Blessed Sacrament may be kept there only; otherwise It may be kept in the principal oratory of the said house of religion or piety (without prejudice to the right of the church, if any), and nowhere else, unless in the same material building there are distinct and separate families, so that formally they constitute distinct houses of religion or piety.[20]

This latter case would exist when separate communities of sisters of the institute dwell in the same house. But one could not hold that in the same institute the Blessed Sacrament may be reserved simultaneously in the principal oratory and the chapel of the infirmary or even in the chapel of the novices, if such chapels are

and whenever he chooses. Cf. Coronata, *Institutiones,* II, n. 767, e; Vermeersch-Creusen, *Epitome,* II, n. 501, 6°.

[18] Cf. canon 1265, § 1, 1°; *Instruction of the Sacred Congregation of the Sacraments on the careful Custody of the Most Holy Eucharist,* (English translation, Philadelphia: American Ecclesiastical Review, 1938), 4.

[19] Cf. canons 1265, § 2; 1267. Cappello, *De Sacramentis,* I, n. 358, 4°; Vermeersch-Creusen, *Epitome,* II, n. 589 (who adds that the petition for this indult for a religious house will be sent to the S. Congregation for Religious or, in mission countries, to the S. Congregation for the Propagation of the Faith).

[20] *P. C. I.,* 3 iun. 1918—*AAS* (1918), 346; Bouscaren, *Canon Law Digest* (Milwaukee: Bruce, 1934), I, 601.

in the same building with the principal oratory.[21] However, one could consider as a separate and distinct family the student body of a boarding school,[22] the general curia, the provincial curia,[23] and, one may add, the nurses residing in a hospital.

The local ordinary is obligated to inquire, especially during his visitation, how the regulations concerning the custody of the Blessed Sacrament are observed in public and private oratories; and, as often as the local ordinary finds that the regulations are not complied with, he can command that they be fulfilled as soon as possible, and a brief time being allowed for this purpose, under penalty of a heavy fine. The institution of the process in case of sacrilegious theft is his reserved obligation. He must inquire for the apostolic indult for reservation in the churches and oratories in which the reservation of the Blessed Sacrament is not permitted by law.[24] Whenever he shall find that this privilege is not supported by legitimate right, he will remove the abuse at once. And he may revoke the faculty of reserving the Blessed Sacrament in churches and oratories, even private, which apostolic privilege they enjoy through indult, as often as he notes that serious abuses have sprung up or that all conditions for the safeguarding of the reverence and the worship due the Blessed Sacrament are not fulfilled.[25]

Article 2: Preaching

Priests who are to fulfill the sacred office of preaching in religious houses of congregations of women religious of pontifical approval are designated and receive their approval from the local ordinary.[26] But the law further prescribes that he who is to preach cannot use this faculty in the religious house without the consent of the religious superioress.[27]

[21] Schaefer, *De Religiosis,* n. 436; Vermeersch-Creusen, *Epitome,* II, n. 592; Fanfani, *De Iure Religiosorum,* n. 400 c.

[22] Vermeersch-Creusen, *loc. cit.;* Fanfani, *loc. cit.*

[23] Schaefer, *loc. cit.*

[24] Cf. canon 1265, § 1, 1°, 2°.

[25] Cf. *"Instruction of 1938,"* n. 10.

[26] Cf. canon 529.

[27] Cf. canon 1338, § 3.

While these two canons may seem at first glance to provide some ground for conflict, the conflict would scarcely arise, for the local ordinary customarily allows the sisters a free choice, at least in occasional sermons, between secular and religious priests that are approved. However, Vermeersch-Creusen observe that the local ordinary, if he so desires, can reserve such choice strictly to himself, particularly in the case of Retreat Masters. But it may be questioned whether the Holy See would not be loathe to approve such action as opportune and prudent.[28]

Article 3: Administration of the Sacraments

Confessors of women religious of congregations of pontifical approval, whether these confessors be secular or religious priests, and no matter what position or office they may hold, generally need *special* jurisdiction for the valid and licit administration of the sacrament of penance to these religious.[29] This requirement of special jurisdiction extends to the hearing of the novices' confessions as well and save for the exceptions just listed in the footnote, must supersede any privilege or particular law to the contrary.[30]

The usual jurisdiction for hearing the confessions of women is not identical with the special jurisdiction for hearing the confessions of women religious. Save for the exceptions expressed by

[28] Cf. Vermeersch-Creusen, *Epitome,* I, n. 508. "Il est rare que les Ordinaires imposent un prédicateur, à moins de raisons toutes spéciales et graves."—Bastien, *Directoire Canonique,* n. 379.

[29] Cf. canon 876, § 1. Three exceptions to the requirement for special jurisdiction are noted in this canon, viz., Cardinals (c. 239, § 1, 1°), occasional confessors (c. 522), and confessors of sisters who are seriously ill (c. 523). Cf. Schaefer, *De Religiosis,* n. 171; Vermeersch-Creusen, *Epitome,* I, n. 590, 3°; Wernz-Vidal, *De Religiosis,* n. 170. Coronata (*Institutiones,* I, n. 546) has misconstrued the sense of canon 876 when he states that this special jurisdiction is *generally* conceded by the local ordinary. It is generally *needed* by confessors of women religious, of course but when it is needed this jurisdiction is conceded by the local ordinary. Cf. Coronata, *Institutiones,* I, n. 551, note 4.

[30] The special faculty, however, is not necessary for hearing the confessions of postulants. Cf. Coronata, *Institutiones,* I, n. 546; Wernz-Vidal, *De Religiosis,* n. 170.

the law,[31] a priest who would attempt to hear the confession of a woman religious of a congregation of pontifical approval, if he had only the general faculties for hearing the confessions of women, and not the special jurisdiction required for hearing the confessions of women religious would act both illicitly and invalidly.[32]

Religious as well as secular priests must have this special jurisdiction before hearing the confessions of women religious. The Code specifically mentions that, save for the privilege of Cardinals, rank or office will justify no exception to the rule. Thus the requirement would seem to extend even to a canon penitentiary as well as to the pastor of a convent that has not been withdrawn from parochial care, both of whom by the very prescription of law enjoy jurisdiction for hearing the confessions of their subjects.[33] This special jurisdiction is to be conceded by the ordinary of the place where the religious house is situated, even though the women religious are subject immediately to the Holy See.[34]

The local ordinary may administer the Sacrament of Confirmation in any part of his diocese, even in places enjoying the privilege of exemption. Definitely he may administer this Sacrament in the chapels of women religious of pontifical approval.[35]

An outside extern bishop, if he should wish to confirm in the chapel of a religious community, should obtain the permission of the local ordinary of the diocese. Of course, this permission could be reasonably presumed. In fact, it would not be required if the

[31] Cf. canons 522 (occasional confessors), canon 523 (confessors of sisters who are seriously ill), canon 239, § 1, 1° (a Cardinal), and canon 882 (any priest in case of danger of death).

[32] Cf. Sobradillo, *Tractatus de Religiosarum Confessariis ad Normam Codicis Iuris Canonici Concinnatus* (Torino: Berutti, 1932), p. 100; Wernz-Vidal, *De Religiosis,* n. 170.

[33] Cf. canons 401, § 1; 873, §§ 1, 3; Sobradillo, *De Religiosarum Confessariis,* p. 110; Wernz-Vidal, *De Religiosis,* n. 170.

[34] Cf. canons 876, § 2; 525. Coronata, *Institutiones,* I, n. 553, b; Wernz-Vidal, *De Religiosis,* n. 170.

[35] Canon 792; Vermeersch-Creusen, *Epitome,* II, n. 68; Augustine, *Commentary,* IV, 117.

outside bishop were administering the Sacrament to his own subjects in a private manner without using the crozier and mitre.[36]

Marriages may not be celebrated in the churches or oratories of women religious except in cases of urgent necessity, for example, if no other church is available, and with permission of the local ordinary, who must ascertain that proper safeguards against disruption of or danger to religious life are employed.[37] Both Cappello and Gasparri state that the local ordinary can extend this prohibition in particular cases to any type of pious house.[38]

[36] Cf. canon 783; Vermeersch-Creusen, *op. cit.*, c., n. 63; Augustine, *op. cit.*, 107.

[37] Cf. canon 1109, § 2; Cappello, *De Sacramentis*, III-II (4. ed., Romae: Marietti, 1939), n. 728; Gasparri, *Tractatus Canonicus de Matrimonio* (Civitas Vaticana: Typis Polyglottis Vaticanis, 1932), II, n. 1065.

[38] Cappello, *loc. cit.; Gasparri, loc. cit.*

Chapter XIV

TEMPORAL GOODS

Article 1. Administration and Alienation of Temporal Goods

Administration of property, in the canonical sense, includes all the acts which are necessary and useful: 1. To keep the property in good condition; 2. To make it productive; 3. To derive benefit from it; 4. To apply, pay out, and use it for legitimate purposes.[1]

Ordiary administration comprises the acts regularly necessary for the upkeep of the property and for supplying its current needs. This may include the collecting of debts or rentals of lands or houses, the receiving of dividends or interest, the ordinary sale of produce, the purchase of supplies needed for daily use, the depositing of money for convenience of security and other similar acts which in themselves are regularly necessary for ordinary administration. Extraordinary administration comprises the special acts, those which do not recur with frequency or regularity, and which imply a major or definite departure in administration.[2]

The Code states that the property of the institute, of the province and the house, is to be administered conformably to the constitutions. In congregations of women religious of pontifical appproval, besides superioresses, those officials also who are so empowered by the constitutions can, within the limits of their

[1] Cf. Vromant, *De Bonis Ecclesiae Temporalibus ad usum praesertim Missionariorum et Religiosorum* (Editions Du Museum Lessianum; Louvain, 1927), n. 172; Vermeersch-Creusen, *Epitome,* I, n. 601; McManus, *The Administration of Temporal Goods in Religious Institutes, The Catholic University of America Canon Law Studies No. 109,* (Washington, D. C.: The Catholic University of America, 1937), p. 79.

[2] Cf. Vromant, *loc. cit.;* Larraona, "Commentarium Codicis"—*CpRM,* XII (1931), 356; McManus, *op. cit.,* p. 80.

office, validly incur expenses and perform the juridical acts of ordinary administration.[3]

While the local ordinary has the right of vigilance concerning the administration of all ecclesiastical property in general within the limits of his territory, this right is restricted by the withdrawal of particular ecclesiastical property from his administration. However, if legitimate prescription ascribes greater rights to him, such prescription stands.[4] And the Code definitely restricts his right and duty of enquiring into the temporal administration of congregations of women religious of pontifical approval, saving the prescriptions of canon 533-535.[5] Hence a particular study of these provisions must be provided for a satisfactory knowledge of the rights and duties of the local ordinary concerning the congregations here treated.

Regarding this right of vigilance, as attributed to the local ordinary, it is necessary to note, as Vromant declares, that it comprises the right of investigation and a right of demanding an account of the property administered (canon 1519, §1) and the right of prescribing a prudent method of administration, provided the method prescribed and prescriptions ordered are in accordance with the sacred canons (canon 1519, §2). Thus the local ordinary, when such a right is attributed to him, could rightfully prescribe: 1. That a proper inventory of the temporal goods be made (canon 1522, 2°, 3°); 2. That the records and documents of purchase or other contracts be properly filed (canons 375-377); 3. That necessary repairs be made to the property; 4. That his general directions and suggestions in the application of the revenue of the property be heeded, provided the will of the donor and the rights of the administrator be safeguarded.

But the right of vigilance must be clearly distinguished from the immediate and direct administration of the temporal goods. It is true that supervision may connote a right to have knowledge of the quantity and value of the temporal goods, to demand an

[3] Cf. canon 532, §§ 1, 2.
[4] Cf. canon 1519.
[5] Cf. canon 618, § 2, 1°.

accounting of the safe investment and the faithful application of donations, etc., and to attain assurance that the administration is orderly and prudent. But it does not give the local ordinary any right to determine specifically the mode of expenditure or to reserve to himself the total expenditure or partial distribution of these temporal goods, for such acts belong to the immediate administration.[6]

Alienation, in the strict sense of the term, is the act by which the direct ownership of property is transferred to another person, whether physical or moral. But in the sense of the Code of Canon Law alienation will include not only the transfer of ownership but also any act by which an administrator, without giving up direct ownership, transmits or remits to another an incorporeal right (*ius in re*), as for example by mortgage or lease, in such manner that the ownership of the property is put under limitations or made less secure.[7]

The Code attributes no right or duty to the local ordinary in the general matter of the alienation of property belonging to congregations of women religious of pontifical approval. When permission for alienation of their property is required by the Code, such authorization must be petitioned directly from the Holy See.[8] However, one could admit that the local ordinary, as guardian of the law in his territory and as authorized by the Holy See to guard against any abuse in the congregations here

[6] Cf. Vromant, *De Bonis Ecclesiae Temporalibus*, n. 174; McManus, *The Administration of Property in Religious Institutes*, p. 88; Fanfani, *De Iure Religiosorum*, n. 452.

[7] McManus, *The Administration of Property in Religious Institutes*, p. 119; Vromant, *De Bonis Ecclesiae Temporalibus*, n. 279; Cleary, *Canonical Limitations on the Alienation of Church Property, The Catholic University of America Canon Law Studies No. 100*, (Washington, D. C.: The Catholic University of America, 1936), p. 94; Larraona, "Commentarium Codicis"—*CpRM*, XIII (1932), 188: "Alienatio in hoc loco est: actus iuridice efficax quo proprietas, iura realia, possessio iuridica personae ecclesiasticae pertinentia, gratuito vel onerose transferuntur, abiiciuntur, minuuntur vel onerantur."

[8] Cf. canon 534, § 1.

treated, would have the right and duty to see that due authorization of the Holy See has been properly petitioned and obtained.

Moreover, the Code prescribes that precious images that are valuable for their antiquity, art, or veneration, and which have been exposed for the public devotion of the faithful in churches and public oratories, must not be renovated, when in need of repair, without the written consent of the ordinary, who shall consult prudent and expert men before giving the permission.[9] But this prescription applies only to images in churches or public oratories, and not to those placed in the semi-public oratories of convents.[10]

Article 2. Investment of the Dowry and of Special Gifts

Canon 533 treats of the investment and change of investment of monies which have been destined for particular purposes in congregations of women religious of pontifical approval and which require the previous consent of the local ordinary. As will be seen, these investments concern three particular funds: 1. The dowries of the professed religious of the congregation (canon 533, §1, 2°); 2. Funds which have been donated or bequeathed to the house for expenditure locally on divine worship or on works of charity (canon 533, §1, 3°); 3. Money that has been given to the parish or the mission, or to religious for the benefit of the parish or the mission (canon 533, §1, 4°).

Canon 533 stipulates that in the investment of money the disposition of canon 532, §1, shall be observed, namely, that the property of the institute, of the province and of the house, is to be administered conformably to the constitutions. Hence the constitution must be consulted relative to the administration of any funds as well as regarding their investment.

By investment of money is meant any relatively permanent disposition that is made of it by means of converting it into other values or securities, which with at least an equal assurance furnish

[9] Cf. canon 1280.

[10] Cf. Blat, *Commentarium Codicis,* Lib. III, pars III, n. 154; Coronata, *Institutiones,* II, n. 859, 3°

guaranty of its continued preservation and make it productive of revenue and fruits.[11]

In every investment there is an element of risk, and even the smallest investment demands business acumen and experience in commercial affairs. This canon, therefore, represents the effort of the Church to safeguard as far as possible the particular funds administered by congregations of women religious of pontifical approval, by adding to the care and diligence of the religious administrator the experience and judgment of the local ordinary. Hence a particular study of the rights and duties of the local ordinary regarding these three categories of funds, when administered by congregations of women religious of pontifical approval, must be provided.

A dowry is the sum of money or property that is entrusted to the religious institute by a new member in order that its revenue may serve for her support.[12] The Code does not impose the obligation of furnishing a dowry upon candidates for a congregation of women religious of pontifical approval, for it simply states that the prescriptions of the constitutions of the particular con-

[11] Cf. Larraona, "Commentarium Codicis"—*CpRM,* XII (1931), 437, 438; Coronata, *Institutiones,* I, n. 559, 2°; Vromant, *De Bonis Ecclesiae Temporalibus,* n. 176; Vermeersch-Creusen, *Epitome,* I, n. 602; Cocchi, *Commentarium,* IV, n. 52.

There are as many ways of investing money as there are ways of spending it. For money may be invested in lands and buildings with the return of a yearly rental, or in bonds, stocks, notes or mortgages, which may be purchased with the expectation of remuneration in the form of interest, dividends, etc.

In past centuries there was some preference, which was in some cases indicated even as a canonical prescription, that investment should be made in immovable property. But, when the course of world events proved that such immovable property could be confiscated so easily, the trend of investment veered towards movable goods. In general, however, the common law of the present day permits investment in either movable or immovable property. Coronata, *Institutiones,* I, n. 559, 2°, note 3; Vromant, *De Bonis Ecclesiae Temporalibus,* n. 176.

[12] Cf. Coronata, *Institutiones,* I, n. 577; Schaefer, *De Religiosis,* n. 228, 2°.

gregation must be followed in this regard.[13] Hence in some congregations of women religious of pontifical approval one may find that the dowry is not required, because the sisters are engaged in active work (teaching, nursing, etc.,) and thus are more or less self-supporting.[14] One must consult, therefore, the constitutions of the particular congregation to ascertain the fact of the requirement of a dowry as well as the minimum amount that must be provided, if a dowry is required. Moreover, when the requirement of a dowry is absolute in congregations of women religious of pontifical approval, then the right to condone this amount, either in whole or in part, is reserved to the Holy See.[15]

Canon 550, §2 stipulates that the vigilance of the local ordinary over the dowries must be exercised with diligence. And, in keeping with this right of vigilance, the local ordinary can demand an account of the administration of the dowries. This account is to be given especially at the time of the visitation (which, as previously mentioned, will be once every five years in the case of congregations of women religious of pontifical approval) and also at any other times that the local ordinary may deem an accounting necessary.[16]

The distinction between vigilance and visitation is not well clarified by any of the authors available for the purpose of this study, for many details of vigilance depend on the prudent judgment of the local ordinary and the gravity of the obligation imposed. Vigilance, in that it is constant and not confined to any one determined period, is more extensive than visitation, which can possibly be fulfilled in one day. Visitation is more thorough, in that the visitor is obligated to review and examine all the details of the matter subject to visitation, and it obliges to an examina-

[13] Cf. canon 547, § 3.

[14] Toso, *Commentaria Minora,* II-II, 108 (ad can. 547); Geser, *The Canon Law Governing Communities of Sisters,* q. 655; Pruemmer, *Manuale Iuris Canonici,* q. 208.

[15] Cf. canon 547, §4; Coronata, *Institutiones,* I, n. 577, 2°. Schaefer *(De Religiosis,* n. 94) notes that the Faculties usually given to an Apostolic Delegate contain provision for dispensation from the dowry.

[16] Cf. canon 535, § 2.

tion undertaken locally at the religious house. Vigilance, on the other hand, can be exercised indirectly, through use of the telephone or any other mode of communication, and the bishop can keep himself informed through communications that have come to him from others, and through denunciations or charges that he has heard. Hence one may say that the act of visitation is related to the exercise of vigilance as a species to its genus. Thus, when through his vigilance the local ordinary has definite grounds for suspicion that the maintenance and conservation of the dowries is being endangered by faulty administration, he has every right, in the opinion of the present writer, to institute a personal visitation for the correction of such abuse as may exist. For the local ordinary has been especially entrusted with the right and charged with the corresponding duty of exercising an alert diligence in his vigilance over this particular administration.

Since, on the one hand, the administration of the dowries is connected with the house at which the superioress-general or the provincial superioress maintains her habitual residence, and since, on the other hand, all local ordinaries must demand an account of the administration of the dowries of the individual sisters, Pruemmer holds that it seems to follow that the general or provincial superioress must remit an account of this administration to every ordinary in whose territory a religious house of her congregation is established. But, as he himself admits, such an interpretation and application of the law could occasion serious inconveniences. Therefore he considers it a better course of action to call for the rendering of the account to only that ordinary in whose diocese the administration of the dowry is transacted.[17]

In the opinion of the writer the sending of an account of the administration to every local ordinary in whose territory there exists a religious house of the congregation can in no way be regarded as contributing to greater efficacy in checking any possible abuse. For what means are accorded by law to a local ordinary for the sake of personally checking an abuse which is extant outside of his diocese? And is canonical vigilance over a

[17] Cf. Pruemmer, *Manuale Iuris Canonici*, q. 208, 3°.

particular point of discipline rendered more effective when it is shared by several authorities when they have but an *equal* competence in the application of remedial measures?[18] In consequence of these considerations it appears that it is the right and duty of the ordinary of the place where the dowries are administered to exercise diligent vigilance over these funds. If other local ordinaries have reliable information or certified knowledge of a faulty administration, then of course they should communicate this information or knowledge to him, unless they have good reason to infer that he is cognizant of the situation.

The common law prescribes that the superioress-general or the provincial superioress, with consent of her council, must place the dowry in a safe, lawful and productive investment. Before the dowry is thus invested she must obtain the consent of the local ordinary. It is the ordinary of the place of the general or provincial house from which this investment is being made—who shall be petitioned for this consent, for as a general rule any reference to a local ordinary links his authority with the place regarding which the mention occurs.

Though the consent of the local ordinary in the investment of the dowry is thus required by the Code, it should be clearly noted that the choice of the investment is left to the religious superioress. For the duty of the local ordinary, as Coronata notes, is merely to judge whether the securities chosen are safe, lawful and profitable, and thus to give his consent to such an investment. And he has no right to force a superioress to invest in any specifically determined security.[19] And if the superioresses and the local ordinary cannot agree on the investment, the matter may be referred to the Holy See.[20]

[18] Coronata (*Institutiones,* I, n. 577, 4°, note 7) cites the opinion of Pruemmer, who acknowledges the right of vigilance as pertaining to all local ordinaries in whose diocese such religious are resident, and simply remarks that this claim remains unproved.

[19] Cf. Coronata, *Institutiones,* I, n. 577, 4.

[20] Vermeersch-Creusen, *Epitome,* I, n. 651, 3°; Larraona, "Commentarium Codicis"—*CpRM,* XXI (1940), 27; Bastien, *Directoire Canonique,* n. 101.

If death comes before the expiration of the novitiate, even though the novice may have made the profession allowed in danger of death,[21] the congregation has no claim to the dowry and the full capital sum must be returned to her legal heirs, if she has made no other disposition.[22] Moreover, the dowry-sum must be returned to even a professed religious, if she leaves the congregation, no matter what may be her reason.[23]

It is the right and duty of the local ordinary to see that this obligation of the return of the dowry is fulfilled. Moreover, the Code expressly states that if a religious superioress, contrary to canon 549, presumes to spend in whatever manner the dowry which a member has brought to the community, or to withhold it contrary to the norms of canon 551, she shall be punished by the local ordinary conformably to the gravity of the offense, even with deposition from office if it be deemed necessary.[24]

Canon 533, § 1, 3°, states that in the investment of money the previous consent of the local ordinary must be obtained by the superioress of every house of a religious congregation of pontifical approval in the case of funds which have been donated or bequeathed to the house for expenditure locally on divine worship or on works of charity.

Funds given for divine worship include such purposes as the celebration of Masses or other ecclesiastical functions, the illumination of votive lights or of the Sanctuary Lamp, etc. Works of charity include such works as the granting of dowries to poor girls, the endowment of orphan asylums, of trade schools, or even of beds in hospitals, the establishment of burses for students, of salaries for teachers, etc., provided such funds were given for a supernatural purpose and not through mere philanthrophy.[25]

[21] Pius X, decr. *Spirituali consolationi,* 10 sept. 1912—*AAS,* IV (1912), 589 sq.; *S. C. de Religiosis,* resp. 29 dec. 1922—*AAS,* XV (1923), 156.

[22] Pruemmer, *Manuale Iuris Canonici,* q. 208, 4°.

[23] Canon 551. Schaefer, *De Religiosis,* n. 231, note 3: "quavis de causa, i.e. libere vel coacte dimissa, licite vel illicite." Vermeersch-Creusen, *Epitome,* n. 652.

[24] Canon 2412.

[25] Vermeersch-Creusen, *Epitome,* I, n. 606; Vromant, *De Bonis Ecclesiae Temporalibus,* n. 146, 2°.

The funds themselves can be of various kinds: land, money, or any other movable or immovable goods that are to be invested for preservation and fruitfulness.[26]

While Blat holds that the use of the word *"fundi"* in the canon is definite evidence that only foundations are included in this prescription—an opinion that is approached or intimated by Pruemmer and Schaefer[27]—it is difficult to conceive of a reason for excluding other funds which are destined to endure for a time which is not sufficiently long in its duration to allow them to be classified as foundations. "Fundi" is a much more general term than "fundatio" and consequently it appears tenable that this term connotes the investment of any or all donations or bequests which are destined for local worship or charity.[28] For if the canon was intended to embrace only foundations, then the more proper term for the identification of that concept could readily have been employed.

Since the wording of the text is explicit, in that it embraces only those funds which are destined for local worship or charity, one must agree that money and temporal goods given to the support of the needs of the religious community itself are not herein included, since such needs definitely pertain to the internal economic order, concerning which the local ordinary has no right to enquire in the case of the congregation here treated.[29] Nor does the prescription include such funds as are destined for divine worship or charity, but which the religious can spend in any place they wish.[30]

[26] Cocchi, *Commentarium,* IV, n. 54; Vermeersch-Creusen, *loc. cit.;* Coronata, *Institutiones, I,* n. 559, b, note 5.

[27] Blat, *De Religiosis,* n. 258, 3°; Pruemmer, *Manuale Iuris Canonici,* q. 194; Schaefer, *De Religiosis,* n. 197.

[28] Since, however, the question is one of investment, the prescription does not include funds that are to be spent at once. Cf. Blat, *De Religiosis,* n. 258, 3°.

[29] Blat, *De Religiosis,* n. 258, 3°; Coronata, *Institutiones,* I, n. 559, 2°. b. note 6; Schaefer, *De Religiosis,* n. 197.

[30] Schaefer, *De Religiosis,* n. 197, a; Fanfani, *De Iure Religiosorum,* n. 155, b, 2°.

Since explicit mention is made of the religious house, Blat and Fanfani hold that the province cannot be included in this prescription.[31] Vermeersch-Creusen exclude from this prescription only those funds which are given to the institute or congregation as such.[32] Schaefer very pointedly concludes that, since the term "house" is used, the province and the congregation are not thereby included. But later he inclines to the opinion that if money be given to the province then the rule of canon 533, § 1, 3° should nevertheless be considered as applying in the case for analogous reasons.[33] As a matter of practice, all such funds destined for divine worship or charity in a determined locality will be expended ordinarily through a particular house and not through such an extended organization as the province or the entire congregation. Since the term "house" is not qualified in the canon by the term "local," there seems to be little, if any, positive reason for assuming that the rule of canon 533, § 1, 3° does not apply in cases wherein the money is donated either to the provincial or the general house.[34]

On the basis of the phrase *"eo ipso loco"* (literally *in that place itself*), as used in the prescription of canon 533, § 1, 3°, canonists find still further reason for a restrictive interpretation relative to the need of consent from the local ordinary for the investment of the funds or money donated to a religious house for the purpose of furthering divine worship or of promoting the works of Christian charity. In his interpretation of this canon Larraona excludes the requirement of the consent of the local ordinary relative to the investment of all funds which are donated that they may be expended outside the very site of the house or outside of the town

[31] Blat, *De Religiosis,* n. 258, 3°; Fanfani, *De Iure Religiosorum,* n. 155, b, 2°. Wernz-Vidal *(De Religiosis* n. 224) accede to this opinion if the congregation of pontifical approval extends to more than one diocese.

[32] *Epitome,* I, n. 606.

[33] Schaefer, *De Religiosis,* n. 107; Cf. canon 20; *AAS,* XII (1920), 252.

[34] Note that the Constitution *"Conditae a Christo,"* on which this prescription is based, used the term *"certae domui,"* which indicates that the legislation pointed to a ***particular*** house and not to a ***particular kind*** of a house. Cf. Const. *"Conditae a Christo,"* § II, IX—*Fontes,* n. 644.

in which the religious house is situated.[35] Coronata accedes to the same opinion, though he also mentions that other canonists include the entire diocese in the territorial connotation of *"locus."*[36] Schaefer and Vermeersch-Creusen extend the connotation of this term to the diocese.[37]

One could rather believe that the phrase *"eo ipso loco,"* as it stands in the canon, refers to what precedes, and therefore points not to the locality of the religious house but to the territory denoted by the term *"locus"* at the beginning of the canon where the *"ordinarius loci"* is mentioned. The word *"locus"* can thus be accepted as comprising a double connotation: 1. That the consent of the ordinary of the place must be obtained for the investment of funds that are destined for the place of which he is the ordinary; 2. That this consent must be obtained from the ordinary of the place for which the expenditure of the funds is destined.[38] Thus, if funds are given to a religious house in the Archdiocese of New York for works of charity in the Diocese of Brooklyn, the consent of the ordinary of the Diocese of Brooklyn must be obtained for the investment of these funds.

In summation, the previous consent of the local ordinary must be obtained by any superioress of a congregation of women religious of pontifical approval if she is to invest any funds that have been given or bequeathed to any house for the determined purpose of divine worship or for the promotion of the works of charity and designated to be expended specifically within the territory of that ordinary. Moreover, that same local ordinary has the right of enquiry concerning the administration of such funds when they are received by a congregation of women religious of pontifical approval.[39]

[35] This author is consistently restrictive in his interpretation of the term *"locus."* Cf. "Commentarium Codicis"—*CpRM,* XIII (1932), 34.

[36] *Institutiones,* I, n. 559, 2°, b, note 7.

[37] Schaefer, *De Religiosis,* n. 197; Vermeersch-Creusen, *Epitome,* I, n. 606.

[38] For this second conclusion cf. Schaefer, *De Religiosis,* n. 197.

[39] Cf. canon 535, § 3, 2°.

The following section of canon 533 states that the same formalities for the investment of money, that is, the method of administration conducted in conformity with the constitutions, are required of a religious when the money has been received for a parish or mission, or when it has been given to religious for the benefit of the parish or mission. For the investing of such money there is furthermore required the previous consent of the local ordinary on the part of every religious, even though he be a member of a regular order.[40]

This clause "funds given to the mission" should not be confused with the more general phrase "mission funds." For, as Larroana remarks, the common opinion of canonists interprets the term "mission," as used in this prescription of canon 533, as connoting a quasi-parish or mission church which has some connection with the religious house.[41]

Since the church of women religious of congregations of pontifical approval cannot be made a parochial church, one would scarcely expect to find even a mission joined to the religious house of such a congregation.[42] But it does happen at times that persons have given or bequeathed money to women religious of the congregations here treated for the benefit of some particular mission or church, and in this case it would be necessary to obtain the consent of the local ordinary for the investment of the money, in the same way as is indicated in the previous section of canon 533 with reference to the funds donated for the furtherance of divine worship or the promotion of the works of Christian charity.

In every change of any of these three investments by congregations of women religious of pontifical approval the regulations of the constitutions of the congregation must be observed and the consent of the local ordinary must be petitioned anew.[43]

[40] Cf. canon 533, § 1, 4°.

[41] Cf. Larraona, "Commentarium Codicis"—*CpRM,* XIII (1932), 93; Blat, *De Religiosis,* n. 258; Vermeersch-Creusen, *Epitome,* I, n. 606, 3°; Coronata, *Institutiones,* I, n. 559, p. 675.

[42] Cf. canon 609, § 2.

[43] Cf. canon 533, § 2.

A change of investment is implied by a change of the form of the investment or of the nature of the securities or property in which the money has been invested. For example, the conversion of a mortgage into shares of stocks or into bonds, the substitution of a borrower or securer in a loan (even though the investment should continue to be a loan), or the purchase of stocks or bonds in another business, and even a change from preferred to common stocks in the same securities, would have to be considered as transactions which properly imply a change in the investments, and none of these can be effected contrary to the constitutions or without the additional consent of the local ordinary.[44]

The religious superioress must keep in mind that this regulation is primarily intended to safeguard the funds and to prevent changes in the investment which may render it unsafe, illicit or unproductive. For safety is the factor that must be preferred even to productivity. And when any change in the investment may render it less safe, in that case, above all, must the constitutions be observed and the consent of the local ordinary be petitioned anew.

However, one could not conclude that this renewal of consent is required in the routine renewal of notes, the repurchase under the same conditions when bonds have matured, or the equal exchange in stocks of the same kind in the same company when the shares have been called for redemption or reissue. Under ordinary conditions such transactions are to be considered as routine, unless there be a substantial reason to fear the financial condition of the company has been weakened or that its directors have become less capable of conducting its management with equal promise of safety and a like assurance of success.

In summary, therefore, one must hold that the administration of the property of a congregation of women religious of pontifical approval pertains to the interior regime of the congregation. But in the three instances here noted, the consent of the local ordinary is required for the investment of monies. A due ac-

[44] Cf. Larraona, "Commentarium Codicis"—*CpRM,* XIII (1932), 98; Blat, *De Religiosis,* n. 258, p. 249.

counting of the dowry is to be given to the local ordinary on the occasion of his visitation and at any other time that he deems such an accounting useful. Moreover, in the congregations here studied, the local ordinary can demand an accounting of the administration of the funds that have been destined by the donor for the purpose of divine worship or for works of charity and also of the funds given for the benefit of a church or a mission within the territory of the local ordinary.

Article 3: Pious Bequests, Trusts and Foundations

As noted in the introduction to this chapter, the right and duty of the local ordinary to inquire into the internal economic affairs of a congregation of women religious of pontifical approval is generally detailed in the provision of canon 618, § 2, 1°, which states that the ordinary possesses this right and duty only in so far as the restrictive provisions and dispositions of canons 533-535 warrant.

Canon 533, as explained in the previous article, treats of the investment of funds and of the change made in such an investment. Only three sections of §1 of this canon (viz. 2° investment of the dowry; 3° investment of funds which have been donated or bequeathed to the house to be expended locally on divine worship or on works of charity; 4° investment of money that has been given to the parish or the mission or to religious for the benefit of the parish or mission) together with the provision of § 2 of the same canon regarding the change made in these investments can be considered as directly applicable to the congregations here studied. Canon 534, in treating of the alienation of property, is of no direct concern for the present study, since the congregations here treated must apply to the Holy See when extraneous permission for the alienation of their property is required. And canon 535, which treats of the account to be rendered concerning the administration, is applicable to the relationship between the local ordinary and the congregations of women religious of pontifical approval in the matter of dowry (§ 2). Finally, this same canon attributes to the local ordinary the right of enquiry into the administration of the funds referred to in canon 533, § -, 3°, 4°.

Must one hold, therefore, that canon 618, § 2, 1°, is so generally restrictive that the local ordinary is excluded from having any part in the administration or the investment of all the other property belonging to or administered by congregation of women religious of pontifical approval? Has he no other rights relative to the devises, donations or bequests made for pious causes, or regarding the trusts and foundations presented to such congregations, save the rights which canon 533 bespeaks for him?

Larraona adheres strictly to the opinion that canons 533-535 constitute the sole express legislation on the administration of the property of religious and that any other principle as found in Book III of the Code regarding administration can be applied to congregations of women religious of pontifical approval primarily only, if not exclusively, through the medium of analogy.[45] A number of other canonists seem to sense little difficulty about the possible connection between canon 618 and the pertinent canons which deal with the question of property administration in Book III of the Code. Perhaps this impression arises from the fact that they seem content simply to quote the text of canon 618 and thereupon make no attempt to explain what is connoted by economic administration. Vromant, however, enumerates the provisions of Book III and then adjoins a definite statement that, in as far as the enumerated cases are found in congregations of women religious of pontifical approval, such congregations are subject to the prescriptions of Book III in the same manner as congregations of men religious of pontifical approval.[46]

[45] "*Hic praecipue* diximus, quia pro Religiosis *haec specialia* locum generatim tenet, illorum quae in tit. XXVIII lib. III de bonis ecclesiasticis administrandis statuuntur. Adsunt aliqua in citato titulo quae Religiosos ex ipso textu Codicis tangunt (can. 1524), alia quae ex iuridica saltem analogia ceterisque regulis can. 20 applicanda ipsis sunt (cfr. cc. 1518, 1519, § 1 col. ad can. 518, § 2; 1523, 1528), sed ceterum ille titulus Religiosos, qua tales, directe non respicit: quod est in mente habendum."—Larraona, "Commentarium Codicis"—*CpRM,* XII (1931), 355.

[46] Vromant, *De Bonis Ecclesiae Temporalibus, n.* 236.

Definitely one should hold that the general prescriptions of Book III regarding pious devises, trusts, foundations, etc., apply equally to congregations of women religious of pontifical approval, for express mention of religious is made in these prescriptions [47] and the administration of the property bequeathed as pious causes is one that pertains not merely to the private internal economic administration of a congregation, but is one of public trust, for the fulfillment of which the Church has seen fit to add the supervision of the local ordinary as the guardian of those who are in need and as the juridically accredited executor of all pious wills.[48] Hence the correct position must be that in the investment and administration of ecclesiastical property congregations of women religious of pontifical approval are subject to the jurisdiction of the local ordinary in accordance with the general principles enumerated in Book III of the Code, as well as to the specific provisions found in canons 533-535.

A. *Pious Bequests*

The Church is most solicitous in her demand that donations or bequests given to charity or religion should be exactly fulfilled in the manner that the donor or testator desired, whether this desire concerned the mode of administration or the mode of distribution of the temporal goods.[49] Canon 1514 definitely stipulates this as

[47] Cf. canons 1516; 1550.

[48] Cf. canon 1515, § 1.

[49] Cf. canon 1514; Vromant, *De Bonis Ecclesiae Temporalibus,* n. 157. A pious cause is anything undertaken with respect to God and a supernatural end, for the purpose of promoting the honor and glory of God, to obtain remission of sin or of the punishment due to it, or to increase grace or the reward in Heaven due to saintliness. Among such pious causes would properly be included: all places or institutes of Christian charity such as churches, religious institutes, confraternities, ecclesiastical hospitals, etc., Masses, or other sacred functions and aid of the poor. But works of mere philanthropy, since they lack a supernatural end, could not be classified as pious causes.

A donation or bequest for a pious intention is any disposition of temporal goods towards a pious cause. Such disposition can be made *"inter vivos," "mortis causa,"* or by testament. A donation *"inter vivos"*

a prescription of law. The Code names the local ordinary as the duly accredited executor of all donations of bequests for pious causes, even if the latter are meant to be of benefit for the congregations of women religious of póntifical approval.[50] And so exact is this prescription that the donor or testator is not permitted to attach a clause to his donation or bequest which would attempt to exclude the ordinary in this right of execution and supervision over such donations or bequests to pious causes.[51]

In virtue of this right and duty as the duly accredited executor, the local ordinary has the obligation and duty of ascertaining, even by visitation, that in the congregations here studied, such pious intentions are properly fulfilled. While the ordinary has no right to substitute an executor for the one so designated by the donor or testator, or to reserve to himself the direct administration of such bequests or donations, he must be considered as an auxiliary (*in subsidium datus*) to the legal or testamentary execu-

is that by which ownership of the temporal goods is transferred during the life of the donor and is effected from the moment of acceptance. A donation *"mortis cause"* is a contract that is revocable until the time of death of the donor, but which is effected at the moment of his death. A testament is an act of disposition revocable until the death of the testator. A legacy is a donation, or a part of the inheritance left at death, and as such is to be fulfilled *(praestanda)* by the heir or executor. Cf. Coronata, *Institutiones,* II, n. 1053; Vermeersch-Creusen, *Epitome,* II, n. 834; Vromant, *De Bonis Ecclesiae Temporalibus,* n. 147 ff.

[50] Cf. canon 1515, § 1. Since this present study is concerned only with congregations of women religious of pontifical approval, it is here noted once for all that any reference to the ordinary in this article will always imply a local ordinary. And the specific local ordinary will be the proper ordinary of the religious person concerned, excepting the case when a particular specification of place has been made, in which case the reference will be to the ordinary of *that* place. Cf. Cocchi, *Commentarium,* VI, n. 195; Vermeersch-Creusen, *Epitome,* II, n. 836, 3°; Couly, "Les Biens Temporels de L'Eglise," *"Le Canoniste Contemporain,* XLV (1922), 119.

[15] Any clause contrary to the rights and duty of the ordinary in this matter, if attached to a last will, is to be regarded as null and void. In other donations such a clause always remains prohibited by ecclesiastical law. Cf. canon 1515, § 3; Coronata, *Institutiones,* II, n. 1055; Vromant, *De Bonis Ecclesiae Temporalibus,* n. 160, 3°.

tors, and, if such executors have not been appointed or are not living at the time that the donation or bequest becomes effective, the right of execution devolves upon him.[52] The delegated executors, however, must render an account to the ordinary, once they have performed their office.[53]

B. *Trusts*

When donations or bequests of temporal goods are left to a person to be transferred to another or expended for some certain work, such an undertaking is called a trust.[54] Thus a trust is constituted whenever any commission is entrusted to the integrity of another. And this is especially true of a donation or bequest given to a person with the accompanying obligation on his part to employ it for a pious use or to convey it to someone else.

The trustee who takes title to the property and acquires a full and real right over such temporal goods can be either a physical or a moral person, but the trustee must distribute the temporal goods in accordance with the intention of the donor. Hence upon this trustee rests the obligation of discharging the duty imposed by his acceptance of the trust.[55]

Though the authors seem not to stress the point, yet the term "fiducia" (a trust in its most generic acceptation) should be understood as comprising the double concept of a trust (in its more specific sense) and of an endowment (fundatio) since both can be constituted by donation or bequest, and since both impose a burden in favor of a work or of a person distinct from the per-

[52] Coronata, *Institutiones,* II, n. 1055, b; Vromant, *De Bonis Ecclesiae Temporalibus,* n. 159.

[53] Cf. canon 1515, § 2; Vromant, *De Bonis Ecclesiae Temporalibus,* n. 160.

[54] "Fiduciarie accipere est ita accipere ut largitio rei acceptae fidei donatarii committatur."—Coronata, *Institutiones,* II, n. 1056, note 7; Claeys Bouuaert-Simenon, *Manuale Iuris Canonici,* III, n. 267; Bondini, "De Fiduciae ad Causas Pias in Foro Externo Probatione," *Ius Pontificium,* VI (1926), 87; Vermeersch-Creusen, *Epitome,* II, n. 836, II.

[55] Couly, "Les Biens Temporels de l'Eglise"—*Le Canoniste Contemporain,* XLV (1922), 108; Vromant, *De Bonis Ecclesiae Temporalibus,* n. 153.

son who is burdened. But, while a trust in the specific sense can be imposed upon both a physical and a moral person, an endowment is entrusted by its very essence to a moral person alone; perpetuity is a formal element of every endowment or foundation, and it is of the essence of such a foundation or endowment that the capital should be preserved and invested, and that the income derived from it should be devoted to the purpose served by it, while perpetuity is not in itself proper to a trust, and any investment of the trust would only connote an incidental factor.[56]

Canon 1516 stipulates a cleric or religious who has, either by way of donation or by last will, received temporal goods in trust for pious causes must notify the ordinary concerning this trust and describe all the goods received, both movable and immovable, with the obligations attached to them.

Hence any person, moral or physical, of the congregations here treated, who has received temporal goods in trust for pious causes, is obligated to this twofold duty towards the local ordinary: 1. Notification of the acceptance of the trust; 2. The presentation of an inventory of all the goods and obligations attached to them.[57] If the property of a trust is to be kept for a notable time, then a safe investment of it is to be made under the direction of the local ordinary. And when the obligations and stipulations inherent in the trust have been carried out, then an account of this compliance with the demands of the trust must be furnished to the local ordinary.[58] If the donor of the trust should endeavor to exclude this right and duty of the local ordinary in his

[56] Hannan, *Canon Law of Wills*, n. 96; Vromant, *De Bonis Ecclesiae Temporalibus*, n. 347.

[57] As noted above, the determination of the local ordinary in regard to whom this duty will be discharged will be thus defined: if the goods in trust have been specifically designated for a certain place, then, by reason of the goods thus to be shared, the ordinary of that place must be notified and a proper inventory presented to him. Otherwise, this duty will be discharged to the proper local ordinary of the religious person.

[58] Cf. canons 1516, § 2; 1515. Vromant, *De Bonis Ecclesiae Temporalibus*, n. 162, 2°.

supervision over it, the religious or cleric shall not accept the trust when so offered.[59]

In order to determine definitely whether a donation or a bequest is a mere gift or a committed trust, one must find some norm that will enable one to discern whether the element of an entrusted commitment (*fides*), so fundamental and essential to every trust (*fiducia*), is actually inherent in such a donation or bequest. In answering a question regarding a donation or bequest which has been made to a clerical congregation of pontifical approval for the purpose of education of their students for the foreign missions, Coyeneche held that, while such a fund could be considered as a trust in the wide sense, it was not properly such in the strict sense of the term. For donations and bequests for this purpose are of the same character as those which are furnished for the aid of the students of the congregation, for the provision of teachers and preachers of the institute, etc., all of which can be considered rightly as pious causes, but not in the technical sense of canon 1516.

It is true, he continues, that when such donations or bequests are made with a definite restriction as to the place for which they are destined and in which they are to be expended, then one must consider that the pious cause is distinct from the proper work and scope of the congregation and is subject to canon 1516. But when the donation or bequest is made simply to be applied to the congregation or to a determined and pious cause within the exclusive ambit and proper scope of the congregation itself, then such a donation or bequest is a mere gift and not a trust, and as such does not come under the supervision of the local ordinary. For

[59] If the donor has expressed this exclusion as a *conditio sine qua non*, then the religious cannot licitly accept the trust. But if the excluding clause was inserted only as an ordinary formula, and the trust was offered by anyone as an outright donation *(actus inter vivos)*, then the donor must be admonished to cancel such a clause, otherwise the trust may not be accepted. If, however, the trust was committed through last will *(ex testamento* or *mortis causa)*, then the clause which gives expression to such an exclusion is simply to be considered as not attached, and consequently the trust may be accepted. Cf. canon 1515, § 3; Vromant, *De Bonis Ecclesiae Temporalibus*, n. 162, 4°.

when a donation or bequest is given as aid to the proper scope of a congregation of pontifical approval, the ordinary has no right of demanding an account of it.[60]

While this distinction as to the proper work and scope of the congregations is admissible, it should be noted that its connotation must be definitely restricted to such work as is of benefit to the congregation itself, and may not be extended to all the work that is proper to the congregation. For all the examples that are offered by Goyeneche in illustration of his statement imply works of a purely internal interest to the congregation in as far as the persons benefitting by the gift are members of the very moral person which received the gift. Hence one could not say that there was a commission in trust confided to the integrity of another for the benefit of a third party, since the donation or bequest is being used for the benefit of the moral person to whom it was given. It is indeed a mere gift for the proper work of the congregation, a work whose achievement or fulfillment will prove to be of benefit to the congregation itself.[61]

But it seems incorrect to admit the general statement of other canonists who have accepted the phrase "opus proprium" as extending in its connotation to every type of work that is proper to the congregation, so that any donation or bequest which is given for the promotion of a work that falls within the sphere of the constitutions of religious congregations of pontifical approval should be considered as a plain gift, and not as a committed trust, provided only that the application of the gift is not restricted to some specific place or locality.[62] In view of this, one cannot admit that a donation or bequest given solely for a specific portion of the work that is proper to a congregation may rightly be regarded as lacking the element of an entrusted commitment when the work so specified has any external influence. Thus, for example, in a congregation of women religious whose work includes both teaching and nursing, a fund may have been entrusted to them

[60] Cf. Goyeneche, "Consultationes"—*CpRM,* III (1922), 266.

[61] Cf. Nebreda, "Studia Canonica"—*CpRM,* VII (1926), 324.

[62] Cf. Vromant, *De Bonis Ecclesiae Temporalibus,* n. 164, p. 177; Hannan, ***The Canon Law of Wills,*** **n. 471.**

solely and expressly for the training of extern lay nurses. Such specification if placed as a *conditio sine qua non* of the donation or bequest, even though no restriction is indicated regarding the place in which the will of the donor is to be fulfilled, vests this donation or bequest with the element of obligatory confidence that the fund will be used for that purpose alone, and thus brings the factor of the ultimate and rightful application of the fund under the watchful supervision of the local ordinary even when such application is to be made by congregations of pontifical approval.

Relative to donations or bequests made to congregations of women religious of pontifical approval one may, in consequence of the previous considerations, advance the determined specification of a gift, either for the promotion of a particular work (as a *conditio sine qua non*), or for the benefit of a particular place, as a sufficient norm for certifying the requisite presence of an entrusted commitment (*fides*), which places the donation within the category of a committed trust. Thus, if the donation or bequest is made with a specific local restriction for its expenditure and use, so that the entrusted commitment must be executed in the place expressly specified, then such a donation or bequest must be considered properly as a trust, and will entail the duty of a proper notification and of a due presentation of its inventory to the ordinary of the place in favor of which the gift was specified.

If only a particular part of the work of the congregation is specified in the donation or bequest, one is obliged to make a further distinction. For, if this specification is merely precatory, then one can rightly consider that the intention of the donor was primarily concerned with the benefit of the congregation and secondarily with the work specified. In such a case, then, it would be permissible to consider the donation or bequest as a mere gift, which leaves it outside the supervisional orbit of the local ordinary with relation to the congregations here studied. But if the specification of the work is a *conditio sine qua non,* in that the donation or bequest is entrusted for that particular work alone, then again the element of an entrusted commitment is found therein, and it seems certain that such a donation or bequest must be considered as properly being a trust, subject in its supervision to the local ordinary also when its execution is committed to a congregation of pontifical approval.

Finally, it is clearly evident that when a donation or bequest is made to a pontifically approved congregation of women religious for work that is not within its proper sphere, then such a donation or bequest must be considered as a trust, for the fulfillment of the obligation engendered must ordinarily be entrusted to some outside person, since the undertaking of work that is foreign to the purpose of a congregation of pontifical approval must be considered as a change in the constitutions, a change that may not be made without an apostolic indult.[63]

It is the duty of the local ordinary to do all in his power to accomplish the proper execution of legacies and donations destined for pious uses. If all other means have been exhausted, he may even impose censures (*ferendae sententiae*) on those who have come into possession of a legacy or donation destined for pious use, even through a trust, and who neglect to fulfill their obligation.[64] And those who presume to usurp or convert to other use such ecclesiastical property are branded with excommunication.[65]

The reduction, mitigation, and commutation of last wills is reserved to the Holy See, and may be effected only for a just

[63] Cf. canon 618, § 2, 1°.

[64] "Any person who either by donation, or last will, or as a trustee comes into possession of a legacy or donation destined for pious institutes, and neglects to fulfill his obligation, shall be forced to do so by the ordinary even with censures."—Canon 2348. "If the ordinary hears that a cleric or religious has been entrusted with a *fiducia,* he can summon witnesses. If the trust is proved by two reliable witnesses [c. 1791, § 2], he can compel proper discharge of it even by censures [c. 2348]. But if there are not witnesses who can submit proof, the ordinary can put the cleric or the religious on oath, and then let the matter to the conscience of the one making the affidavit."—Hannan, *The Canon Law of Wills,* n. 783. Cf. Vromant, *De Bonis Ecclesiae Temporalibus,* n. 165; Coronata, *Institutiones,* II, n. 1056; Bondini, "De Fiduciae ad Causas Pias in Foro Externo Probatione"—*Ius Pontificium,* VI, (1926), 87.

[65] Cf. canon 2346.

and necessary cause. The local ordinary has no power to modify last wills, unless the founder has explicitly conceded this power to him. If, however, through no fault of the executors, the execution of the imposed obligation has become impossible in view of a decrease in the revenue or for some other reason, the ordinary, after having heard all interested parties and adhering, in so far as this is possible, to the will of the founder, may reduce the obligations according to the laws of equity. But the reduction of Masses is always reserved exclusively to the Holy See.[66]

C. *Foundations*

By a foundation, as treated here in the canonical sense, is meant the temporal goods given to some moral ecclesiastical person in any manner with the obligation to say a certain number of Masses, to hold other specified ecclesiastical functions, or to perform some works of piety or charity perpetually or for an extended period in return for the revenue of these goods.[67] Hence

[66] Cf. canon 1517. Reduction is a legitimate decrease of the burdens imposed, without changing their nature. Thus the obligation of one hundred Masses might be decreased to fifty. Mitigation is a modification of an accessory or secondary part of the burden. Thus five solemn high Masses might be modified to five high Masses *(missae cantatae)*. Commutation is a substitution of the obligation or of the destination of the benefit. Thus in place of a hospital, which was intended, a school might be built. Cf. Vromant, *De Bonis Ecclesiae Temporalibus,* n. 166; Coronata, *Institutiones,* II, n. 1057; Cocchi, *Commentarium,* VI, n. 196; Blat, *Commentarium Codicis, De Rebus,* Lib. III, Pars VI, n. 437; Hannan, *The Canon Law of Wills,* n. 795. But it should be noted that the reduction, mitigation or commutation of a donation *inter vivos* must be arranged with the donor. Cf. Claeys Bouuaert-Simenon *Manuale Iuris Canonici,* III, n. 268.

[67] Cf. canon 1544. "Thus a foundation is marked by five essential elements. First, there is temporal property, personalty or realty, given by donation or testamentary disposition. Second, a canonically established moral person is the beneficiary. Third, the purpose is religious or charitable. Fourth, there is an arrangement whereby the annual revenue of the endowment is to be devoted to a precise purpose, the income being derived from the capital fund invested for the period of the foundation. Fifth, the obligation is perpetual, or at least for a long period of time."—Hannan, *The Canon Law of Wills,* n. 751; Vromant, *De Bonis Ecclesiae Temporalibus,* n. 347.

a pious foundation is neither a collegiate nor a non-collegiate moral person, but rather a fund that has been entrusted to a moral ecclesiastical person. And such a fund can be entrusted to any moral personality in a congregation of women religious of pontifical approval.[68] The property of a pious foundation must always be considered as ecclesiastical property. As such it is subject to the special provisions inculcated by the law of the Code relative to ecclesiastical property.[69].

Since a foundation is a bilateral contract, acceptance of the obligation is necessary.[70] And acceptance of a pious foundation by a congregation of women religious of pontifical approval is permitted on three conditions: 1. The consent of the local ordinary must be obtained; 2. The moral person must be able to

[68] Coronata, *Institutiones,* II, n. 1079. It is to be well noted that a foundation, as understood here in the canonical sense, is not a non-collegiate ecclesiastical institution, since foundations and non-collegiate ecclesiastical institutions are distinct and separate canonical concepts. For a foundation is the canonical consideration of a burden which is left or joined to a moral person. And this moral person to which the foundation is adjoined can be preexistent or coexistent. Thus a foundation could be attached to a preexisting institution, such as a hospital, or the local ordinary could incorporate a new juridical entity especially for the foundation itself, thus joining the foundation to this special juridical entity for the constitution of which the foundation itself furnished the necessary material basis. Hence one may say that the Code in its concept apprehends an institution in the light of its being established in reality of existence *(ratione constitutionis in esse),* and a foundation from the viewpoint of its being burdened with an obligation *(ratione oneris).*

[69] The property of lay foundations, namely of such foundations as are established without ecclesiastical authority, is not ecclesiastical property, but is nonetheless subject to the ordinary by virtue of canon 1515, in as much as the ordinary must be recognized as the accredited executor of all pious causes, in virtue of which capacity he has the right and duty of ascertaining that all pious intentions and bequests are fulfilled. The acquisition of this certainty in turn presupposes the right of receiving an accounting relative to this fulfillment on the part of the delegated executors.

[70] Vromant, *op. cit.,* n. 346, 6°

discharge the obligations; 3. The fund must be adequate. The consent of the local ordinary is to be given in writing.[71]

But the local ordinary is obliged to withhold this consent until he has duly ascertained that the moral person through its agents can satisfy the obligation imposed by the new foundation and can continue at the same time to fulfill all the other obligations created for it by the acceptance of foundations in the past. And he shall especially ascertain that the income from the foundation corresponds fully to the imposed obligations, according to the custom of the respective diocese.[72]

Regarding the substantial element of the foundation the local ordinary has two rights. One is the establishment of a definite sum below which no one may accept a pious foundation validly and licitly. The other is the establishment of a plan of distribution when the founder made no express disposition, for instance, in a case wherein the founder merely expressed a wish to have the foundation devoted to several charitable purposes.[73]

In the matter of custody and investment the local ordinary has the right of designating the place for the immediate safe-deposit of money and movable property of a pious foundation, and passes final judgment on the safety and utility of the subsequent investment. But this final judgment is to be formulated after he has taken counsel with the diocesan council of administration, the founder, the superioress of the moral person, in the case of the congregations here treated, and all other persons interested.[74]

[71] Cf. canon 1546. Acceptance of the foundation is made by the religious superioress *ad normam constitutionum vel legitimae consuetudinis.* Cf. Vromant, *De Bonis Ecclesiae Temporalibus,* n. 349. Acceptance without the due permission of the local ordinary would in itself most probably be valid, but definitely rescissible by the ordinary. Cf. Wernz, *Ius Decretalium,* III, n. 200; Vromant, *loc. cit.*

[72] Cf. canon 1546, § 1; Vromant, *op. cit.,* n. 349, II.

[73] Cf. Hannan, *The Canon Law of Wills,* n. 756; Vromant, *De Bonis Ecclesiae Temporalibus,* n. 348.

[74] Cf. canon 1547. "Realty and chattels annexed to realty, as well as securities, are to be retained in the form given by the founder. If they are to be sold, it can only be with the permission of the Holy See or the proper Superior, according to the provisions of canons 534, 1530, 1532.

The articles of foundation should be put in writing with one copy deposited in the diocesan chancery and another in the archives of the moral person to whom the fund has been entrusted. These articles should contain mention of the amount of the foundation funds, of the burdens to be fulfilled, of the manner in which they are to be fulfilled, of the person to fulfill them, of the provisions to be made if the fund fails, and of the eventual allocation of the fund if the moral person to which it has been entrusted should ultimately lapse from existence. It would also be provident to attach to the copy deposited in the archives of the moral person the copy of the permission given by the local ordinary for the acceptance of the fund which constitutes the foundation.[75]

In conclusion it may be stated that pious foundations which have been entrusted to congregations of women religious of pontifical approval are subject to the local ordinary under three aspects: 1. As a pious cause; 2. As a trust, and 3. As a pious foundation. With reference to the first of these aspects the local ordinary is the accredited executor, who must ascertain, even through the medium of his canonical visitation, that the pious intention and will of the donor is properly fulfilled. To this end the local ordinary is rightfully entitled to demand from the delegated executors the rendering of an account. With relation to the second of these considerations the local ordinary can exact due notification concerning the accepted trust and can moreover require that an inventory of the various elements of the trust be presented to him. With respect to the third of these distinct elements the local ordinary has rights and duties not only with regard to the substantial content and acceptance of a pious foundation, but also in relation to its investment, custody and conservation.[76]

As in the case of other trusts, the reduction of obligations attached to the pious foundation is reserved exclusively to the

Other chattels, however, should be sold, and the proceeds devoted to the purposes of the fund."—Hannan, *The Canon Law of Wills,* n. 761. Cf. Vromant, *op. cit.,* n. 350; Blat, *De Rebus,* Lib. III, Pars VI, n. 473.

[75] Cf. Vromant, *De Bonis Ecclesiae Temporalibus,* n. 352, 2°.

[76] Cf. canons 1549; 1546; 1547 ff.

Holy See, unless the document of foundation explicitly gives the local ordinary certain specified powers to reduce the obligations.[77]

[77] Pious foundations of Masses, however, can never be reduced without permission of the Holy See. Cf. canon 1517.) And the indult to reduce the foundations of Masses does not extend to other Masses due by contract or to other works of the pious foundations. Moreover, a general indult to reduce the obligations of foundations must be understood in the sense that the person possessing the indult shall, unless the contrary is apparent, reduce other obligations rather than the Masses. Cf. canon 1551.

Chapter XV

OTHER RIGHTS AND DUTIES

Article 1. Censorship of Books

Censorship of books has been instituted by the Church as a safeguard against the possible spread of error or moral corruption. It consists in the due examination and judgment of a work by ecclesiastical authority with the consequent concession or refusal of permission for its publication.

The works and articles which women religious of congregations of pontifical approval must subject to previous ecclesiastical censorship and authorization will include such books, brochures and articles of which mention is made in canon 1385, § 1. The religious of these congregations must obtain the proper authorization of the local ordinary as well as of their major superioress when they wish to publish books or public writings of the above specified character.[1]

This authorization (commonly called the *Imprimatur*) shall be given in writing, and it shall be printed either at the beginning or end of the book or paper, or on the front or back of the picture, with the name of the ordinary and the date and the place of the concession.[2] Such authorization may be conceded by the proper local ordinary of the religious, by the ordinary of the place of publication, or by the ordinary of the place in which the work or article is printed.[3]

[1] Cf. canon 1385; Coronata, *Institutiones,* II, n. 955; Fanfani, *De Iure Religiosorum,* n. 282.

[2] Cf. canon 1394.

[3] Cf. canon 1385, § 2. The proper ordinary of a religious of the congregations here treated is the ordinary of the diocese in which is situated the religious house with which the particular religious is definitely affiliated. Cf. Coronata, *loc. cit.;* Fanfani, *loc. cit.;* Vermeersch-Creusen, *Epitome,* II, n. 726; Augustine, *Commentary,* VI, 441, note 12.

Hence the religious is free to choose between the three ordinaries, but it must be noted that she cannot legitimately petition the consent of one of these local ordinaries, when consent has been refused by another, unless she makes explicit mention of the refusal. If she made no mention of this refusal, she would be guilty of a moral fault, but it seems that the consent given by the second ordinary would be validly given though it was illicitly obtained.[4]

Aside from these requirements of previous censorship and authorization, canon 1386, § 1, states that religious of the congregations here treated are forbidden to write any books, even those that have no religious character, without the previous permission of the major superioress and the local ordinary. Though, at first glance, this prescription may seem to be applicable only to those books which require no censorship, Coronata and Vermeersch-Creusen adhere to the strict view and hold that the prescription applies to all books. Thus, even though the religious may plan on obtaining the *Imprimatur* from another of the three local ordinaries of her choice, it seems that she must obtain the permission of her proper ordinary for the writing of the book.[5] This same consent is also required for the religious when writing in newspapers, magazines, or periodicals of any kind, as well as for undertaking the direction of such work.[6]

Most probably this prescription does not extend to the writing of one or two articles of minor moment, but is intended principally for an habitual writing or collaboration. Nor is it necessary to obtain a renewal of permission for each time of writing; a

[4] Cf. canon 1385, § 2; Coronata, *Institutiones,* II, n. 955.

[5] Coronata *(Institutiones,* II, n. 955, 2°) writes: "Vi huius paragraphi requiritur licentia proprii Ordinarii auctoris . . . nec sufficit licentia Ordinarii loci publicationis seu editionis. . . . Hanc interpretationem, quae serverior primo intuitu videtur, suadet coniunctio *quoque,* quae hac paragrapho abhibetur. Consensus Ordinarii in hoc casu non necessario requirit examen praevium libri, nec etiam necessario scripto dandum est."

[6] Cf. canon 1386, § 2.

general permission, *semel pro semper,* would suffice until it is revoked.[7]

A religious of a congregation of pontifical approval should never, except for a just and reasonable cause that is approved by the local ordinary, publish anything in those newspapers or periodicals which combat religion or morality.[8] This prescription includes even single cases of writings and extends to all articles, interviews and similar literary contributions. Even though the texts of advertisements and announcements (official notices, etc.,) would not properly be comprised under this positively specified obligation, yet their publication in such newspapers or periodicals would most probably in the larger majority of cases be prohibited by the natural law.[9]

Again, it would be utterly futile for a sister to seek to avoid submitting to the requirement of previous censorship, or to proceed without the consent and permission required in these prescriptions, in view of the article's anonymous authorship or in consideration of its publication under a pseudonym, for in these instances also the same prescriptions must be observed. The thing forbidden by the law of canon 1386 is the unauthorized writing and publishing of articles in newspapers, brochures and periodicals. The law abstracts entirely from the point whether or not the written article can be identified in its authorship by a religious.

Finally, particular attention must be paid to the special norms to be observed for the publication of whatever pertains to the beatification or canonization of Servants of God; for the publication of books, booklets and leaflets containing grants of indulgences; for the publication of new collections of the decrees of the Roman Congregations, and for the production of new editions of liturgical books either in whole or in part, of litanies, and of versions of the Sacred Scriptures.[10]

[7] Coronata, *Institutiones,* II, n. 955, 2°b.

[8] Cf. canon 1386, § 2.

[9] Cf. Coronata, *Institutiones,* II, n. 955,3°; Ayrinhac, *Administrative Legislation in the New Code of Canon Law* (New York: Longmans Green, 1930), n. 233, 3°.

[10] Cf. canons 1387-1931.

ARTICLE 2. TAXES

When there is not sufficient revenue for the establishment or upkeep of the diocesan seminary, the local ordinary is empowered by the Code to impose a tax in his diocese for this purpose. In the congregations of women religious of pontifical approval this tax can be imposed on hospitals that have been established by ecclesiastical authority and provided with funds of their own, for instance by foundations, and upon every religious house, unless the religious live solely on alms or have actually in maintenance a college for the training of students or teachers for the promotion of the common welfare of the Church.[11]

This assessment must be general throughout the diocese, proportionate to the needs of the seminary, and of the same percentage for all who are liable for the payment of this tax.[12] Moreover, this assessment must not exceed five percent of the taxable income, namely, of what is left after all obligations and expenditures have been deducted. This general principle must be applied to all who are liable for the tax.[13]

Hospitals operated by the congregations here treated are not subject to this tax if they are only pious institutions, having been erected without ecclesiastical approval, for only ecclesiastical institutions are included in the prescriptions of the canon. Nor would the assessment be applicable to hospitals which subsist on the generosity of voluntary contributors or on alms. And any expense for the upkeep of free wards (charity patients) in the

[11] Cf. canon **1356, § 1.**

[12] Cf. canon 1356, § 2. "Tributum si imponantur debet esse *generale,* i.e., omnibus personis physicis aut moralibus a iure expressis impositum, seposita qualibet personarum acceptione; ideo nequit Ordinarius loci aliquem a tributo solvendo dispensare: debet esse eiusdem proportionis pro omnibus, unde nequit Ordinarius tributum trium centenarum partium pro una, quatuor pro altera, quinque pro tertia persona imponere, sed vel trium vel quatuor vel quinque, at pro omnibus aequali taxatione."—Coronata, *Institutiones,* II, p. 282; Augustine, *Commentary,* VI, 385.

[13] Cf. canon 1356, § 3.

hospital, plus the interest to be paid on capital or mortgage could be deducted.[14]

In arriving at the definite figure or amount of taxable income, religious houses which operate schools, hospitals, orphanages, etc., would evidently be permitted to deduct any revenues of their own which are expended on such institutions. While the term *"collegium"*, as used in the text, is not defined, authors extend the term not only to seminaries but to any Catholic college for youth or for teachers. Augustine, however, is inclined to exclude from this classification, and thus to consider as not exempt from the payment of this tax, those colleges which are intended only for the members of the respective religious family, scholasticates for example, in that such institutions are primarily destined for the benefit of the respective order or congregation, and not for the Church at large. But this argument, with slight adaptation, could be applied to any college.[15] Again, this deduction would likewise apply to the case of a house taxed by the mother house of the congregation, according to constitutions or statute, for the support of the school of the congregation.[16]

The Code insists that any custom contrary to the imposition of this seminary tax is reprobated, every contrary privilege revoked, and every appeal withdrawn.[17]

Any other tax for the benefit of the diocese can be imposed on ecclesiastical institutions only at the time of their foundation or consecration.[18]

[14] Augustine, *Commentary,* VI, 387; Coronata, *Institutiones,* II, p. 282; Vermeersch-Creusen, *Epitome,* II, n. 690.

[15] Augustine, *Commentary,* VI, 385. *Contra,* Coronata, *Institutiones,* II, p. 283; "Responsa S. C. Concilii ab R. P. Augustine allata illi conclusioni non favent."—Vermeersch-Creusen, *Epitome,* II, n. 690.

[16] Coronata, *Institutiones,* II, p. 283; Vermeersch-Creusen, *Epitome,* II, n. 690.

[17] Cf. canon 1356, § 1. "Excluditur igitur etiam appellatio in devolutivo. Recursus tamen ad S. Sedem semper manet apertus. Haec potest imperare restitutionem soluti tributi."—Vermeersch-Creusen, *Epitome,* II, n. 690; Pruemmer, *Manuale Iuris Canonici,* q. 410; Coronata, *Institutiones,* II, p. 280.

[18] Cf. canon 1506.

Article 3. Dispensation

In the general norms for dispensation, the Code states that local ordinaries cannot dispense from the general laws of the Church, even in a particular case, unless this power has been granted them either explicitly or implicitly, or unless recourse to the Holy See is difficult and simultaneously there is a danger of grave harm in delay and the dispensation is one which the Holy See is wont to grant.[19]

While the Code does not grant to the local ordinary the power of dispensing from the obligations of the constitutions in the congregations here treated, it states that every indult lawfully granted by the local ordinary in dispensing from the obligation of the common law avails likewise for all the religious of the congregations here treated who are living in the diocese, but without prejudice to the vows and particular constitutions of their own institute.[20] Thus, by virtue of canon 1245, the local ordinary can dispense in a particular case from the obligation of the common law regarding fast and abstinence, and by virtue of such dispensation the obligation of the common law ceases also for the members of a congregation of women religious of pontifical approval who are living within his diocese.

However, if the constitutions of the congregation impose the same obligation as that imposed by the common law, then the members of the congregation may make use of the dispensation granted by the local ordinary only if the superioress likewise can and does dispense from the obligation of the constitution.[21]

[19] Cf. canon 81; Reilly, *The General Norms of Dispensation, The Catholic University of America Canon Law Studies, No. 119,* (Washington, D. C.: The Catholic University of America, 1939), p. 65.

[20] Cf. canon 620.

[21] The superioress has power to dispense an individual subject from one or another point of the rule and constitutions, but only in a particular case, for the time being, and for a just cause. But the superioress has no power to grant to the whole community a dispensation from the rule and constitutions, except in cases in which the rule and constitutions give her such power. Thus the superioress may at times and for a just cause dispense the whole community from the obligation of silence

Article 4: Trials

In congregations of women religious of pontifical approval, if any controversy arises between the religious of the congregation, between physical or moral persons of different religious organizations, or between a religious and a secular cleric or lay person, the local ordinary will be the judge of the first instance.[22] Hence any judicial process, either contentious or criminal, that concerns the religious treated in this study will be taken for trial to the court of the local ordinary as the court of first instance. For the major superioresses of the congregations here treated are not "ordinaries" and have no judicial power.[23]

The local ordinary who is competent to act in first instance may be either the one in whose diocese is situated the religious house to which the religious person is legitimately assigned (canon 1563); the one in whose diocese the thing contested is located (canons 1560, 1 °, 1564); the one in whose territory the contract under dispute has been made or is to be fulfilled (canon 1565, §1); the one in whose territory the crime was committed (canon 1566, §1); or, finally, either one of the local ordinaries who by law has jurisdiction over a matter connected with, or contained in, the matter contested (canon 1567).[24]

If the controversy involves a province that extends into several diocese, any one of the local ordinaries, who have authority within the territory of the province is competent to judge the case.

at table on certain occasions, or from the observance of a fast day prescribed by the rule and constitutions, but not from the obligation of fast and abstinence prescribed by the Church. Geser, *The Canon Law Governing Communities of Sisters,* qq. 937, 939; Augustine, *Commentary,* III, 345; Pruemmer, *Manuale Iuris Canonici,* q. 187.

[22] Cf. canon 1579, § 3. Religious may be involved in the controvery as private persons or as administrators and superioresses of the religious house. Cf. Blat, *De Processibus,* (Tom. IV of his *Commentarium Codicis,* Romae, Apud Angelicum, 1927), n. 37.

[23] Blat, *loc. cit.*

[24] Coronata, *Institutiones,* III, n. 1120; Gallik, *The Rights and Duties of the Local Ordinary Regarding Diocesan Sisterhoods,* p. 126.

And in all these cases as outlined, the court of second instance will be that which the tribunal of the first instance uses.[25]

However, it should be noted that in the matter of cases for which the law establishes a necessary forum judicial actions to regain possession or quasi-possession of property or property rights, of which one was wrongfully deprived either by force or secretly, must be brought before the local ordinary where the property is located. Cases concerning administration must be tried before the local ordinary in whose territory the administration was conducted. And cases concerning inheritances or pious legacies must be tried before the local ordinary of the domicile of the testator, except when there is a question merely of the execution of a legacy, which is to be settled according to the ordinary rules of competency.[26]

Moreover, canonical legislation expressly stipulates that if religious have not obtained the consent of their superiors, they shall have no standing in court, except in the following cases: 1. If the suit is concerned with vindicating, against the religious organization, rights which they have acquired by profession; 2. If they legitimately live outside the religious house, and the defense of their rights becomes urgent; 3. If they wish to institute a denunciation of their superioress.[27]

The superioresses and the duly authorized officials who have been so designated by the constitutions have the right and duty, within the limits of the constitutions, of vindicating and defending the rights of the community in court. For the Code states that the rector or administrator shall have the right of representing a moral person in court, with the one restriction that religious superioresses cannot act in court in the name of their community, except in the manner prescribed in their constitutions. And if conflict should arise between the rights of the moral person and those of the rector or administrator, then the local ordinary shall designate a procurator to represent the moral person.[28]

25 Coronata, *loc. cit.*
26 Cf. canon 1560, 1°, 3°, 4°.
27 Cf. canon 1652.
28 Cf. canons 532, § 2; 1649; 1653, § 6.

Article 5: Penalties

The coercive power of the local ordinary over congregations of women religious of pontifical approval is proportionate to his jurisdictional power over the congregation. For canon 619 states that, in all matters in which religious are subject to the local ordinary, he can coerce them even with penalties.[29]

While this power of the local ordinary will generally be exercised by applying the penalties prescribed in the common law, special reasons may justify an increase of the penalty or, again, circumstances may warrant the attaching of penalties to universal or particular laws which lack penal sanctions.[30] The local ordinary may not, however, attach a reserved censure to a law that already carries the sanction of a censure reserved to the Holy See.[31]

Moreover, if grave scandal has been given, or if the special gravity of the transgression require it, the local ordinary may; even without previous threat of punishment, punish transgressors of the law with some just penalty, even though the law has no penalty attaced.[32]

Since a detailed study of the penalties that apply to religious in particular is beyond the scope of this study, the reader may be referred to the Fifth Book of the Code and to the specific study of the subject already made.[33]

[29] Cf. Coronata, *Institutiones,* I, n. 626; Vermersch-Creusen, *Epitome,* I, n. 722; Blat, *De Religiosis,* n. 582.

[30] Cf. canons 2220, § 1; 2221. "Vicarius Generalis sine mandato speciali non habet potestatem infligendi poenas."—Canon 2220, § 2.

[31] Cf. canon 247, § 1; Vermeersch-Creusen, *Epitome,* III, n. 446; Chelodi, *Ius Poenale* (4. ed., Tridenti: Ardese, 1935), n. 33; Ayrinhac, *Penal Legislation* (New York: Benziger, 1936), n. 88.

[32] Cf. canon 2222, § 1; Vermeersch-Creusen, Epitome, III, n. 412; Blat, *De Delictis* et Poenis, n. 40.

[33] Cf. Canons 2323; 2324; 2325; 2331; 2344; 2347; 2348; 2355; 2360; 2361; 2362; 2380; 2389; 2390; 2391; 2411; 2412; 2413; 2414. Smith, *The Penal Law for Religious, The Catholic University of America Canon Law Studies, No. 98,* (Washington, D. C.: The Catholic University of America, 1935).

CONCLUSIONS

1. Congregations of women religious with simple vows were neither approved nor recognized until the time of the Constitution *"Conditae a Christo"* of Pope Leo XIII.

2. In the election of the superioress-general, the Code of Canon Law does not empower the local ordinary to break a tie vote.

3. Visitation by the local ordinary to congregations of women religious of pontifical approval will ordinarily be made only once each five years. In this visitation, the semi-public oratories of the religious house will be included.

4. The local ordinary has the right and duty of specifically determining the limits of the enclosure of these congregations and of making any specific changes in these limits.

5. The right of vigilance and the right of visitation differ as genus and species.

6. In canon 533, § 1, 3°, the phrase *"eo ipso loco"* has a double connotation: 1. That the consent of the ordinary of the place must be obtained for the investment of funds that are destined for the place of which he is the ordinary; 2. That this consent must be obtained from the ordinary of the place for which the expenditure of the funds is destined.

7. In addition to the temporal goods detailed in canon 618, § 2, 1°, any pious bequests, trusts or endowments made to these congregations and which have the nature of an entrustment are subject to the local ordinary.

BIBLIOGRAPHY

Sources

Acta Apostolicae Sedis, Commentarium Officiale, Romae, 1909—

Acta et Decreta Concilii Plenarii Americae Latinae, Romae, 1902.

Acta et Decreta Concilii Plenarii Baltimorensis III (1884), Baltimorae, 1886.

Acta et Decreta Sacrorum Conciliorum Recentiorum, Collectio Lacensis, 7 vols., Friburgi Brisgoviae, 1870-1890.

Acta Sanctae Sedis, 41 vols., Romae, 1865-1908.

Bullarium Diplomatum et Privilegiorum Sanctorum Romanorum Pontificum Taurinensis Editio, 25 vols., Augustae Taurinorum, 1857-1872.

Canones et Decreta Sacrosanctai Oecumenici Concilii Tridentini, Taurini: Marietti, 1913.

Canonical Legislation concerning Religious, Authorized English Translation, Rome: Vatican Printing Office, 1929.

Codex Iuris Canonici Pii X Pontificis Maximi iussu digestus Benedicti Papae XV auctoritate promulgatus, Romae: Typis Polyglottis Vaticanis, 1917.

Codicis Iuris Canonici Fontes cura Emi. Petri Card. Gasparri editi, 9 vols. Romae [later Civitate Vaticana]: Typis Polyglottis Vaticanis, 1923-1939. (Vols VII-IX *ed. cura et studio Emi. Iustiniani Card. Serédi*).

Collectanea in usum Secretariae Sacre Congregationis Episcoporum et Regularium, ed. Bizzarri, Romae, 1885.

Collectanea S. Congregationis de Propaganda Fide, 2 vols., Romae: Typographia Polyglotta S. C. de Propaganda Fide, 1907.

Corpus Iuris Canonici, editio Lipsiensis secunda post Aemilii Richteri curas . . . instruxit Aemilius Freidberg, 2 vols., Lipsiae, 1879-1881.

Corpus Iuris Civilis, vol. III, *Novellae Constitutiones,* ed. R. Schoell. Opus Schoellii morte interceptum absolvit G. Kroll, Berolini apud Weidmannos, 1928-1929.

Decreta Authentica Congregationis Sacrorum Ritum, 6 vols., Romae, 1898-1927.

Decretales D. Gregorii Papae IX una cum Glossis Restitutae, Romae, 1582.

Harduin, Jean, *Acta Conciliorum et Epistolae Decretales ac Constitutiones Summorum Pontificum,* 12 vols., Parisiis, 1715.

Instruction of the Sacred Congregation of the Sacraments on the Careful Custody of the Most Holy Eucharist, English Translation, Philadelphia: American Ecclesiastical Review, 1938.

Liber Sextus Decretalium una cum Clementinis et Extravagantibus Earumque Glossis Restitutis, Romae, 1582.

Mansi, Joannes, *Sacrorum Conciliorum Nova et Amplissima Collectio,* 53 vols., Parisiis, Arnhem, Lipsiae, 1901-1927.

Normae secundum quas S. Cong. Ep. et Reg., procedere solet in approbandis Novis Institutis Votorum Simplicium, Typis S. Cong. de Propaganda Fide, 1901.

Rules and General Constitutiones of the Friars Minor, Paterson, N. J.; St. Anthony Guild Press, 1936.

AUTHORS

Appletern, Victor, *Compendium Praelectionum Iuris Regularis Adm. R. P. Piati Montani ad Recentissimas Leges Ecclesiasticas Redactum,* 2. ed., Parisiis: Casterman, 1913.

Ayrinhac, H. A., S. S., *Administrative Legislation in the New Code of Canon Law,* New York: Longmans, Green & Co., 1930.

——— *Penal Legislation in the New Code of Canon Law,* Revised by P. J. Lydon, New York: Benziger, 1936.

Bachofen Augustinus, *Compendium Iuris Regularium,* Neo-Eboracensis: Benziger, 1903.

[Bachofen], Charles Augustine, *A Commentary on the New Code of Canon Law,* 8 vols. (vol. III, *Religious,* 5. ed., 1938; vol. VI, *Administrative Law,* 3. ed., 1931), St. Louis: Herder.

——— *Liturgical Law, A Handbook of the Roman Liturgy,* St. Louis: Herder, 1931.

Balmes, Hilaire, O.M.I., *Les Religieux à voeux simples d'aprés le Code,* Bruxelles: Action Catholique, 1921.

Barrett, John, S. S., *A Comparative Study of the Third Plenary Council of Baltimore and the Code of Canon Law, The Catholic University of America Canon Law Studies, N. 83,* Washington, D. C.: The Catholic University of America, 1932.

Bastien, Pierre, *Constitution "Conditae a Christo" de Leon XIII sur les Instituts à Voeux Simples et Leurs Relations avec l'Authorité Diocesaine,* Bruges, 1902.

——— *Directoire Canonique a l'Usage des Congrégations à Voeux Simples,* 3. ed., Bruges: Beyaert, 1923.

Battandier A., *Guide Canonique pour les Constitutions des Instituts à Voeux Simples,* 6. ed., Paris, 1923.

Benedictus XIV, *De Synodo Dioecesana,* 2 vols., Romae, 1806.

Beste, U., O.S.B., *Introductio in Codicem,* Collegeville, Minn.: St. John's Abbey, 1938.

Blat, A., O.P., *Commentarium Textus Codicis Iuris Canonici,* 6 vols., (lib. II, II-III, *de Religiosis,* 3. ed., 1938; lib. III, *de Rebus,* Partes II-VI, 2. ed., 1934; lib. V, *de Delictis et Poenis,* 1. ed., 1924), Romae: Apud "Angelicum."

Boffa, Conrad, *Canonical Provisions for Catholic Schools, The Catholic University of America Canon Law Studies, N. 117,* Washington, D. C.: The Catholic University of America, 1939.

Bondini, Aloisius, O.M.C., *De Privilegio Exemptionis seu de Regularium Immunitate ab Ordinariorum Locorum Iurisdictione prout in Novo Iuris Canonici Codice Sancitur,* Romae: Desclée, 1919.

Bougard, Louis, *St. Chantal and the Foundation of Visitation,* translated from the 11th French edition by a Visitandine, 2 vols., New York, 1895.

Bouix, Dominicus, *Tractatus de Iure Regularium,* 3. ed., 2 vols., Parisiis, 1882.

Bouscaren, T. L., S.J., *Canon Law Digest,* 2 vols., Milwaukee: Bruce, 1934-1937.

Cappello, Felix M., S.J., *De Vistatione SS. Liminum et Dioeceseon ac de Relatione S. Sedi Exhibenda,* 2 vols., Romae: Pustet, 1913.

——— *Summa Iuris Canonici,* 2. ed., 3 vols., (Vol. III, 1. ed., 1936), Romae: Apud Aedes Universitatis Gregorianae, 1932-1936.

——— *Tractatus Canonico-Moralis de Sacramentis vol. I, de Sacramentis in Genere, de Baptismo, Confirmatione et Eucharistia,* Romae: Marietti, 1928.

Chelodi, Ioannes, *Ius de Personis iuxta Codicem Iuris Canonici, Praemisso Tractatu de Principiis et Fontibus Iuris Canonici,* ed. altera, a Sac. Ernesto Bertagnolli recognita et aucta, Tridenti: Libr. Edit. Tridentum, 1927.

——— *Ius Poenale et Ordo Procedendi in Iudiciis Criminalibus iuxta Codicem Iuris Canonici,* 4. ed., recognita et aucta a Vigilio Dalpiaz, Tridenti: Ardesi, 1935.

Cicognani, Amleto, *Canon Law,* Authorized English Version by J. O'Hara and F. Brennan, 2. ed., Philadelphia, Dolphin Press, 1935.

Claeys Bouuaert F.—Simenon, G., *Manuale Iuris Canonici ad usum Seminariorum,* 4. ed., 3 vols., (vol. II, 2. ed., 1935), Gandae et Leodii, 1934.

Cleary, Joseph F., *Canonical Limitations on the Alienation of Church Property, The Catholic University of America Canon Law Studies, N. 100,* Washington, D. C.: The Catholic University of America, 1936.

Cocchi, G., *Commentarium in Codicem Iuris Canonici,* 8 vols., (tom. IV, *de Religiosis,* 3. ed., 1932; tom. V, *de Rebus,* 3. ed., 1932; tom. VI, *de Rebus,* 3. ed., 1933), Romae: Marietti.

Coronata, P. Matthaeus Conte a, O.F.M. Cap., *Institutiones Iuris Canonici ad usum Utriusque Cleri et Scholarum,* 5 vols., Taurini: Marietti. 1928-1936.

Creusen, Joseph, S.J., *Religieux d'après le Droit Ecclésiastique,* 3. ed., Paris: Beauchesne, 1924.

——— *Religious Men and Women in the Code,* First translation by Edward F. Garesche, Third English Edition, revised and edited to conform with the first French edition, by Adam C. Ellis, Milwaukee: Bruce, 1940.

Currier, Charles, *History of Religious Orders,* New York, 1913.

D'Angelo. Sosio. *La Esenzione dei Religiosi,* Torino: L.I.C.E., 1929.

Fanfani, Ludovicus, *De Iure Religiosorum ad Normam Codicis Iuris Canonici,* Taurini: Marietti, 1925.

Ferraris. F. Lucius, *Prompta Bibliotheca Canonica, Iuridica, Moralis, Theologica, necnon Ascetica, Polemica Rubricistica, Historica,* 9 vols., Romae, 1885-1899.

Frey, Wolfgang, *The Act of Religious Profession, The Catholic University of America Canon Law Studies, N. 65,* Washington, D. C.: The Catholic University of America, 1931.

Funk, Francis X., *A Manual of Church History,* Translated from the 5. German edition, 2 vols., St. Louis: Herder, 1910.

Gallik, George A., *The Rights and Duties of Bishops Regarding Diocesan Sisterhoods,* St. Paul, Minn.: Wanderer Printing Co., 1939.

Gasparri, Petrus (Card.), *Tractatus Canonicus de Matrimonio,* 4. ed., Romae: Marietti, 1939.

Gerster a Zeil, Thomas Villanova, O.F.M. Cap., *Ius Religiosorum in Compendium Redactum,* Taurini: Marietti, 1935.

Geser, Fintan, O.S.B., *The Canon Law Governing Communities of Sisters,* St. Louis: Herder, 1938.

Hannan, Jerome D., *The Canon Law of Wills, an Historical Synopsis and Commentary,* Philadelphia: Dolphin Press, 1935.

Hefele, Charles,—LeClercq, Henry, *Histoire des Conciles,* 10 vols., Paris, 1907-1938.

Heimbucher, Max, *Die Orden und Kongregationen der katholischen Kirche,* 3. ed., 2 vols., Paderborn, 1933-1934.

Kearney, Raymond *The Principles of Delegation, The Catholic University of America Canon Law Studies, N. 55,* Washington, D. C.: The Catholic University of America, 1929.

Leverett, E. P., *Latin Lexicon,* Philadelphia: Lippencott.

Lucidi, Angelus, *De Visitatione Sacrorum, Liminum,* 3. ed., 3 vols., Romae, 1883.

Maroto, Philippus, *Institutiones Iuris Canonici ad Normam Novi Codicis,* 2 vols., tom. I, 3. ed., Romae, 1921.

Martin, Victor, *Les Congrégations Romaines,* Paris: Bloud et Gay, 1930.

McCormick, Robert E., *Confessors of Religious, The Catholic University of America Canon Law Studies, N. 33,* Washington, D. C.: The Catholic University of America, 1926.

McManus, James E., *The Administration of Religious Property, The Catholic University of America Canon Law Studies, N. 109,* Washington, D. C.: The Catholic University of America, 1937.

Melo, Antonius, O.F.M., *De Exemptione Regularium, The Catholic University of America Canon Law Studies, N. 12,* Washington, D. C.: The Catholic University of America, 1921.

Michiels, P. Gomarrus, *Normae Generales Iuris Canonici,* 2 vols., Lublin in Polonia: Universitas Catholica, 1929.

Montelambert, Count de, *The Monks of the West,* 2 vols., Boston: Noonan, 1872.

Mouthon, Joseph, O.P., *Institutions Canoniques a l'Usage des Curies Episcopales, du Clerge Paroissial, et des Familles Religieuses,* 2 vols., Paris, 1922.

——— *Traite sur l'Etat Religieux Considere au Point de Vue de la Theologie Morale et de Droit Canonique,* Paris: Desclée, 1922.

Nervegna, Joseph, *De Institutis Votorum Simplicium Religiosarum et Monialium,* Romae, 1904.

Ojetti, B., *Synopsis Rerum Moralium et Iuris Pontificii,* Romae, 1899.

Orth, Clement Raymond, *The Approbation of Religious Institutes, The Catholic University of America Canon Law Studies, N. 71,* Washington, D. C.: The Catholic University of America, 1931.

Ottaviani, Alaphridus, *Institutiones Iuris Publici Ecclesiastici,* 2. ed., 2 vols., Civitate Vaticana: Typis Polyglottis Vaticanis, 1935-1936.

Papi, Hector, S.J., *The Government of Religious Communities,* New York: Kennedy, 1919.

Parsons, Anscar, O.F. M. Cap., *Canonical Elections,* The Catholic University *of America, Canon Law Studies, N. 118,* Washington, D. C.: The Catholic University of America, 1939.

Pejska, Joseph, C.SS.R., *Ius Canonicum Religiosorum,* 3. ed., Friburgi in Brisgovia: Herder, 1927.

Piatus, F. Montensis, O.F.M., *Praelectiones Iuris Regularis,* 3. ed., 2 vols., Tornaci: Casterman, 1906.

Prümmer, Dominicus M., O.P., *Manuale Iuris Canonici in Usum Clericorum praesertim Illorum Qui ad Instituta Religiosa Pertinent,* 3. ed., Friburgi Brisgoviae: Herder, 1922.

Raus, I. B., C.SS.R., *De Sacrae Obedientiae Virtute et Voto secundum Doctrinam Divi Thomae et S. Alphonsi, iuxta Normas ac Codicem Iuris Canonici Tractatus Canonico-Moralis,* 2 vols., Lugduni: Vitte, 1923.

——— *Institutiones Canonicae,* 2. ed., Parisiis: Vitte, 1931.

Reilly, Thomas F., C.SS.R., *The Visitation of Religious, The Catholic University of America Canon Law Studies, N. 112,* Washington, D. C.: The Catholic University of America, 1938.

Reilly, Edward M., *The General Norms of Dispensation, The Catholic University of America Canon Law Studies, N. 119,* Washington, D. C.: The Catholic University of America, 1939.

Romani, Sylvius, *Summa Iuris Canonici Lineamenta,* Romae: apud Auctorem, 1939.

Schaaf, Valentine, O.F.M., *The Cloister, The Catholic University of America Canon Law Studies, N. 13,* Washington, D. C.: The Catholic University of America, 1921.

Schaefer, Timotheus, O.M.Cap., *Compendium de Religiosis ad Normam Codicis Iuris Canonici,* Münster in W.: Ex Officina Libraria Aschendorff, 1927.

Sister Saint Ignatius,D.C., *Across Three Centuries, A History of the Congregation of the Daughters of the Cross, 1625-1930,* New York: Benziger, 1932.

Smith, I. Gregory, *Christian Monasticism from the Fourth to the Ninth Century of the Christian Era,* London, 1802.

Smith, Mariner T., O.P., *The Penal Law for Religious, The Catholic University of America Canon Law Studies, N. 98,* Washington, D. C.: The Catholic University of America, 1935.

Sobradillo, A. M. de, O.F.M.Cap., *Tractatus de Religiosarum Confessariis ad Normam Codicis Iuris Canonici Comcinnatus,* Torino: Berruti, 1932.

Suarezius, Franciscus, *Opera Omnia,* 26 vols., Parisiis, 1856-1861.

Thomas Aquinas, S., O.P., *Summa Theologica,* Romae, 1894.

Thomassinus, Ludovicus, *Vetus et Nova Ecclesiae Disciplina circa Beneficia et Beneficiarios,* 3 vols., Venetiis, 1730.

Toso, Albertus, *Ad Codicem Iuris Canonici Commentaria Minora,* 5 vols., Romae: Marietti, 1920-1934.

Vasto, P. Bernardus A., O.F.M.Cap., *De Communicatione Privilegiorum praesertim inter Religiones,* Aquilae in Vestinis, Italia, 1936.

Vermeersch, Arthurus, S.J., *De Religiosis Institutis et Personis,* 2 vols., tom, I, 2. ed., 1907; tom. II, 4. ed., 1909.

Vermeersch, Arthurus—Creusen, Josephus, *Epitome Iuris Canonici cum Commentariis ad Scholas et ad Usum Privatorum,* 3. ed., 3 vols., Romae: Dessain, 1927.

Vromant, G., *De Bonis Ecclesiae Temporalibus ad usum praesertim Missionarium et Religiosorum,* Lovanii: Editione de Museum Lessianum, 1927.

Wernz, Franciscus X., S.J., *Ius Decretalium ad usum Praelectionum in Scholis Textus Iuris Canonici, sive Iuris Decretalium,* 6 vols., Romae, 1899-1904.

——— *Ius Decretalium,* 2. ed., 6 vols., Romae, 1906-1913.

Wernz, Franciscus X.,—Vidal, Petrus, S.J., *Ius Canonicum ad Codicis Normam Exactum,* 7 toms. in 8 vols., tom. III, *de Religiosis,* Romae: Apud Aedes Universitatis Gregorianae, 1933.

Woywod, Stanislaus, O.F.M., *A Practical Commentary on the Code of Canon Law,* 4. ed., New York: Wagner, 1932.

Periodicals

American Ecclesiastical Review, The, (later, *The Ecclesiastical Review*), Philadelphia, 1889—

Analecta Ecclesiastica, (Originally *Analecta Iuris Pontificii,* Romae, 1852-1868, Parisiis, 1869-1891), Romae, 1893-1911.

Archiv für katholisches Kirchenrecht, Innsbruck, 1857-1861; Mainz, 1862—

Commentarium pro Religiosis (later, *Commentarium pro Religiosis et Missionariis*), Romae, 1920—

Le Canoniste, (originally *Le Canoniste Contemporain,* 45 vols., Paris, 1878-1922), vols. 46-48, 1924-1926.

Jus Pontificium, Romae, 1921—

Periodica de Re Canonica et Morali utili praesertim Religiosis et Missionariis, Brugis, 1905—

Articles

[Anonymous], "Midnight Mass in Religious Houses"—*AER,* LXXXVII (1932) 628-633.

Bondini, "De Fiduciae ad Causas Pias in Foro Externo Probatione,"—*J. P.*, VI (1926), 87.

Couly, "Les Biens Temporels de l'Eglise,"—"*Le Canoniste Contemporain,* XLV (1922), 14-410.

Goyeneche, "Consultationes,"—*CpRM,* I (1920)—

——— "Quaenam sunt attributiones Directoris Congregationis dioecesanae."—*CpRM,* XIV (1933), 357.

Larraona, Arcadius, "'Commentarium in Partem Secundam Libri II Codicis, quae est de Religiosis,"—*CpRM,* I (1920),—

Maroto, Philippus, "Annotationes,"—*CpRM,* II (1921)—

——— "De Unione Plurium Monasteriorum Muliebrium in Religiosam Congregationem sub Communi Regimine,"—*CpRM,* III (1922), 305-317.

Schiewietz, Stephan, "Geschichte und Organisation der Pachomianischen Klöster im vierten Jahrhundert,"—*AKKR,* LXXXII (1902), 454-475.

Steiger, A. P., "De Propagatione et Diffusione Vitae Religiosae Synopsis Historica,"—*Periodica,* XIII (1924), (29)-(60), (73)-(100), (153)-(180).

Tabera, "De Dimissione Religiosorum,"—*CpRM,* XIV (1933), 53-59.

Abbreviations

AAS—Acta Apostolicae Sedis

AER—The American Ecclesiastical Review (later *The Ecclesiastical Review*).

AKKR—*Archiv für katholisches Kirchenrecht*
ASS—*Acta Sanctae Sedis*
Bull. Rom. Taur.—*Bullarium Romanum ed. Taurinensis*
Bull. Rom. Cont.—*Bullarii Romani Continuatio*
Coll. S. C. Ep. et Reg.—*Collectanea Sacrae Congregationis Episcoporum et Regularium*
Coll. S.C.P.F.—*Collectanea Sacrae Congregationis de Propaganda Fide*
CpRM—*Commentarium pro Religiosis et Missionariis*
Fontes—*Codicis Iuris Canonici Fontes cura . . . Gasparri editi . . .*
J.P.—*Jus Pontificium*
Mansi—*Sacrorum Conciliorum Nova et Amplissima Collectio*
MPG—Migne, *Patrologia Graeca*
MPL—Migne, *Patrologia Latina*
P.C.I.—*Pontifical Commission for the Interpretation of the Code*
Periodica—*Periodica de Re Canonici et Morali utili praesertim Religiosis et Missionariis*
S.C.C.—*Sacra Congregatio Concilii*
S.C. de Rel.—*Sacra Congregatio de Religiosis*
S. C. Ep. et Reg.—*Sacra Congregatio Episcoporum et Regularium*
S.C.R.—*Sacra Congregatio Rituum*
S. C. super Statu Reg.—*Sacra Congregatio super Statu Regularium*

ALPHABETICAL INDEX

BIOGRAPHICAL NOTE

Benjamin Francis Farrell was born in Littleton, West Virginia, April 22, 1905. He attended St. Mary's School in Clarksburg, West Virginia, and St. Charles College, Catonsville, Maryland. After completing the philosophical course at St. Mary's Seminary, Baltimore, Maryland, where he received the degree of Master of Arts, he entered the North American College in Rome, Italy, and was ordained to the priesthood on December 20, 1930. His theological studies were made at the University of the Propaganda, Rome, Italy, where he received the degree of Licentiate in Theology. In September, 1938, he entered the Catholic University of America to pursue a graduate course of studies in the School of Canon Law. In June, 1939, he received the degree of Bachelor of Canon Law. In the same month of the following year he received the Licentiate in Canon Law.

CANON LAW STUDIES

1. Freriks, Rev. Celestine A., C.PP.S., J.C.D., Religious Congregations in Their External Relations, 121 pp., 1916.
2. Galliher, Rev. Daniel M., O.P., J.C.D., Canonical Elections, 117 pp., 1917.
3. Borkowski, Rev. Aurelius L., O.F.M., J.C.D., De Confraternitatibus Ecclesiasticis, 136 pp., 1918.
4. Castillo, Rev. Cayo, J.C.D., Disertacion Historico-Canonica sobre la Potestad del Cabildo en Sede Vacante o Impedida del Vicario Capitular, 99 pp., 1919 (1918).
5. Kubelbeck, Rev. William J., S.T.B., J.C.D., The Sacred Pentitentiaria and Its Relations to Faculties of Ordinaries and Priests, 129 pp., 1918.
6. Petrovits, Rev. Joseph J.C., S.T.D., J.C.D., The New Church Law On Matrimony, X-461 pp., 1919.
7. Hickey, Rev. John J., S.T.B., J.C.D., Irregularities and Simple Impediments in the New Code of Canon Law, 100 pp., 120.
8. Klekotka, Rev. Peter J., S.T.B., J.C.D., Diocesan Consultors, 179 pp., 1920.
9. Wanenmacher, Rev. Francis, J.C.D., The Evidence in Ecclesiastical Procedure Affecting the Marriage Bond, 1920 (Printed 1935).
10. Golden, Rev. Henry Francis, J.C.D., Parochial Benefices in the New Code, IV-119 pp., 1921 (Printed 1925).
11. Koudelka, Rev. Charles J., J.C.D., Pastors, Their Rights and Duties According to the New Code of Canon Law, 211 pp., 1921.
12. Melo, Rev. Antonius, O.F.M., J.C.D., De Exemptione Regularium, X-188 pp., 1921.
13. Schaaf, Rev. Valentine Theodore, O.F.M., S.T.B., J.C.D., The Cloister, X-180 pp., 1921.
14. Burke, Rev. Thomas Joseph, S.T.D., J.C.D., Competence in Ecclesiastical Tribunals, IV-117 pp., 1922.
15. Leech, Rev. George Leo, J.C.D., A Comparative Study of the Constitution, "Apostolicae Sedis" and the "Codex Juris Canonici," 179 pp., 1922.
16. Motry, Rev. Hubert Louis, S.T.D., J.C.D., Diocesan Faculties According to the Code of Canon Law, II-167 pp., 1922.
17. Murphy, Rev. George Lawrence, J.C.D., Delinquencies and Penalties in the Administration and Reception of the Sacraments, IV-121 pp., 1923.
18. O'Reilly, Rev. John Anthony, S.T.B., J.C.D., Ecclesiastical Sepulture in the New Code of Canon Law, II-129 pp., 1923.

19. Michalicka, Rev. Wenceslas Cyrill, O.S.B., J.C.D., Judicial Procedure in Dismissal of Clerical Exempt Religious, 107 pp., 1923.
20. Dargin, Rev. Edward Vincent, S.T.B., J.C.D., Reserved Cases According to the Code of Canon Law, IV-103, pp., 1924.
21. Godfrey, Rev. John A., S.T.B., J.C.D., The Right of Patronage According to the Code of Canon Law, 153 pp., 1924.
22. Hagedorn, Rev. Francis Edward, J.C.D., General Legislation on Indulgences, II-154 pp., 1924.
23. King, Rev. James Ignatius, J.C.D., The Administration of the Sacraments to Dying Non-Catholics, V-141 pp., 1924.
24. Winslow, Rev. Francis Joseph, A.F.M., J.C.D., Vicars and Prefects Apostolic, IV-149 pp., 1924.
25. Correa, Rev. Jose Servelion, S.T.L., J.C.D., La Potestad Legislativa de la Iglesia Catolica, IV-127 pp., 1925.
26. Dugan, Rev. Henry Francis, A.M., J.C.D., The Judiciary Department of the Diocesan Curia, 87 pp., 1925.
27. Keller, Rev. Charles Frederick, S.T.B., J.C.D., Mass Stipends, 167 pp., 1925.
28. Paschang, Rev. John Linus, J.C.D., The Sacramentals According to the Code of Canon Law, 129 pp., 1925.
29. Pointek, Rev. Cyrillus, O.F.M., S.T.B., J.C.D., De Indulto Exclaustrationis necnon Saecularizationis, XIII-289 pp., 1925.
30. Kearney, Rev. Richard Joseph, S.T.B., J.C.D., Sponsors at Baptism According to the Code of Canon Law, IV-127 pp., 1925.
31. Bartlett, Rev. Chester Joseph, A.M., LL.B., J.C.D., The Tenure of Parochial Property in the United States of America, V-108 pp., 1926.
32. Kilker, Rev. Adrian Jerome, J.C.D., Extreme Unction, V-425 pp., 1926.
33. McCormick, Rev. Robert Emmett, J.C.D., Confessors of Religious, VIII-266 pp., 1926.
34. Miller, Rev. Newton Thomas. J.C.D., Founded Masses According to the Code of Canon Law, VII-93 pp., 1926.
35. Roelker, Rev. Edward G., S.T.D., J.C.D., Principles of Privilege According to the Code of Canon Law, XI-166 pp., 1926.
36. Bakalarczyk, Rev. Richardus, M.I.C., J.U.D., De Novitiatu, VIII-208 pp., 1927.
37. Pizzuti, Rev. Lawrence, O.F.M., J.U.L., De Parochis Religiosis, 1927. (Not printed).
38. Bliley, Rev. Nicholas Martin, O.S.B., J.C.D., Altars According to the Code of Canon Law, XIX-132 pp., 1927.
39. Brown, Mr. Brendan Francis, A.B. LL.M., J.U.D., The Canonical Juristic Personality with Special Reference to Its Status in the United States of America, V-212 pp., 1927.

40. Cavanaugh, Rev. William Thomas, C.P., J.U.D., The Reservation of the Blessed Sacrament, VIII-101 pp., 1927.
41. Doheny, Rev. William J., C.S.C., A.B., J.U.D., Church Property: Modes of Acquisition, X-118 pp., 1927.
42. Feldhaus, Rev. Aloysius H., C.PP.S., J.C.D., Oratories, IX-141 pp., 1927.
43. Kelly, Rev. James Patrick, A.B., J.C.D., The Jurisdiction of the Simple Confessor, X-208 pp., 1927.
44. Neuberger, Rev. Nicholas J., J.C.D., Canon 6 or the Relation of the Codex Juris Canonici to the Preceding Legislation, V-95 pp., 1927.
45. O'Keefe, Rev. Gerald Michael, J.C.D., Matrimonial Dispensations, Powers of Bishops, Priests and Confessors, VIII-232 pp., 1927.
46. Quigley, Rev. Joseph A.M., A.B., J.C.B., Condemned Societies, 139 pp., 1927.
47. Zaplotnik, Rev. Johannes Leo, J.C.D., De Vicariis Foraneis, X-142 pp., 1927.
48. Duskie, Rev. John Aloysius, A.B., J.C.D., The Canonical Status of the Orientals in the United States, VIII-196 pp., 1928.
49. Hyland, Rev. Francis Edward, J.C.D., Excommunication, Its Nature, Historical Development and Effects, VIII-181 pp., 1928.
50. Reinmann, Rev. Gerald Joseph, O.M.C., J.C.D., The Third Order Secular of Saint Francis, 201 pp., 1928.
51. Schenk, Rev. Francis J., J.C.D., The Matrimonial Impediments of Mixed Religion and Disparity of Cult, XVI-318 pp., 1929.
52. Coady, Rev. John Joseph, S.T.D., J.U.D., A.M., The Appointment of Pastors, VIII-150 pp., 1929.
53. Kay, Rev. Thomas Henry, J.C.D., Competence in Matrimonial Procedure, VIII-164 pp., 1929.
54. Turner, Rev. Sidney Joseph, C.P., J.U.D., The Vow of Poverty, XLIX-217 pp., 1929.
55. Kearney, Rev. Raymond, A., A.B., S.T.D., J.C.D., The Principles, of Delegation, VII-149 pp., 1929.
56. Conran, Rev. Edward James, A.B., J.C.D., The Interdict, V-163 pp., 1930.
57. O'Neil, Rev. William H., J.C.D., Papal Rescripts of Favor, VII-218 pp., 1930.
58. Bastnagel, Rev. Clement Vincent, J.U.D., The Appointment of Parochial Adjutants and Assistants, XV-257 pp., 1930.
59. Ferry, Rev. William A., A.B., J.C.D., Stole Fees, V-135 pp., 1930.
60. Costello, Rev. John Michael, A.B., J.C.D., Domicile and Quasi-domicile, VII-201 pp., 1930.
61. Kremer, Rev. Michael Nicholas, A.B., S.T.B., J.C.D., Church Support in the United States, VI-1930.

62. Angulo, Rev. Luis, C.M., J.C.D., Legislation de la Iglesia sobre la intencion en la application de la Santa Misa, VII-104 pp., 1931.
63. Frey, Rev. Wolfgang Norbert, O.S.B., A.B., J.C.D., The Act of Religious Profession, VIII-174 pp., 1931.
64. Roberts, Rev. James Brendan, A.B., J.C.D., The Banns of Marriage, XIV-140 pp., 1931.
65. Ryder, Rev. Raymond Aloysius, A.B., J.C.D., Simony, IX-151 pp., 1931.
66. Campagna, Rev. Angelo, Ph.D., J.U.D., Il Vicario Generale del Vescovo, VII-205 pp., 1931.
67. Cox, Rev. Joseph Godfrey, A.B., J.C.D., The Administration ot Seminaries, VI-124 pp., 1931.
68. Gregory, Rev. Donald J., J.U.D., The Pauline Privilege, XV-165 pp., 1931.
69. Donohue, Rev. John F., J.C.D., The Impediment of Crime, VII-110 pp., 1931.
70. Dooley, Rev. Eugene A., O.M.I., J.C.D., Church Law On Sacred Relics, IX-143 pp., 1931.
71. Orth, Rev. Raymond Clement, O.M.C., J.C.D., The Approbation of Religious Institutes, 171 pp., 1931.
72. Pernicone, Rev. Joseph M., A.B., J.C.D., The Ecclesiastical Prohibition of Books, XII-267 pp., 1932.
73. Clinton, Rev. Connell, A.B., J.C.D., The Paschal Precept, IX-108 pp., 1932.
74. Donnelly, Rev. Francis B., A.M., S.T.L., J.C.D., The Diocesan Synod, VIII-125 pp., 1932.
75. Torrente, Rev. Camilo, C.M.F., J.C.D., Las Processiones Sagradas, V-145 pp., 1932.
76. Murphy, Rev. Edwin J., C.PP.S., J.C.D., Suspension Ex Informata Conscientia, XI-122, pp., 1932.
77. Mackenzie, Rev. Eric F., A.M., S.T.L., J.C.D., The Delict of Heresy in its Commission Penalization, Absolution, VII-124 pp., 1932.
78. Lyons Rev. Avitus E., S.T.B., J.C.D., The Collegiate Tribunal of First Instance, XI-147 pp., 1932.
79. Connolly, Rev. Thomas A., J.C.D., Appeals, XI-195 pp., 1932.
80. Sangmeister, Rev. Joseph V., A.B., J.C.D., Force and Fear as Precluding Matrimonial Consent, V-211 pp., 1932.
81. Jaeger, Rev. Leo A., A.B., J.C.D., The Administration of Vacant and Quasi-vacant Episcopal Sees in the United States, IX-229 pp., 1932.
82. Rimlinger, Rev. Herbert T., J.C.D., Error Invalidating Matrimonial Consent, VII-79 pp., 1932.
83. Barrett, Rev. John D.M., S.S., J.C.D., A Comparative Study of the Third Plenary Council of Baltimore and the Code, IX-221 pp., 1932.

84. Carberry, Rev. John J., Ph.D., S.T.D., J.C.D., The Juridical Form of Marriage, X-177 pp., 1934.
85. Dolan, Rev. John L., A.B., J.C.D., The Defensor Vinculi, XII-157 pp., 1934.
86. Hannan, Rev. Jerome D., A.M., S.T.D., LL.B., J.C.D., The Canon Law of Wills, IX-517 pp., 1934.
87. Lemieux, Rev. Delisle A., A.M., J.C.D., The Sentence in Ecclesiastical Procedure, IX-131 pp., 1934.
88. O'Rourke, Rev. James J., A.B., J.C.D., Parish Registers, VII-109 pp., 1934.
89. Timlin, Rev. Bartholomew, O.F.M., A.M., J.C.D., Conditional Matrimonial Consent, X-381 pp., 1934.
90. Wahl, Rev. Francis X., A.B., J.C.D., The Matrimonial Impediments of Consanguinity and Affinity, VI-125 pp., 1934.
91. White, Rev. Robert J., A.B., LL.B., S.T.B., J.C.D., Canonical Ante-Nuptial Promises and the Civil Law, VI-152 pp., 1934.
92. Herrera, Rev. Antonio Parra, O.C.D., J.C.D., Legislation Ecclesiastica sobra el Ayuno y la Abstinencia, XI-191 pp., 1935.
93. Kennedy, Rev. Edwin J., J.C.D., The Special Matrimonial Process in Cases of Evident Nullity, X-165 pp., 1935.
94. Manning, Rev. John J., A.B., J.C.D., Presumption of Law in Matrimonial Procedure, XI-111 pp., 1935.
95. Moeder, Rev. John M., J.C.D., The Proper Bishop for Ordination and Dismissorial Letters, VII-135 pp., 1935.
96. O'Mara, Rev. William A., A.B., J.C.D., Canonical Causes For Matrimonial Dispensations, IX-155 pp., 1935.
97. Reilly, Rev. Peter, J.C.D., Residence of Pastors, IX-81 pp., 1935.
98. Smith, Rev. Mariner T., O.P., S.T.L., J.C.D., The Penal Law For Religious, VII-169 pp., 1935.
99. Whalen, Rev. Donald W., A.M., J.C.D., The Value of Testimonial Evidence in Matrimonial Procedure, XIII-297 pp., 1935.
100. Cleary, Rev. Joseph F., J.C.D., Canonical Limitations on the Alienation of Church Property, VIII-141 pp., 1936.
101. Glynn, Rev. John C., J.C.D., The Promoter of Justice, XX-337 pp., 1936.
102. Brennan, Rev. James H., S.S., A.M., S.T.B., J.C.D., The Simple Convalidation of Marriage, VI-135 pp, 1937.
103. Brunini, Rev. Joseph Bernard, J.C.D., The Clerical Obligations of Canons, 139 and 142, X-121 pp., 1937.
104. Connor, Rev. Maurice, A.B., J.C.D., The Administrative Removal of Pastors, VIII-159 pp., 1937.
105. Guilfoyle, Rev. Merlin Joseph, J.C.D., Custom, XI-144 pp., 1937.
106. Hughes, Rev. James Austin, A.B., A.M., J.C.D., Witnesses in Criminal Trials of Clerics, IX-140 pp., 1937.

107. Jansen, Rev. Raymond J., A.B., S.T.L., J.C.D., Canonical Provisions for Catechetical Instruction, VII-153 pp., 1937.
108. Kealy, Rev. John James, A.B., J.C.D,, The Introductory Libellus in Church Court Procedure, XI-121 pp., 1937.
109. McManus, Rev. James Edward, C.SS.R., J.C.D., The Administration of Temporal Goods in Religious Institutes, XVI-196 pp., 1937.
110. Moriarity, Rev. Eugene James, J.C.D., Oaths in Ecclesiastical Courts, X-115 pp., 1937.
111. Rainer, Rev. Eligius George, C.SS.R., J.C.D., Suspension of Clerics, XVII-249 pp., 1937.
112. Reilly, Rev. Thomas F., C.SS.R., J.C.D., Visitation of Religious, VI-195 pp., 1938.
113. Moriarty, Rev. Francis E., C.SS.R., J.C.D., The Extraordinary Absolution from Censures, XV-334 pp., 1938.
114. Connolly, Rev. Nicholas P., J.C.D., The Canonical Erection of Parishes, X-132 pp., 1938.
115. Donovan, Rev. James Joseph, J.C.D., The Pastor's Obligation in Prenuptial Investigation, XII-322 pp., 1938.
116. Harrigan, Rev. Robert J., M.A., S.T.B., J.C.D., The Radical Sanation of Invalid Marriages, VIII-208 pp., 1938.
117. Boffa, Rev. Conrad Humbert, J.C.D., Canonical Provisions for Catholic Schools, X-211 pp., 1939.
118. Parsons, Rev. Anscar John, O.M. Cap., J.C.D., Canonical Elections, XII-236 pp., 1939.
119. Reilly, Rev. Edward Michael, A.B., J.C.D., The General Norms of Dispensation, X-156 pp., 1939.
120. Ryan, Rev. Gerald Aloysius, A.B., J.C.D., Principles of Episcopal Jurisdiction, XII-172 pp., 1939.
121. Burton, Rev. Francis James, C.S.C., A.B., J.C.D., A Commentary on Canon 1125, X-222 pp., 1940.
122. Miaskiewicz, Rev. Francis Sigismund, J.C.D., Supplied Jurisdiction according to Canon 209, XII-340 pp., 1940.
123. Rice, Rev. Patrick William, A.B., J.C.D., Proof of Death in Prenuptial Investigation, VIII-156 pp., 1940.
124. Anglin, Rev. Thomas Francis, M.S., J.C.L., The Eucharistic Fast.
125. Coleman, Rev. John Jerome, J.C.L., The Minister of Confirmation.
126. Downs, Rev. John Emmanuel, A.B., J.C.L., The Concept of Clerical Immunity.
127. Esswein, Rev. Anthony Albert, J.C.L., Extrajudicial Penal Powers of Ecclesiastical Superiors.
128. Farrell, Rev. Benjamin Francis, M.A., S.T.L., J.C.L., The Rights and Duties of the Local Ordinary Regarding Congregations of Women Religious of Pontifical Approval.

129. Feeney, Rev. Thomas John, A.B., S.T.L., J.C.L., Restitutio in Integrum.
130. Findlay, Rev. Stephen William, O.S.B., A.B., J.C.L., Canonical Norms Governing the Deposition and Degradation of Clerics.
131. Goodwine, Rev. John, A.B., S.T.L., J.C.L., The Right of the Church to Acquire Property.
132. Heston, Rev. Edward Louis, C.S.C., Ph.D., S.T.D., J.C.L., The Alienation of Church Property in the United States .
133. Hogan, Rev. James John, S.T.L., J.C.L.,, Judicial Advocates and Procurators.
134. Kealy, Rev. Thomas M., A.B., Litt. B., J.C.L., Dowry of Women Religious.
135. Keene, Rev. Michael James, O.S.B., J.C.L., Religious Ordinaries and Canon 198.
136. Kerin, Rev. Charles A., S.S., M.A., S.T.B., J.C.L., The Privation of Christian Burial.
137. Louis, Rev. William Francis, M.A., J.C.L., Diocesan Archives.
138. McDevitt, Rev. Gilbert Joseph, A.B., J.C.L., Legitimacy and Legitimation.
139. McDonough, Rev. Thomas Joseph, A.B., J.C.L., Apostolic Administrators.
140. Meier, Rev. Carl Anthony, A.B., J.C.L., Penal Administrative Procedure Against Negligent Pastors.
141. Schmidt, Rev. John Rogg, A.B., J.C.L., The Principles of Authentic Interpretation in Canon 17 of the Code of Canon Law.
142. Slafkosky, Rev. Andrew Leonard, A.B., J.C.L., The Canonical Episcopal Visitation of the Diocese.
143. Swoboda, Rev. Innocent Robert, O.F.M., J.C.L., Ignorance in Relation to the Imputability of Delicts.
144. Dubé, Rev. Arthur Joseph, A.B., J.C.L., The Generol Principles for the Reckoning of Time in Canon Law.
145. McBride, Rev. James T., A.B., J.C.L., Incardination and Excardination of Seculars.